IN

ITALY

THE
SECRET WAR
IN
ITALY

Operation Partridge and No. 1 Special Force

WILLIAM FOWLER

Ian Allan

THE
SECRET WAR
IN
ITALY

Operation Herring and No 1 Italian SAS

WILLIAM FOWLER

Ian Allan
PUBLISHING

The Secret War in Italy
William Fowler

First published 2010

ISBN 978 0 7110 3528 7

Published by Ian Allan Publishing

an imprint of Ian Allan Publishing Ltd, Hersham, Surrey KT12 4RG.
Printed in England by CPI Mackays, Chatham, Kent ME5 8TD.

Visit the Ian Allan Publishing website at www.ianallanpublishing.com

Distributed in the United States of America and Canada by
BookMasters Distribution Services.

No 1 Italian Special Air Service
The Secret War in Italy 1943-1945

'SAS operations rarely went according to plan. I can't remember one that ever did, but one has to make up ways to get round that. Which we did.'

Captain Anthony Greville-Bell, 2 SAS,

Stirling's Men by Gavin Mortimer

'Action Stations!'

'Red On!'

The bulky figures standing stooped in the cramped fuselage of the Dakotas were bathed in a satanic red light and the noise became deafening as the dispatcher slid back the aircraft door.

'Green On!'

'Go! Go! Go!'

Now as the darkened interior turned a lurid green and as the first paratrooper dived out of the door, he seemed to pull the others behind him out into the roaring darkness of the short spring night of 20 April 1945.

The young soldiers felt the violent impact of the slipstream, static lines snaked out, the parachutes deployed with a pistol-shot crack and as they seemed to hang suspended, below them they could see the terrifying blazing streaks of tracer as German anti-aircraft gunners ripped off bursts of fire at the departing aircraft and now desperately vulnerable paratroops. Alone for a few moments in the moonlight, there was sufficient time to wonder if they were on a one-way suicide mission.

What they did not know was that they were jumping into history. They were making the last operational parachute jump of World War 2 in Europe and the only one by a unique British-trained and directed Special Forces formation.

They were the men of No 1 Italian Special Air Service on Operation HERRING – a mission to create mayhem behind German lines for 36 hours, but one that for some would last several days longer.

In individual leg bags and the containers floating down beside them was the equipment for the mission - plastic explosives, booby-trap pressure switches, detonators, grenades, automatic weapons, ammunition and rations.

The 210 men, combat-hardened volunteers from the Allied Italian forces, had received intense training in ambush, night fighting and demolitions tactics at a secret Special Operations Executive centre in northern Italy.

They were to disrupt the German withdrawal following the Allied spring offensive with ambushes that would create traffic jams that could be hit by Allied fighter bombers, and attacks on bridges and other key facilities to prevent them being demolished by the Germans.

As they began the run-in on to their Drop Zones (DZs) some of the USAAF Dakota pilots were met by heavy flak and reported afterwards that some DZs were not obvious, and so some of the sticks of paratroops were dropped miles off target and one over 30 miles from its designated DZ.

However these misdrops did not significantly hinder these determined men. A few, wounded in the air, were captured upon landing and clubbed to death, but the rest went into action almost immediately.

One group, who barricaded themselves inside a farmhouse, fought a short but violent siege in which only two men escaped.

Life was brutally cheap in Italy in 1945.

However, other patrols from No 1 ISAS were more successful, inflicting heavy damage for light casualties. Two patrols linked up with local partisans and seized the small towns of Ravarino and Stuffione, capturing 451 Germans and holding out until the arrival of the Allied ground forces. Though some of the war-weary, demoralised Germans were cracking under the Allied land and air offensive, many were intent on evading capture and were prepared to fight ferociously to reach the safety of the Austrian Alps. No 1 Italian SAS and other formations like Major Roy Farran's SAS team in Operation TOMBOLA and Major Walker-Brown's in operation GALIA, working with partisans behind German lines, were to play a significant part in ensuring that the German withdrawal in 1945 collapsed into a rout and never made it to the security of Austria.

This is their story.

Contents

Introduction

'To be ignorant of what occurred before you were born is to remain always a child. For what is the worth of human life, unless it is woven into the life of our ancestors by the records of history?'

Cicero in *Imperium* by Robert Harris

To untie the white tape around the buff document folders held at the National Archives, Kew, is for a researcher, to rediscover something of the excitement of a childhood Christmas or birthday. Instead of tearing away the colourful wrapping paper to reach the wonders inside, the folder or box is carried carefully to a designated desk space in the Reading Room. Will it contain merely routine correspondence between staff officers and headquarters – or unique documents and reports of genuine historical value and intense immediacy? For a few seconds there is an almost childlike thrill of anticipation.

My first encounter with what was then the Public Record Office in Kew on the western outskirts of London, and universally known as the PRO, was early in 1990. I was a very small cog in a larger machine that was using the model of history to test concepts for an operational analysis programme for the British Ministry of Defence.

I delved into war diaries and after-action reports from World War 2 to find examples of human reactions to 'A Rapidly Approaching Threat' or 'Shock and Surprise' and, most fascinatingly, how a single soldier could inspire a group – the 'Hero Factor' in war. Some of these concepts

I would test in a modest way less than a year later when as a reserve officer I volunteered for service with British forces in Operation GRANBY – the first Gulf War of 1990-1 – and became another small cog, albeit in a very much bigger machine.

Since that first visit to Kew almost 20 years ago the busy staff at the National Archive have always been wonderfully helpful and patient with me and other researchers – veterans and novices alike.

It was at Kew that I discovered the story of No 1 Italian SAS. Like researchers before and since, it was a silent 'Eureka!' moment in the quiet of the Reading Room. Here was a piece of unusual history from World War 2 that had never been recorded for English readers. Some of the documents inside were routine correspondence but others, like the critical pieces of a jigsaw, helped to build up a picture of the recruitment and training of this unique special forces formation.

The staff at Romsey Public Library, a branch of the Hampshire County Library Service, worked wonders tracking down invaluable reference works on Special Forces operations in Italy as well as *'F' Squadron* by Carlo Bonciani, the colourful account of this unique Italian combat unit.

In Sandy Sandersone MBE I found a kindred spirit who shared my passion for history and research but crucially provided invaluable background on World War 2 explosives, incendiaries and booby-trap mechanisms.

My thanks to Brigadier General Luciano Portolano, the Italian Army Attaché at the Italian Embassy in London, who put me in touch with Colonel Antonino Zarcone of *Stato Maggiore Dell'Esercito V Reparto Affari Generali.*

Colonel Zarcone provided copies of the original after-action reports by Captain Carlo Gay, the commanding officer of 'F' Recce Squadron, as well as the section covering the squadron in the history of the *Cremona, Friuli, Folgore, Legnano, Mantova* and *Piceno* Combat Groups published in Rome in 1973. Colonel S. G. Salavatore, Director of the *Direzione Generale per il Personale Militare* forwarded the biographical background and citations for *S. Ten* Franco Bagna and *Parac* Amelio de Juliis, the two men awarded the Gold Medal for Military Valour (MOVM). I am grateful to Francesca Hughes for translating these documents.

I am particularly indebted to Daniel Battistella – grandson of Sergeant Major Modesto Dall'asta who jumped over DZ 23 with Patrol 'C' of 'F' Recce Squadron commanded by Captain Carlo Gay. Daniel has been more than generous with his time and the mass of documents and photographs he has collected about 'F' Recce Squadron. His enthusiasm for the subject has been inspirational.

Amassing this information would have been pointless without Nick Grant of Ian Allan Publishing, who shared with me my interest in this little-known episode in World War 2 and saw its potential as a book.

Living in Hampshire, my work at the National Archives would have been impossible without the hospitality of old friends Stephan and Siân Pyle and Diana and Dorian Lovell-Pank, who, living near Kew, not only generously provided bed and board but also shared my interest in the project.

Finally, as always, my gratitude to Carol, who over the months has listened patiently to my increasing enthusiasm for the story of No 1 Italian SAS, and without whose love and support this book would not have been possible.

William Fowler,
Romsey, Hampshire, 2010

Chapter 1

The Tough Old Gut

In landing operations, retreat is impossible.

General George S. Patton
General Order to the US 7th Army,
Operation HUSKY, 1943

Operation HERRING was a small part of a long campaign that began with the Allied invasion of the Italian mainland in early September 1943. Following the defeat of German and Italian Axis forces in North Africa, the British Prime Minister, Winston Churchill, had optimistically promised the American Allies that Italy would be the 'soft underbelly' of Europe. The landings, he was sure, would precipitate the fall of the Italian leader Benito Mussolini and give the Allies a southern route north into the heartland of Nazi Germany. For the soldiers on the ground this 'soft underbelly' would, over two gruelling years of fighting, come to be known as the 'tough old gut'.

The first move in the assault on mainland Europe began on 28 May 1943 when men of 2 Special Air Service Regiment (2 SAS), veterans of covert operations in North Africa, launched Operation SNAPDRAGON, the reconnaissance of the heavily-fortified Italian island of Pantelleria. Mussolini had boasted that the tiny 32-square-mile island would be a second Malta, resisting the Allied bombardment and landings. The SAS landed by submarine, suffering no casualties, but gained little information. Then in 100 hours the RAF and USAAF flew 5,000 sorties against Pantelleria and dropped 6,000 tons of bombs. This was then followed by a naval bombardment so concentrated that the garrison quickly surrendered to a seaborne assault by the British 1st Division on 11 June.

The Daily Telegraph reporter K. Hooper gleefully reported from the island under the headline:

Comic Opera of Pantelleria Landing

Thousands of Italian prisoners forming the bulk of the 15,000 garrison wound their dusty tattered way from the surrounding hills into a foul ruin which once bore the name of Pantelleria... One of the most outstanding facts about the reduction of this Mediterranean stronghold is that the attacking forces suffered no casualties whatsoever. The only man to suffer any sort of injury was bitten by a donkey.

A day later the tiny Italian island of Lampedusa was bombarded from the air and sea. When the fighter flown by Sergeant Jack Cohen of the RAF developed engine trouble and he was forced to land on the island, the desperate garrison rushed out from their shelters waving white flags and shouting, 'Can't you stop this?' He could not, and along with the garrison took cover for another two hours of bombardment. Italian Army engineers then managed to repair his aircraft and he flew off to tell the Royal Navy and US Navy that the garrison wished to surrender.

The surrender of the garrisons of Linosa, Lampedusa and Pantelleria cleared the way for Operation HUSKY, the invasion of Sicily. At this stage in the war many Italian troops were demoralised and reluctant to fight for a cause in which they no longer believed. If obsolescent equipment and poor leadership is added to this toxic brew, it is easy to understand why men would not fight and were eager to surrender. Courage and military prowess comes from a mixture of good training, effective leadership, decent equipment and a belief in the cause for which a soldier is asked to fight and perhaps die. In 1945 the men of No 1 Italian SAS would give a striking demonstration of courage in battle.

Back in 1943 Sicily was defended by the Italian Sixth Army, a force of about 230,000 men under General Alfredo Guzzoni, who had his HQ at Enna. There were coastal batteries covering likely invasion beaches and airfields along the southern and eastern shore; many of the crews of these guns were older men who lived on the island. In addition to the Italian garrison, the island had part of the *15th Panzer Grenadier Division* and the battered and under-strength *Panzerdivision Hermann Göring*, which was refitting. The key to the island was the port of Messina, on the straits between Sicily and the Italian mainland. Held by the Germans and Italians, it allowed the island to be reinforced or evacuated; in Allied hands it trapped the Axis forces on the island and was a jumping-off point for an attack on the Italian peninsula.

Two minor SAS raids, MARIGOLD and HAWTHORN, were launched against Sardinia in 1943. In MARIGOLD, a joint SAS and SBS operation carried out on 30 May, the plan was to snatch a prisoner. The eight

SAS and three SBS men were landed at night from a submarine; however, an alert garrison opened fire and the team was forced to withdraw. HAWTHORN, launched on 7 July, was strictly an SBS operation but since John Verney, the officer who led it, later transferred to the SAS, it is often listed as an SAS operation.

Of the two SAS Regiments formed in North Africa, No 1 and No 2 SAS, 2 SAS survived in Algeria as a recruit training and selection organisation, but 1 SAS was disbanded at the end of the campaign in North Africa. Major Blair Mayne's A Squadron was combined with the remnants of B and became the 250-strong Special Raiding Squadron (SRS). Mayne, a tough Ulster Scot, was universally known by the nickname 'Paddy'.

Lt Derrick Harrison joined the SRS in their training camp in Palestine. Harrison, who was to serve with the SAS in Sicily, Italy and France described his experiences in training under Mayne in *These Men are Dangerous*. Mayne went back to basics, even though '...not a man in the unit who could by the greatest stretch of imagination be called a recruit. It was typical of the training. Nothing was taken for granted. What can be learned can be forgotten, so we started from scratch.

'It was this thoroughness that accounted in great measure for the success of our undertakings and our remarkably low casualty rate in operations to come.'

Like any special forces formation, the most severe punishment was to be Returned To Unit or RTU'd. As James Dunning, who served with No 4 Commando, explained, the power of a Commanding Officer to RTU men who did not match up to the demanding standards of special forces ensured that officers and men were of the highest calibre.

The men on these raids were not to know that they were part of a larger Allied deception operation designed to deflect German attention away from Sicily and convince the *Oberkommando der Wehrmacht* (OKW) – the German High Command – that shipping massing in North Africa was destined for an invasion of Sardinia, the south of France or even Greece.

Following a stormy night on 9-10 July 1943 British and American airborne forces landed on Sicily; they were the advance guard for the US Seventh and British Eighth Armies. Of the 137 gliders released some 69 landed in the sea, and though the amphibious invasion force managed to rescue some of the soldiers about 200 were drowned. The British 1st Airlanding Brigade was tasked with the capture of the Simeto Bridge north of the town of Primasole. The glider-borne British troops were widely scattered, and of the men in the 12 gliders that landed near the bridge, the troops removed demolition charges but were forced to withdraw. The troops who forced them out were men of *Fallschirmjäger Regiment 3 (FJR 3)* and the machine-gun and engineer battalions and other elements of *FJR 4*. They had flown from bases in southern France via Italy to Sicily and jumped at Catania airport on 12 July as part of a rapid reinforcement for the island.

US airborne forces were also badly scattered and 2,781 men were spread over a 50-mile radius.

The Anglo-American amphibious landings by the Fifteenth Army Group, commanded by General Harold Alexander, were in the southeast tip of Sicily. The US Seventh Army under General George Patton landed at Licata and the US II Corps under General Omar Bradley between Gela and Scoglitte. Here they were faced respectively by the Italian 207 Coastal Division and 18 Coastal Brigade.

Aboard the luxury liner the SS *Strathnaver* – now a troopship carrying men of the British 50th Division to Sicily – Christopher Buckley, a veteran correspondent who had covered the Spanish Civil War and who would survive World War 2 but be killed in Korea, observed his fellow passengers.

> *'If one talked to the officers about the invasion one found them ready and eager to discuss it with the same intense but dispassionate interest that a keen player might give to a particularly enthralling chess problem. To talk to the men was to discover an attitude which might be summed up in the single phrase, 'Glad to be getting on with the job; we've got to clean up this show before we can go home.' Nothing more. No animosity and heroics. The enemy was merely 'Jerry' or 'The Ities', regarded respectively with grudging admiration and with more than humorous contempt ... this very dispassionate quality in the British soldier is his strength. For essentially he thinks in unemotional terms of the job ahead and his approach is always scientific rather than emotional. Which on the whole is an advantage in the ugly business of killing people whom you have never seen before and whom you might not dislike if you were ever to meet them.'* [1]

On the night of 11-12 July, tanks of the *Panzerdivision Hermann Göring* launched a counterattack against the American 1st Infantry Division at Gela and some had actually reached the coastal dunes before the attack was broken up by heavy naval gunfire. It is estimated that over 5,000 naval shells rained down on the 60 tanks of *Panzerregiment Hermann Göring*, knocking out 40 PzKpfw III and IV and 17 tanks of the Army *Tiger-Kompanie* 2/504.

The British Eighth Army under Montgomery, composed of the XXX Corps under General Oliver Leese and the XIII under General Miles Dempsey, landed respectively at Pachino and between Avola and Cassible. They were faced by the Italian 204 Coastal Division.

As well as the newly-established US and British Airborne Forces, US Rangers and British Commandos (SAS and SRS) played a significant part in the invasion of Sicily. As part of HUSKY on 10 July the SRS and the SAS were tasked with disrupting Axis movement on the island and neutralising two Italian coastal artillery positions at Capo Murro di Porco ('Pig's Snout Headland') on the southeast coast. The assault on the artillery positions was more of a conventional sea-borne commando attack than a covert 'behind the lines' operation.

The battery consisted of three 155mm guns, three 20mm anti-aircraft guns, machine-gun positions and fire control equipment. As the Land Craft Assault (LCA) carrying the SRS started the run-in to the shore, one hove to and picked up Brigadier Hicks, the commanding officer of the 4 Airborne Brigade. He was clinging to the wing of his glider, which had been released too early over the sea. Of the 137 Waco and Horsa gliders committed to the operation, 82 failed to reach the coast and Derrick Harrison recalls that the SRS picked up only five survivors.

The Italian gunners were either 'too shell-shocked or too scared to offer resistance'. Captain Johnny Wiseman, who was in radio contact with Mayne, reported that prisoners were leaving the position. 'Get your men off the site', said Mayne, 'The REs [Royal Engineers] are ready to blow the guns'.'

Roy Bradford and Martin Dillon's fascinating study of Mayne, *Rogue Warrior of the SAS*, describes the conversation that followed: 'Sorry sir,' mumbled Wiseman. 'I've lost my false teeth.' 'Don't be so bloody silly,' roared Paddy. It was true, but by great good luck I found them, God knows how, in the dark." Wiseman, who would survive the war and who would later laugh as he recalled the incident, had lost his front teeth in a university cricket match.

Derrick Harrison remembered taking cover as the charges detonated. 'There was a sharp concussion and flying pieces of metal whined eerily above our heads. As the sound of the explosions rolled away, from the signaller's wireless set came the strains of 'Land of Hope and Glory' as a broadcasting station crashed in on our frequency.'[2]

Bunkers were cleared with the bayonet and grenades, and by dawn at 06.00 hours Mayne pushed his men on to capture an anti-aircraft gun site which the SRS 3-inch mortars had engaged, destroying the ammunition dump [see Appendix 3]. For the loss of one man killed and two wounded, they had destroyed two batteries, taken 500 prisoners and killed or wounded 200 of the enemy.

Two days later the SRS was tasked with the capture of the port and town of Augusta. The SRS had been briefed to expect limited opposition and that they would be 'mopping up' dispirited Italian soldiers. Instead they were faced by tough German soldiers of the *Hermann Göring*

Division who were backed up by 15.5cm guns sited in the hills. In daylight the LCAs ran in under machine-gun and artillery fire and once ashore the SRS 'leap-frogged' through the town, giving covering fire to one another and clearing buildings with grenades. When the Germans pulled back, the SRS celebrated in some style in Augusta. Mayne commented in a letter to his sister that as the date was the anniversary of the Battle of the Boyne and the high point of the Protestant marching season in Ulster, 'All we needed was some drums and banners and we would have felt right at home.' The operations in Sicily would earn Mayne his first DSO and he would go on to win two bars for this decoration. While undoubtedly very brave and a natural soldier, Mayne was a complex man who made enemies easily. It was this that may have denied him a Victoria Cross at the end of the war. Mayne would die in a car crash in his native Northern Ireland after a night of heavy drinking on 13 December 1956.

Two SAS operations, CHESTNUT and NARCISSUS, were part of the diversionary attacks to support the main landings on Sicily. In CHESTNUT two ten-man patrols from 2 SAS, 'Pink' under Captain Philip Pinckney and 'Brig' under Captain Bridgemann-Evans were parachuted into the northern part of the island. 'Pink' was tasked with severing roads and telephone lines in the north-east as well as the Catania-Messina railway line. 'Brig' was to attack convoys and an enemy HQ near Mount Etna. In the original plan they were to have been landed from a submarine, which would have put them closer to their target and in a formed group. In the first parachute operation by 2 SAS the two groups were dropped on the night of 12 July but almost immediately had problems.

'Pink''s radios were damaged, the party widely scattered and stores and equipment lost. 'Brig' disastrously landed amongst buildings, alerting the enemy, and Bridgemann-Evans was captured, though he later escaped. With no radio contact the RAF cancelled a reinforcement drop scheduled for the 13th. On the ground the groups achieved little but managed to make their way back to Allied lines.

In *The Special Air Service*, Philip Warner reports that though local people were pleased to see the CHESTNUT team, in one community SAS men and villagers were subjected to an Allied air attack. The patrol 'had to reassure the inhabitants that no harm was meant as the bombs were aimed at German military targets only. In order to reinforce this view they stood in the open when the bombs fell but did not enjoy the experience as some of the bombs came very close.' In the after-action analysis the failure was attributed to changed plans and lack of rehearsal.

Tragically, Major Geoffrey Appleyard, the former CO of the Small Scale Raiding Force was lost when the aircraft on which he was the drop supervisor for the 'Pink' team failed to return to base.

Operation NARCISSUS was a full-scale assault on 10 July by 40 men of A Squadron 2 SAS against what was thought to be a fortified lighthouse with coastal artillery and fire control equipment. It was the operational début in the SAS of Major Roy Farran.[3] The men were transported to the coast by landing craft, but discovered that except for three terrified Italian soldiers, the lighthouse was deserted; and so since it posed no threat to the HUSKY landings they returned without firing a shot.

Kesselring moved the *XIV Panzer Korps* onto the island

to bolster the Italian garrison. As the Allies piled on the pressure following their landings, Kesselring did not wait for clearance from Hitler before he began to withdraw his forces across the Straits of Messina into mainland Italy.

On 19 July the Fascist Party Secretary Carlo Scorza broadcast from Rome to the population of Sicily and urged the island's population to resist the invasion. 'This is a war of religion, institutions and bread. Italy is defending her Catholic faith. Italy is defending her traditional and modern institutions.

'The Italians know that this is a war of distributive justice, and therefore a war for bread. Italy is battling desperately because she wants to save herself.'

In less than two years the war would be over and Italians would have executed Scorza and hung his body alongside that of his leader Mussolini from the roof of a garage forecourt in Milan.

On 29 July the German press saluted Mussolini on his 60th birthday. It was a public demonstration of Hitler's loyalty to the leader of this increasingly unreliable Fascist ally.

In Sicily the Germans, assisted by a hard core of dedicated Italian soldiers, put up a strong resistance and their demolitions and rearguard actions meant that Messina did not fall until 17 August. It seemed to some Allied commanders that its capture had become a race between the British, under Montgomery, and the US Army, under Patton, both very competent commanders but also men with huge egos. The Germans, who had realised that Messina was critical, fought hard against the Eighth Army. At 10.15 hours the US 3rd Division entered Messina – Patton and the Americans had won by 50 minutes. However, it was a Pyrrhic victory since in the six days prior to its capture the German and Italian naval forces had evacuated 40,000 German troops, 60,000 Italian troops, nearly 10,000 German vehicles and 47 tanks to the Italian mainland. For the Allies Sicily was a tactical victory – however, for the Germans it was arguably a strategic triumph, as some of the men who had crossed the straits would live to fight for another two years, delaying the Allies and inflicting casualties.

The cost of the Sicilian campaign had been high. The British and Canadians had lost 2,721 killed, 2,183 missing and 7,939 wounded, while the Americans had suffered 2,811 killed, 686 missing and 6,471 wounded. Axis losses were estimated at 164,000 killed or captured.

1   *Road to Rome*, Christopher Buckley, Hodder and Stoughton, London 1945

2   *These Men are Dangerous*, Derrick Harrison, Cassell & Co, London 1957

3   Roy Farran, who was one of the towering figures of the SAS in World War 2, was born in India on 2 January 1921 and died in Canada on 1 June 2006.
      He joined 3rd King's Own Hussars in Egypt and first saw action between December 1940 and February 1941 in the battle of Sidi Barrani and in the battle for Crete in 1941, but while leading a tank attack he was wounded and captured. For these actions he received his first MC. After several attempts, he escaped under the perimeter fence of a PoW hospital near Athens and, with Greek help, secured a caicque (a Greek fishing boat). Along with a motley group of British and Australians, he sailed for Egypt. After a stormy nine-day passage, in which they ran out of water, they were picked up by a destroyer north of Alexandria, and Farran received a bar to his MC.
      Early in 1943, after parachute training, he joined 2 SAS. He led the raid on the lighthouse on Cape Passero in Sicily and reconnaissance patrols and sabotage in the south. One of the most spectacular of these was in October 1943 when Farran dropped with a 2 SAS detachment north of the River Tronto behind

German lines. In five days his force destroyed transport, cut communications and blew up railway lines. A third MC followed.

In France, between 19 August and 17 September 1944, Farran, aged 23 and now a Major, led a column of 60 men and 20 Jeeps from the 2 SAS in Operation WALLACE. Suffering few casualties, it inflicted 500 on the Germans, destroyed 95 vehicles, a train and 100,000 gallons of fuel. Returning through France, Farran's squadron took illicit leave in Paris.

Following WALLACE, Farran returned to Italy and led Operation TOMBOLA in 1945. He anticipated a court-martial for disobeying orders by 'falling' from the aircraft, but the Americans later awarded him the Legion of Merit and the incident was forgotten.

His postwar military career was marred by an accusation of murder of a 16-year-old Jewish youth in covert anti-terrorist operations in the then British-administered mandate of Palestine. Court martialled, he was found not guilty since no body could be produced and a witness failed to pick out Farran in an identity parade.

Out of the army, Farran, like many of his generation and background, drifted. He worked as a quarryman in Scotland, went to Africa and, in 1950, stood as the Conservative candidate for Dudley and Stourbridge against George Wigg, a future Labour minister who would later use Parliamentary Privilege to pursue the Conservative Minister John Profumo in what would be known as the Profumo Affair. In 1945, as a Lt Colonel, Profumo played a small but significant part in Operation HERRING.

Farran then emigrated to Alberta, Canada, where he farmed, worked as a journalist, starting the weekly *North Hill News* in 1954, and from 1961 to 1979 served in the provincial legislature. He established a foundation in the French Vosges, providing Franco-Canadian student exchanges. For this he was awarded the Legion d'Honneur in 1994 to add to the Croix de Guerre he had received from the French in 1946.

Cancer led to the loss of his larynx but he learned to speak through an incision in his throat. Roy Farran published a number of books which included two about his wartime experiences in the SAS – *Winged Dagger* and *Operation Tombola*.

Chapter 2

Ashore in Europe

We Polish soldiers, for our freedom and yours, have given our souls to God, our bodies to the soil of Italy and our hearts to Poland.

Inscription at the Polish Cemetery, Monte Cassino

Secret negotiations between the Allies and Italy had confirmed that the Italians wanted to surrender and planned to arrest Mussolini. The negotiations reached their conclusion on 3 September when a surrender document was signed in a simple ceremony in a tent in Sicily, General Bedell Smith of the US Army signing for the Allies and General Giuseppe Castellano for the Italians. However, they agreed that the surrender would remain a secret until 8 September.

On the day of the secret surrender, advanced formations of the Eighth Army began crossing the narrow Strait of Messina to the Italian mainland. On the same day the SRS launched the first operation on the European mainland against the port of Bagnara in southern Italy. Code-named BAYTOWN, it was to disrupt German lines of communication and expedite their retreat up the toe of Italy. It started off badly when one of the US Navy Landing Craft Infantry (LCI) broke down and the other ran aground. Men and equipment had to be transferred to four much smaller craft that then landed on the wrong side of the bay. Initially there was only light resistance, but the Germans reacted quickly with machine-gun and mortar fire. The SRS fought a series of actions for three days before Allied forces advancing from Reggio made contact with them. At one point during fighting in a gully north of the town, Mayne, leading from the front, picked up an abandoned German MP40 submachine gun and killed the three-man machine-gun crew who had held up the advance. German casualties were 47 with 35 prisoners, but the SRS suffered five killed and 17 wounded.

In Operation AVALANCHE, commanded by US General Mark Clark, the US VI Corps, under Major-General Ernest Dawley, and the British X Corps, under Lt General Richard McCreery, with British Commandos and US Rangers landed at Salerno on 9 September. As a jumping-off point for the capture of the city of Naples it was ideal, being only 40 miles to the south of that city. With Italy's withdrawal from the war, it was assumed that the landings would be unopposed.

A Jeep reconnaissance was undertaken by 2 SAS, who had landed at the southern port of Taranto, and by October it had pushed up to Termoli. 'A complication was the enthusiastic welcome which the Italians gave their liberators. Jeep crews were literally pelted with presents. The enthusiasm of the liberators soon wore off after they had been struck several times with grapes, walnuts, apricots and even, on one occasion, with wet fish.'[4]

Staff officers in the German Tenth Army under General Heinrich von Vietinghoff had made an assessment of likely Allied beachheads and reacted quickly to the Salerno landings. The 16th Panzer Division and 29th Panzergrenadier Division attacked, supported by the Luftwaffe, and put the Anglo-American force under such pressure that on 14 September, when the Germans put in a particularly intense attack, there was some debate about evacuation. Clark ordered every man who could carry a rifle to man the front line as it was pushed back two miles. Naval gunfire and the deployment of the Mediterranean strategic air force proved critical in defeating the German assaults. By 13 September General Mark Clark's Fifth Army had held tenaciously to the Salerno beachhead for four days but needed immediate assistance, otherwise they were in danger of being pushed back into the sea. Realising the precariousness of his situation, General Clark sent a message to Major-General Matthew Ridgway of the 82nd Airborne Division requesting a drop that night.

A plan was quickly drafted to drop the 504th PIR several miles from the embattled beachhead. Pathfinders jumped first, to mark the DZ with burning petrol in sand-filled cans arranged in the shape of a 'T'.

Meanwhile, on standby at airfields in Sicily, the 1st and 2nd Battalions of the 504th were alerted, issued parachutes, and loaded on aircraft without knowledge of their destination. Briefed aboard the aircraft, the men were told that the Fifth Army beachhead was in danger and they were needed to jump in behind friendly lines. Flying in columns of battalions, they exited over the flaming 'T' in the centre of the DZ. The regiment assembled quickly and within an hour had moved off towards the sounds of artillery and small-arms fire. The plan worked nearly flawlessly, with the exception of one company that landed ten miles off target. By dawn, all the units of the 504th were dug-in in defensive positions. The next night the 505th PIR, led by Colonel James Gavin, arrived in a similar manner.

For Corporal John Hunter with 2 Ptn, Company C, 1st Ranger Bn there was a grim memory of the effect of 4.2-inch mortars firing white phosphorus (WP) shells at a German position at Salerno. Officially WP was a smokescreen round that produced dense clouds of thick white smoke. In reality gobs of burning phosphorus were scattered randomly around the target area. It could not be extinguished and if it landed on human flesh would burn through to the bone. Hunter recalled;

'The 4.2s had clobbered the knoll with white phosphorus shells – it just tore up the trees and shrubs and tore up a platoon of Germans to pieces. That was a mess and one of the ugliest scenes I ever saw up there.'[5]

In the end the Eighth Army's XIII Corps and the 1st Airborne Division advancing from the south forced the Germans to break off the siege and retire northwards to the Gustav Line. On 10 September German troops occupied Rome and five days later the Fifth Army at the Salerno beachhead linked up with the Eighth Army near Vallo di Lucania.

Clark's experience at Salerno would colour his advice to General John Lucas prior to his landing at Anzio a year later.

Meanwhile, by ingenious signals intercepts and analysis, the Germans were able to locate Mussolini's secret prison. It was the Campo Imperiale, a remote winter-sports hotel in the Gran Sasso d'Italia area of the Abruzzo Apennines. Since the hotel was at 7,000 feet and could only be reached by a funicular railway, an airborne assault was the only viable rescue option. On 12 September 1943 108 paratroops of the 1st Company of the *Fallschirmjäger Lehrbataillon* commanded by Lt von Berlepsch and 26 *Waffen-SS* men commanded by *Hauptsturmführer* Otto Skorzeny[6] lifted off from an airfield in southern France in 12 DFS 230 troop-carrying gliders.

Eight of the gliders reached the rocky landing zone by the hotel, and for no German or Italian casualties Mussolini was rescued. Skorzeny greeted the Italian leader; 'Duce, the Führer has sent me. You are free!' and the deposed Italian leader replied, 'I knew my friend Adolf Hitler would not leave me in the lurch'. Paratroops had seized the funicular railway, but Skorzeny and the Duce made their exit in a hazardous flight in a two-seater Fieseler Fi 156 *Storch* (Stork) observation and liaison aircraft that took off from an improvised landing strip close to the hotel with not only the stocky Duce and pilot aboard but also Skorzeny crammed into the little cockpit.[7] It was the culmination of a superb *coup de main* operation that is still studied today.

On 13 September Mussolini was reunited with his wife and then made the journey by train to Bavaria where he met Hitler. On 25 September the Duce then declared a new *Repubblica Sociale Italiana* – Italian Socialist Republic (RSI) – also known as the Saló Republic, based at Gargnano on Lake Garda in northern Italy and allied to Nazi Germany. Hitler was shocked by how pale and gaunt Mussolini looked, but this was not helped by his clothing – a dark civilian overcoat and broad-brimmed dark hat – that he was wearing at the time of his rescue.

Following a rising that began in the city on 27 September, by 1 October Naples had become the first major city in southern Europe to be liberated. The city had been wrecked by systematic demolitions by the Germans and the harbour was choked with sunken ships and cranes. The city stank since both the sewerage system and the water supply had been demolished. Worse still, huge explosive charges fitted with time fuses had been concealed at key points and caused casualties and fear amongst both the Allies and the civilian population.

The campaign in southern Italy had cost British and US forces 12,000 casualties. As the German defences hardened along the Gustav Line south of Rome, the SAS collaborated with local resistance forces along the Adriatic coast and in the mountainous interior. In September 1943 Operations SPEEDWELL and JONQUIL were launched.

Following the Italian surrender the Germans were quick to secure the Allied PoWs who had been held in Italy and began to transfer them northwards to camps in Germany. However, many escaped and contacted friendly Italians. Operation JONQUIL was intended to collect these PoWs and evacuate them south. It called for four patrols from B Squadron 2 SAS to land between Ancona and Pescara on the Adriatic coast and guide PoWs to waiting navy-crewed civilian fishing vessels. The German counterattack at Termoli led to the boats being moved to Bari, and then it emerged that the Germans had banned Italian fishermen from sailing, thus removing a cover for the PoW evacuation. In addition the *Luftwaffe* had local air superiority and would have attacked the boats. When the boats did reach the coast, lack of ship-to-shore communications meant that the PoWs were not at the designated pick-up points, and later when they were, the boats had departed. Few men were evacuated and though

JONQUIL was not planned by the SAS, this did little to mitigate a feeling of frustration and disappointment.

Farran noted that '...most of the prisoners were so demoralised that they were not prepared to exert themselves. Contrary to popular opinion at home, many of them preferred to stay in comparative safety in an Italian farm than to risk their necks in a hazardous escape.'[8]

In contrast, Operation SPEEDWELL, launched on 7 September was not only a success but also a vindication of the tactics devised by David Stirling that emphasised small formations using stealth to attack high-value targets like parked aircraft or road and rail communications. However, it was a victory won at a grim price. With gallows humour Bill Stirling, David's brother, had said to Lt Greville-Bell just before he boarded the aircraft for the flight from North Africa, 'If you don't come back I'll have your sleeping bag'. All soldiers appreciate good kit, and the superior camel-hair sleeping bag had been coveted by Greville-Bell's brother officers.

Two seven-man patrols from 2 SAS under the command of Captains Pinckney (who had earlier led Operation CHESTNUT) and Dudgeon were parachuted into the La Spezia/Genoa area. After they had landed and split down into smaller parties they derailed several trains and cut the railway lines. The men suffered from a combination of bad diet and harsh weather but sustained their attacks over a period of 73 days before they returned to Allied lines. One man, Sergeant 'Tanky' Challenor, lived up to his robust nickname. Along with Wedderburn, a Scots officer with the unlikely nickname of 'Tojo', he stayed behind enemy lines for seven months and destroyed two trains and a tunnel on the Bologna-Genoa line, surviving bouts of malaria and two escapes following capture - one from hospital. Incredibly he was back in action in 1944-5 in Operation WALLACE.

Recalling his attack on the La Spezia-Bologna line, Challenor said, 'We laid our first charge on the outside line of the down-line to La Spezia. We then walked for a considerable distance and planted another charge on the up-line.' As they were strolling back towards the entrance to the tunnel, writes Gavin Mortimer in *Stirling's Men*, 'they heard a train approaching. Running and falling, we just cleared the tunnel mouth as the train thundered in,' said Challenor. There was a 'boom', then a 'crashing, smashing, banging, screeching sound.' As they climbed the mountainside, they heard the faint sound of a train coming down the up-line. There was a second 'boom', as Challenor and Wedderburn congratulated one another on their good fortune.'[9]

There were losses in SPEEDWELL, including Pinckney, whose death remains something of a mystery. His body was found after the war in Baigno in the Emilia Romagna region of northern Italy. It may have been that on landing he was dazed and in pain after aggravating a spinal injury he had suffered in CHESTNUT, wandered away and was caught by the enemy. However, whether he died from his injuries or was shot is unclear.

The death of the towering 6ft 3in Philip Pinckney was a loss to the SAS, since he was an expert on natural foods and 'delighted in collecting slugs, snails, grass-hoppers, and strange, unhealthy-looking leaves and insects which many men would dislike to touch, let alone eat. Few commanders have ever inspired such awe and terror in their men, who never knew what they might be required to swallow next.'[10]

Sergeant Bill Foster and Corporal James Shortall, who were part of the SPEEDWELL team, were captured around 25 September. They were briefly interrogated and then five days later taken to a disused pottery factory. The charge that they were members of a sabotage party and were to be shot on orders of the Führer was read out in English and German. Foster was taken to a lone tree where, according to Lance Sergeant Fritz Bost, a German eyewitness, he refused to be blindfolded but asked for a priest. Lt Emil Grether, the interpreter, snapped back, 'We have no time for that'. Foster was shot, cut down and Shortall, who had been held only yards away, was then led to the tree. Grether would tell a British war-crimes investigator of the young corporal, 'His impassive attitude is pictured in my memory.' Both men were buried in an unmarked grave in the grounds of the factory.

In October a similar fate befell 23-year-old Captain Pat Dudgeon and 21-year-old Bernie Brunt. They had managed to hijack a German vehicle but were stopped at a checkpoint. Like Shortall and Foster, they were dressed in their British Army uniforms. They were interrogated by the local divisional commander General von Ziehlberg but this produced no result. When the General told the two men that they would be shot Dudgeon replied that he wanted to be tried by a proper court, while Brunt remained silent. Later that day orders came down from a higher HQ that the men were to be shot. Posts were hammered into the ground and a firing squad of older, steadier men was selected. The two men were shot in succession. As a last wish Captain Dudgeon was given a brief moment to kneel and pray before he stood by the post. Brunt was then led out from the guardroom, twice refused a last wish, and was shot.

The lonely courage of these men, and many others in the SAS, only came to light after the war when British war-crimes investigators interviewed the German witnesses in 1947.

The German Gustav or Winter Line had been built in the Apennines running from the mouth of the Garigliano to a point south of Ortona. It was held by 15 divisions of the German Tenth Army. The battle for the Gustav Line and its key position, the sixth-century mountaintop Benedictine monastery of Monte Cassino, became an epic of endurance by the *Fallschirmjäger* who held the position.

On 3 October Operation DEVON took 207 men of the SRS with two Commandos of the Special Service Brigade to Termoli, a port on the Adriatic coast. They were tasked with capturing the town to assist the Eighth Army in its assault on the forward line of German defences known as the Termoli Line. They cleared the town and had contacted the advancing reconnaissance patrols of the Lancashire Fusiliers and 2 SAS, when on the morning of the 5th, as the SRS were about to re-embark, the Germans put in a massive counterattack. It was supported by Focke Wulf Fw 190 ground-attack fighters that bombed shipping in the harbour. After heavy fighting around the cemetery and astride the railway line, which lasted all day, the situation was saved by the arrival of Canadian M4 Sherman tanks and men of the Royal Irish Fusiliers.

At one point Captain Alex Muirhead, who had been ordered by Paddy Mayne to site his 3-inch mortars by the railway cutting, came under heavy shellfire. He had withdrawn the mortar line to a ditch behind a building when Mayne appeared and demanded why he had moved. 'Are you scared?' he shouted. Muirhead explained that he did not wish to expose his men to unnecessary risk and Mayne accepted this. 'Several officers had been 'Returned to Unit' by him because in Augusta, they had abandoned their position on the peninsula between the town and the mainland. But, explained Muirhead, 'Mayne always listened to reason'.

Farran recalled 'We were short of rations and the nights were bitterly cold. It was the only pure infantry battle I fought in the war and I never want to fight another'. After this operation the SRS withdrew from Italy.

On 9 October the Fifth Army closed on the River Volturno but skilful German demolitions and the appalling weather delayed the US forces, who were unable to advance until 24 October.

The disarmingly-named SAS Operations CANDYTUFT and SAXIFRAGE, launched on 27 October 1943, were commanded respectively by Roy Farran and Lt Grant Hibbert and were intended to cut the railway line between Ancona and Pescara. Four parties were landed by Motor Torpedo Boats (MTB), expertly crewed by men of the Italian Navy, and after six days behind enemy lines in heavy rain were able to cut the track in seventeen places as well as placing Hawkins mines [See Appendix 3] on the road.

Farran, describing the rain and mud, explained how prior to the attack his group took shelter in a small farm. 'There was a ramshackle cottage a short way off the track - a high, barn-like affair with a dilapidated roof and worm-eaten doors. It is an infallible rule that if one is seeking shelter, the poorest dwellings will always give refuge. Rich houses are unreliable.'[11] Throughout the operation Italian peasants offered shelter and hospitality to the little group.

Though two men were captured, the rest were safely evacuated by MTB.

On the front line, between 5-14 November, men of the British 56th and US 3rd Infantry Divisions closed up to the Bernhard Line in front of the Gustav Line and fought a tough battle to seize Monte Camino, which dominated the River Garigliano. On the eastern side of the Italian peninsula, the Eighth Army under Montgomery had reached the River Sangro on 8 November.

On 15 November Alexander ordered General Clark to halt his attacks south of the Garigliano. The men of the Fifth Army were exhausted and had suffered heavy casualties. Five days later the Eighth Army crossed the Sangro and on 28 November began the assault on the Gustav Line. Though the V Corps overran it at its eastern end, casualties mounted and the advance slowed.

On 2 December Clark resumed his attacks and in four days of heavy fighting the British 56th Division captured Monte Camino; two days later the US II Corps seized Monte la Difensa and Monte Maggiore. Opposite them the German Tenth Army withdrew to the Gustav Line. From 6 December to 17 December the US 143rd Infantry Regiment fought to drive German forces from the town of San Pietro. A company of *Panzergrenadiers* inflicted 1,500 casualties on the US forces, in a pointer of what was to come in street fighting in Italy.

In Operation SLEEPY LAD, launched on 18 December, several parties from 2 SAS were landed by the Royal Navy on the Italian Adriatic coast. Their orders were to cut road and rail links between Ancona and Pescara. The railway line was cut in several places and mines disrupted the road traffic. The Royal Navy failed to make the rendezvous at the close of the operation, but most of the men in SLEEPY LAD reached Allied lines after acquiring a local fishing boat.

Two days after Christmas, following fierce house-to-house fighting, the 1st Canadian Division captured Ortona. The Germans had prepared it for defence with considerable ingenuity, with bunkers under buildings that had been deliberately demolished for added protection and concealment. Italian towns were not laid out in a regular grid pattern, the stone walls were thick and there were very few doors or windows. The Canadians learned that the most effective way to clear a house was to break in on the top floor and work downwards, noting that 'for every German killed going up the stairs it cost us one of our own men.' Heavy casualties and the onset of winter slowed the advance of the Eighth Army.

Montgomery relinquished his command to General Sir Oliver Leese on 8 January and returned to Britain to join the senior command group for Operation OVERLORD, the invasion of Normandy planned for summer 1944.

On 17 January the Fifth Army attacked across the River Garigliano and the British X Corps, commanded by General Richard McCreery, established bridgeheads. The US II Corps attacked on 20 January and the US 34th Infantry Division succeeded in getting across the Rapido but was halted below Monte Cassino. The 36th Division was repulsed as it attempted to cross the swollen river, suffering heavy casualties.

On 24 January tough North African troops of the *Corps Expeditionnaire Français* (French Expeditionary Corps) attacked across the Rapido north of Monte Cassino but were stopped short of the abbey by fierce German counterattacks.

After considerable discussion among the Allied commanders, the USAAF was ordered to bomb the monastery of Monte Cassino. In a daylight raid 142 B-17s, B-25s and B-26s dumped 453 tons of bombs onto the buildings. The Allies were convinced that the Germans were at the least using its commanding position for artillery observation posts and at worst had fortified it. Once the building had been reduced to ruins the German paratroops moved in and fortified them. Their stubborn defence earned them a unique tribute from Hitler, who would assert that they were harder than the *Waffen-SS*. The New Zealanders and men of the 4th Infantry Division who attacked following the bombing were halted by stubborn German resistance.

The Germans made considerable propaganda mileage out of the destruction of the Benedictine monastery, which had a long and distinguished history. Founded in 529 AD by St Benedict of Nursia on the site of an Apollonian temple, it became the home of the Benedictine Order and was for many centuries the leading monastery in western Europe. It was destroyed by Lombards in 590, by Saracens in 884 and by an earthquake in 1349, and rebuilt each time. During the 11th and 12th centuries it became a centre of learning, particularly in the field of medicine. The famous Salerno medical school was established by monks from Monte Cassino. In 1866, when monasticism was abolished in Italy, Monte Cassino was made a national monument. In pre-war staff exercises Italian officers had identified it and the surrounding mountains as the key defensive area blocking an approach to Rome from the south. The Germans were quick to realise this as well in 1943. After the war an exact copy of the monastery was rebuilt on the site by German PoWs held in Italy.

In 1944 the Germans and had taken the precaution of removing over 70,000 books and 1,200 original documents to safety in the Vatican. The operation was undertaken by Lt Colonel Julius Schlegel of the *Hermann Göring Panzer Division* who as an art lover realised that the works were at risk. The Bishop and Abbot of Monte Cassino, Gregorius Diamare, presented Schlegel with an illuminated manuscript to express his gratitude and thanks. Allied propaganda suggested that Schlegel had looted the monastery and after the war Field Marshal Alexander intervened to confirm the monks' assertion that the art treasures had been saved and not stolen. However, elsewhere in Italy art treasures and buildings were vandalised or destroyed as revenge for Italy's perfidy in joining the Allies.

Almost a month after the first air attacks on the monastery, renewed attacks by the IV Indian Corps and the New Zealand 6th Infantry Brigade were preceded by four hours of bombardment. Some 755 bombers attacked – two aircraft for every 350 German paratroopers or five tons of high explosive for each soldier. The air attacks were backed by an artillery bombardment in which 195,969 shells were fired into the town and defences of the monastery. Incredibly, the Germans hung on, though Gurkha soldiers achieved the deepest penetration, reaching the exposed position of Point 435 or 'Hangman's Hill' only 440 yds from the monastery. The Gurkhas, Essex Regiment and Rajput Rifles were to hang on here under German fire, supplied only by night until they were finally evacuated on 25 March.

The fighting had cost the 2nd New Zealand Division 63 officers and over 800 men killed, wounded or missing from an all-volunteer army drawn from the small island community. The 4th Indian Division had lost 1,000 men and 65 officers.

Kesselring's tactical genius was amply demonstrated on 22 January 1944. In Operation SHINGLE, an attempt to outflank the Gustav Line was made by the US VI Corps, composed of the US 3rd and British 1st Infantry Division, who landed on a 15-mile stretch of Italian beach near the pre-war resort towns of Anzio and Nettuno.

The area was defended by two battalions and the Allies under US General John P. Lucas achieved the dream of all commanders – complete tactical surprise. However, because of lack of clarity in his orders and indicators from ULTRA that the Germans would counterattack, Lucas did not exploit his advantage and Kesselring ordered the Fourteenth Army into the area, setting in motion Operation RICHARD, the contingency plan to counter an Allied amphibious attack. In the weeks that followed, ULTRA intelligence that had stifled Lucas' initiative would eventually save the beachhead. The ability to decode mechanically-encrypted German radio signals that had been given the classification 'Ultra Secret' by the Allies would allow the commanders on the beachhead to anticipate German attacks. Raw ULTRA intelligence was available only at Army commander level. Officers further down the chain of command received a cover story to explain how the intelligence had been acquired – this might be a captured map, aerial reconnaissance flight or interrogation of a captured senior German officer, all designed to protect the fact that the Allies had broken the German codes.

However, when Churchill, who was an enthusiastic advocate of the operation, cabled Alexander, 'Am glad you are pegging out claims rather than digging in,' he had no inkling of how disastrously the operation would shape up. In fact Clark, who was aware of RICHARD through ULTRA intercepts, had warned Lucas 'not to stick his neck out' and so Lucas set up his HQ in a wine cellar in the port and concentrated on building up his strength on the beachhead rather than pushing inland.

Sergeant Burgess Scott, a correspondent for the US Army weekly magazine *Yank* who landed in the first wave at Anzio, was an acute observer.

'From the debris littering the beach, it's quite evident that Anzio and Nettuno were, in days past, the resort towns the guidebooks make them out to be. The Tyrrhenian Sea's mild surf tosses up strips of faded canvas and broken sticks that once were bright beach chairs; on the sand are battered hulls of runabouts and sailboats; the bathing beaches are littered with Italian suntan lotion bottles.'But more and more the sea washes up equipment that wasn't made for peacetime pleasure but for war. And sometimes what looked like a piece of driftwood turns out to be a corpse.'[12]

In January a series of SAS raids were launched to take the pressure off the Allied beachhead. The men of Operation MAPLE were dropped by parachute on the night of 7 January to attack railway links north of Rome. It would prove a partial success. The mission was split into two; 'Thistledown', four groups of four men under Lt David Worcester, and 'Driftwood', made up of eight men in two groups commanded by Captain Gunston. 'Thistledown' was to cut the road and railway links between Terni and Orvieto, while 'Driftwood' would cut the track between Urbino-Fabriciano and Ancona-Rimini. 'Thistledown' successfully attacked its targets, destroying 25 vehicles in ten days, but all the patrols were subsequently captured. No one from 'Driftwood' arrived at the beach pick-up point and their fate is unknown. There are reports of the group launching a 22-foot boat south of Porto San Giorgio; they may have drowned, been shot up by Allied aircraft or captured and shot. Plans to reinforce MAPLE were cancelled because of severe weather and the troops tasked for this mission were assigned to Operation BAOBAB.

In Operation POMEGRANATE on 12 January a team of four men from 2 SAS under command of Major Widdrington and Lt Hughes parachuted into northern Italy near Perugia. They were tasked with attacking an airfield at San Egidio from which German reconnaissance aircraft were operating. It was the only airfield attack of the campaign. As the party approached the target they were challenged by a sentry and scattered. The troopers made their way back to Allied lines, where they were RTU'd for failing to engage the enemy. The two officers waited until the night of January 17 when they penetrated the airfield and seven aircraft were attacked with Lewes blast incendiary bombs. Tragically Widdrington was killed afterwards as he was disarming unused bombs and Hughes was wounded. While he was being treated in a German hospital Hughes escaped and made his way back to Allied lines in March.

In BAOBAB on 30 January a small group from 2 SAS

under Captain Grant Hibbert landed on the Italian Adriatic coast between Pesaro and Fan, tasked with the demolition of a railway bridge. Interestingly the operation resembled modern Special Forces attacks with an advanced party providing 'feet on the ground' before the main group arrived. In this case Lt Laws and Signalman Dowell had landed by canoe north of the objective, laid up in a cave and reconnoitred the bridge, which they found to be heavily patrolled by the Italian Carabinieri. They signalled that the target should not be attacked until after 23.00 hours. They identified a building close to the bridge as the guardroom for the 19 men of the Carabiniere garrison and Dowell quietly placed a large rock against the door, so blocking them inside the house. The main party of eight men landed and found that the bridge was now unguarded, and so 160 lbs of plastic explosives was placed against the buttresses. The charges were on a ten-minute fuse, but as the men sprinted for the beach they could hear the Carabinieri struggling to push open the door of their guardroom. To discourage them Corporal McGuire fired a burst through the door with his sub-machine gun and the men made off to their craft. As they paddled out to rendezvous with the 1,730-ton destroyer HMS *Troubridge* they came under heavy but inaccurate fire. Ten minutes had now elapsed and there had been no explosion – to the horror of the group Hibbert said that they would have to return to finish the task. Two minutes later, as the craft were starting back to the alert and hostile shore, there was an explosion which in the after-action report 'resembled the petals of an orange flower opening, while fragments of incandescent material were thrown through the air'. The damage to the bridge took a week to repair.

On 29 January the VI Corps attempted to break out of the Anzio beachhead. The 3rd Division advanced towards Cisterna and the 1st towards Albano in the Alban Hills but both attacks were held by the German Fourteenth Army. Two days later US Rangers waded four miles through flooded drainage ditches in the dark to attack the village of Cisterna but were detected at the last moment; only six men survived the brutal weight of fire from German tanks and infantry.

On the night of 29-30 January the British 24 Guards Brigade attacked the village of Carroceto, where the 29th *Panzergrenadier Regiment* was dug in, and in the fighting the British suffered heavy casualties. On 3 February the Germans counterattacked, hitting the British 1st Division and driving it back in nine days of savage fighting. The Germans were, however, exhausted, having suffered heavy casualties, and paused for four days.

Thirteen days later the I *Fallschirm Korps* under General Schlemm and the *LXXVI Panzer Korps* (General Herr) a total of ten divisions among which was the élite *Panzerdivision Herman Göring*, had been assembled around the 'Anzio abscess', as Hitler called the besieged beachhead. Von Mackensen launched a fierce attack against the battered British sector. Yelling the battle cries of the victory years of World War 1, German infantry supported by tanks crashed into the 1st Division and there was a real danger that the beachhead would be split in two. Only the massive firepower of ships, artillery and bombers halted the attack at Carroceto Creek.

Sapper Stanley Fennell of 23rd Field Company, Royal Engineers recalled encounters with the US Army and later with his enemies.

'The Yankees went rolling past in their Shermans, which brewed up [caught fire and exploded] very easily. They used to wave at us, throw us tins of food. If they were going into action, they wanted to get rid of it anyway. We used to look at them and say 'You poor devils!' – and they used to look down at us, clearing mines, and say 'Wouldn't do that for a fortune.'

When I was captured, the Germans treated us very reasonably – they kept saying, 'We are the frontswine. You are the frontswine.' And we laughed. They seemed to have a very simple kind of humour – very straightforward.'[13]

In North West Europe the operation in Italy was closely followed by the German staff officers since it was seen as a testing ground for tactics that might be employed when the Allies launched the Second Front. It appeared that an aggressive counter attack of the beachhead had failed.

On 22 February Lucas was replaced by the more combative General Lucian Truscott Jr as commander at Anzio.[14] A week later he received a baptism of fire when the US 3rd Division came under attack by four divisions. Once again air power and artillery saved the Allies and on 3 March von Mackensen called a halt to attacks.

On 23 May, following stalemate and siege, the US VI Corps broke out of the Anzio beachhead. German resistance was fierce but a day later the Allies cut Route 7, creating a wedge between the 10th and 14th Armies. On 25 May the US II and VI Corps linked up on Route 7, marking the end of the four-month isolation of the Anzio beachhead that had in places taken on the character of the trenches of World War 1.

During the Anzio campaign the Allied VI Corps had suffered over 29,200 casualties (4,400 killed, 18,000 wounded, 6,800 prisoners or missing). Two-thirds of these losses, amounting to 17 percent of VI Corps' effective strength, were inflicted between the initial landings and the end of the German counter-offensive on 4 March . German combat losses were estimated at 27,500 (5,500 killed, 17,500 wounded, and 4,500 prisoners or missing) – figures very similar to those of the Allies.

Among the German soldiers killed at Anzio was a young officer, Alexander Paulus, the son of Field Marshal Paulus who with the *6th Army* had surrendered to Soviet forces at Stalingrad a year earlier and was now in captivity in the Soviet Union.

The final battle for the Gustav Line, Operation DIADEM, opened on 13 May when 2,000 guns bombarded the German positions and 3,000 aircraft flew sorties against the front line and depth positions. The Polish II Corps isolated the Monastery as the British crossed the River Liri west of Cassino to cut Route 6 west of the town and the US and French Corps attacked south of the river. The tough French Goumiers (Moroccan mountain troops) of General Alphonse Juin's *Corps Expeditionnaire Français* took Monte Faito, where the German 71st Division had followed Hitler's orders and fought with no plan for withdrawal. The 8th Indian and 4th British crossed the fast-flowing River Rapido where they hit well-sited bunkers and defences. The Poles attacked the monastery from the east and north.

On May 18 the red-and-white Polish flag was hoisted over the ruins of the monastery of Monte Cassino. The Polish II Corps under General Wladyslaw Anders had been losing 30 men a day in the fighting before the main assault, in which it lost a fifth of its strength. In the first 90 minutes of the final battle communications broke down and the Poles were forced to withdraw. They then went back and, supported by 200 air strikes, stormed into the ruined monastery.

The four-month battle for Monte Cassino had cost the Allies 21,000 casualties including 4,100 killed. German losses were comparable.

A combination of Kesselring's tactical skill and General Clark's ambition to see the US Fifth Army liberate Rome allowed the German Tenth Army to evade encirclement after the capture of Cassino. Rome had been declared an 'Open City' by Kesselring on 4 June, with German troops ordered to withdraw and not to fight in the streets.

Clark entered the city on June 5, 1944. It was a moment he savoured. He loathed the British so it was an opportunity to score points. The American general was photographed relaxing in a Jeep being driven around the city and visiting the major monuments. Perhaps Clark was not a classicist and did not know that in ancient Rome, when the Senate granted a general a triumphal entry into the capital with a parade of prisoners and booty, a slave was required to stand beside him in the chariot. At intervals he would whisper in the general's ear:

'All glory is fleeting...'

Within twenty-four hours of Clark's entry into Rome Operation OVERLORD, the Allied landings in Normandy, had been launched. Now D-Day became the big story on radio and grabbed the headlines in the newspapers in the United States and Great Britain. Clark and the Fifth Army had become yesterday's news.

Following the fall of Rome the German forces in Italy fell back on the intermediate Albert Line that ran from Grosseto on the west coast, past the historic battleground of Lake Trasimene to the River Chienti and the Adriatic east coast.

This was one of a series of defensive switch lines including the Hitler Line until, for propaganda and morale reasons, the name was changed to the Caesar Line – reports of an Allied breakthrough of the Hitler Line would not have read well in Germany or among the neutral countries. The Germans were then able to join other forces on the formidable 10-mile-deep Gothic Line that ran from La Spezia on the west coast to the Adriatic between Pesaro and Cattolica. By June 16 they were consolidated in their new positions.

As early as 1 June 1944 Kesselring had decided to make a stand on the line of the northern Apennines. He knew that he would need until autumn to prepare the positions and so it was necessary to fight a series of delaying actions through the summer. Italy lent itself to defensive fighting since it is a narrow peninsula with steep mountains, narrow winding roads, deep river valleys and grim winter weather that produced ribald jokes about the tourist brochures' descriptions of 'Sunny Italy'.

In addition to the Albert Line the Germans had established blocking positions on the main roads from Rome to Sienna and Perugia to Arezzo. North of these positions they established the Arno Line along the valley of the River Arno. In Florence German engineers blew up every bridge across the Arno but spared the historic Ponte Vecchio; even so, they fired charges that cratered its approaches and then planted *S Minen* anti-personnel mines in the rubble. Like Rome, Hitler had ordered that the city not be contested and though there was fighting around Florence, it was spared the grim fate of house-to-house combat. However, the city was littered with lethal hazards.

A British report on German booby-trapping operations in Florence noted; 'Rubble from demolitions was trapped with shrapnel and anti-tank mines, some being set as anti-personnel booby traps with pull switches and trip wires. The presence of other metal in the rubble added to the difficulty of detection with either mine detectors or prodders... Booby traps were skilfully laid, many types of explosives and mines used. Trip wires were cleverly concealed by leaves and the use of coloured wire out of doors, and by scattered clothing, documents, etc indoors. Many shutters, door handles, floors and pieces of furniture were efficiently trapped...'[15]

The Germans might have been masters of the delaying tactics of demolitions, booby traps and minefields; however, they had to contend with Allied air attacks and the constant threat of ambush by partisans. While medium bombers struck road and rail communications, fighters attacked convoys and vehicles. Night-time was no cover against the partisans, who, based in the Apennines, attacked isolated vehicles and small groups of troops. The local resistance also gave invaluable help recovering Allied aircrew shot down behind enemy lines.

In the dusty dawn of 25 August 1944 British, Canadian and Polish troops launched the first probing attacks on the Gothic Line, the defences based on the Apennines and the rivers Foglia and Pesaro. Alexander was convinced that the

Gothic Line could be quickly forced and had the benefit of ULTRA intelligence about German dispositions. However it was not until 12 September that the battle began in earnest.

The first move was Operation OLIVE, an attack on the right flank along the Adriatic coast by the three corps, the British V, Canadian I and the Polish II. By 29 August they had reached the Foglia and the Gothic Line. A day later the Canadians managed to break through the defences and reached the River Conca, while the British were held in front of Clemente. Kesselring moved reinforcements to block these moves and they and heavy autumn rain brought the attacks to a halt.

On 12 September the US II and British XIII Corps were launched against the centre of the Gothic Line high on the Apennines. They were attacking at the junction between the German 10th and 14th Armies just east of the Il Giorgio Pass. On the west coast the US IV Corps kept the pressure on the Germans and prevented reinforcements moving to the mountains. In the Apennines the Americans became involved in a desperate fight for the two peaks, Montecelli and Monte Altuzzo, that dominated Il Giorgio Pass; the features were not secured until 17 September.

On the coast the British Eighth Army resumed its attacks on the night of September 12, captured Cariano and looked close to a major breakthrough. However, heavy autumn rains prevented tanks from being brought forward and the advance was not resumed until a day later. A week's hard fighting followed and the Germans were forced back to the Rimini Line.

Up in the mountains American troops captured Fiorenzuola on 21 September, which presented Kesselring with the threat that they might break through to Route 9, the 'Via Emilia', and sever his east-west link. On the right flank, the Eighth Army front, the Greek Brigade took Rimini and the Canadians crossed the River Marecchia. The next obstacle was the River Po, about 62 miles to the north; however, there were nine rivers to be assaulted before the Eighth Army reached this obstacle.

On 24 September General Clark's forces began to push towards Bologna. The German Army had fought hard but three days later it appeared that the Allies were through the Gothic Line.

By 7 October the Eighth Army began to attack towards the River Rubicon and in five days were across this symbolic river. General Sir Henry Maitland Wilson, the Allied Mediterranean C-in-C, sent congratulations saying 'I hope that the crossing of the Rubicon will lead, as with a famous commander in the past, to a decisive victory and the destruction of Kesselring's army'.

At the end of October the Fifth Army closed down its offensive in the mountains. In one month it had suffered 15,700 casualties and was still not out of the mountains.

On 24 November Clark handed command of the Fifth Army to General Truscott and succeeded Alexander as the C-in-C of the Fifteenth Army Group and commander of Allied ground forces in Italy. Alexander was promoted to Supreme Allied Commander in the Mediterranean.

On the coast the advance continued and Canadian troops captured Ravenna on 5 December. The bald facts of the liberation of this historic town, famous for its architecture and art treasures, conceal a fascinating story of co-operation between the United States Office of Strategic Services (OSS), the Communist partisans of the 28th Garibaldi Brigade, the 1st Canadian Division and Popski's Private Army.

Popski's Private Army, or more correctly, No 1 Demolition Squadron PPA, took its name from its multi-lingual and widely travelled commanding officer Major (later Colonel) Vladimir Peniakov, a Belgian of Russian ancestry. PPA was one of the 'Private Armies' that had been nurtured by the British during the campaign in North Africa. In Africa it had been tasked with the destruction of fuel stocks vital for the *Afrika Korps*. In Italy PPA had become a Jeep-mounted reconnaissance force; the Browning HMGs on the Jeeps would provide mobile heavy fire support for the lightly-equipped Partisans.

Ravenna was held by three German infantry divisions; about 2,500 men supported by tanks and Flak 8.8-cm guns that could be used either as AA guns or lethal anti-tank guns. In conventional planning, to defeat such a strong defence would necessitate a heavy air and land bombardment before ground troops were committed. However, Arrigo Boldrini, the skinny 29-year-old commander of the 28th Garibaldi Brigade, whose tactical skill had earned him the *nom de guerre* of Bulow after the Prussian general of the Napoleonic Wars, believed that the city could be taken without such a destructive conventional assault. Using his OSS liaison officer's radio link, he contacted the Eighth Army HQ at Cattolica and proposed a daring plan. The 1st Canadian Division were tasked with organising a submarine to pick up Bulow but instead of waiting, the young Italian and some of his staff were rowed by a dozen fishermen 30 miles down the coast to the

Canadian HQ at Cervia. At Cervia he met Colonel Tiehle of the OSS, who passed Bulow up the line to the Eighth Army HQ. Here, living up to his code name and using clearly marked operational maps, the Italian partisan leader gave a detailed presentation of his plan to the commander of the Eighth Army the gaunt, modest 47-year-old cavalry officer General Sir Richard L. McCreery, along with his chief of staff and chief of operations. McCreery could see a good plan and had the courage to endorse an original but highly risky operation to capture the city. It was a pointer to the future.

Bulow explained to the British officers that his partisans would launch a surprise attack on the rear of Ravenna while his Garavini detachment led in the Allied attack from the south and PPA came in from the east. More partisans would attack across the flatland north of Ravenna. Meanwhile, the townspeople, led by clandestine action groups in neighbouring cities, would harass the Germans' flank along their only route of escape.

Two days later, with McCreery's blessing, Bulow, accompanied by an official Eighth Army observer, Captain Healy of the Canadian Army, was back with his partisans in the marshland north of Ravenna. On the night of 29 November Bulow, who had split his forces into three sections, began moving them along pre-arranged routes where the farmers had been warned to lock up their dogs but leave their doors unlocked in case the partisans needed to take refuge. Bulow's plan called for a concentration of 650 partisans in the valley north of Ravenna, and of 1,250 more near the Reno River. Supported by local action squads from Alfonsine and Ravenna, they would be armed by OSS parachute drops. On 3 December, the Eighth Army transmitted a signal to Bulow confirming a parachute drop that night. The next message Bulow received over the OSS radio was simple and direct: 'ATTACK. GOOD LUCK!'

A day later, at 03.00 hours, 823 partisans of the 28th Garibaldi Brigade, armed with one 47mm gun, four mortars, and a dozen heavy machine-guns set off along sandy footpaths to their jumping-off positions to attack the heavily armed, dug-in German troops protecting Ravenna. Two and a half hours later the attack went in and Bulow's men took the enemy by surprise. All across the area north of Ravenna partisan units attacked German strong points, many of which surrendered after finding themselves surrounded. As Bulow had predicted, the Germans began pulling their forces out of Ravenna to counterattack the partisans. At that point, the Canadian 12th Royal Lancers, led by one of Bulow's detachments, entered the city from the south as Popski's men roared in from the east to find the Germans fleeing. With the exception of one section of blown aqueduct, the city had been captured intact. At 16.30 hours, the OSS radio transmitted a succinct message: 'British in Ravenna. Regards to all.'

The Germans, again as Bulow predicted, evacuated along the road to Ferrara and their exposed flanks came under attack from the partisans who were in position. Arrigo Boldrini, who was personally decorated with the *Medaglia d'oro al Valore Militare*, the Gold Medal for Military Valour (MOVM), Italy's highest award for bravery,[16] by General McCreery, obtained official permission from the Eighth Army for his 800-man brigade to join the line as a regular fighting unit under his command, armed and equipped by the Allies.

Fighting slowed down with the onset of winter and the Eighth Army reached the line of the River Senio south of Lake Comacchio by 29 December.

For Private William Wright of the Royal Irish Fusiliers, a veteran of North Africa, Sicily and Cassino, the bitter weather and brutalising experience of frontline combat would remain a lasting memory – however, there was one particularly grim experience that he would remember. 'There was a wine tank near us, in the Po valley. It was about 15 feet high, and it stood out in the yard of a deserted farmhouse. By this time we were virtually alcoholics - every time we went out, a sniper would have a go at the barrel and we would go out and get the wine under cover of darkness. It was rough, but good. One night, the blinking wine stopped – just like that. By this time, I had a stripe – I was a Lance Corporal, so I could give orders. I said to this bloke 'Nip up and find out what's happened'. He came back and said 'You're not going to like this. There's an old woman's body in there.'[17]

Kesselring knew that the valleys of the Rivers Po and Adige could be held as intermediate defence lines as his forces fell back to strong positions in the southern Alps. Both he and Alexander knew that it would be hard to dislodge German forces in the mountains. With short supply lines and strong positions they could fight for months. The British general knew that it was critical therefore to keep the pressure on the Germans. In Berlin Hitler refused Kesselring permission to withdraw and insisted that Army Group C should stand and fight. It was the same irrational passion not to give ground that in 1945 would see German armies destroyed on the west bank of the Rhine.

4 Philip Warner, *The Special Air Service*

5 *Forgotten Voices of the Second World War*, Max Arthur, Ebury Press, London, 2004

6 Born in Vienna on 12 June 1908, Otto Skorzeny was a striking figure nearly two metres (6ft 6in) tall. He had originally trained as an engineer and joined the Freikorps and the NSDAP in 1930. In the years before the war he worked as the business manager for a building contractor. In 1939 he joined the SS 'Leibstandarte Adolf Hitler' and in 1940 the *Waffen-SS* Division 'Das Reich' serving on the Eastern Front. On 12 September 1943 he led the glider-borne raid that liberated Mussolini. He assisted in putting down the attempt to seize Berlin following the July Plot of 1944. In October 1944 he led a raid to kidnap the son of the Hungarian Regent, Admiral Miklós Horthy, and in this way Germany was able to pressurise the Hungarians to stay in the war up to 1945. In December 1944, in Operation *Greif*, he commanded a force of English-speaking German soldiers who penetrated American lines dressed in US Army uniforms as part of the Ardennes offensive. Many of these men were caught and subsequently shot. After the war Skorzeny was tried by an American military court and acquitted. He fled from an internment camp in Darmstadt in 1948 and, based in Spain and Ireland, worked to assist former *Waffen-SS* members escape from Germany. He died in Madrid on July 5, 1975.

7 The Fieseler Fi 156 *Storch* was a two-seat aircraft with a 240 hp Argus As 10c-3 8-cylinder inverted Vee piston engine that produced a maximum speed of 175 kph and a range of 385 km. It first flew in 1936 and was immediately recognised as a unique aircraft. With little more than a slight breeze to give lift it could take off in 60 metres and land in one third of that distance.

8 *Winged Dagger*, Roy Farran

9 *Stirling's Men*, Gavin Mortimer

10 Warner

11 *Winged Dagger*

12 *Yank, the Army Weekly*, Steve Kluger

13 *Forgotten Voices of the Second World War*

14 Truscott, a hard-driving cavalryman whose distinctive voice had earned him the nickname 'Old Gravel Guts' had commanded the US 3rd Infantry Division through campaigns in Sicily and southern Italy. After the Anzio breakout in May, he led the VI Corps through to Rome, then in the invasion of southern France (Operation ANVIL-DRAGOON), and finally in pursuit of German forces in the Rhone Valley and northward. In 1945 in Italy he commanded the US Fifth Army with flair and distinction.

15 Field Engineering and Mine Warfare Pamphlet No 7, Booby Traps 1952

16 The Gold Medal of Military Valour (*Medaglia d'oro al Valore Militare*) (MOVM) is one of the oldest gallantry awards in the world. Established on 21 May 1793 by King Victor Emanuel III of Sardinia '....per bassi ufficiali e soldati che avevano fatto azioni di segnalato valore in guerra' – for deeds of outstanding gallantry in war by junior officers and soldiers. The Silver Medal for Military Valour (MAVM) is awarded to courageous actions that are just below the criteria for the MOVM.

17 *The War Years 1939-1945: Eyewitness Accounts*, Marshall Cavendish Books

Chapter 3

Italy Divided

I offer neither pay, nor quarters, nor food: I offer only hunger,
thirst, forced marches, battle and death. Let him who loves his
country with his heart, and not merely with his lips, follow me.
Giuseppe Garibaldi to his troops besieged in Rome,
1849

The two years that followed the Italian surrender on 9
September 1943 would see the already impoverished country
turned into a battleground and torn apart in a civil war – Italian
Fascists and some units of the Italian Army sided with the
Germans, while other formations joined the Allies. Some
Italian soldiers who had been taken prisoner by the Germans
were murdered. Brutal Fascist militia the *Brigata Nere* (also
known as the *Banda Nere*) – the Black Brigades – would hunt
their fellow nationals who had become partisans, destroying
the villages they believed had harboured them. As the tide of
war moved progressively against Germany, the cruelty of both
the Germans and Fascist troops increased. SAS troops
attached to the partisans would see terrible vengeance being
taken against Fascists and the ultimate partisan revenge
would be the death of Mussolini and the humiliating
treatment of his body in Milan.

On 25 July 1943 King Victor Emmanuel III, with the
backing of the Fascist Grand Council, had ordered

Mussolini to resign as leader of Italy. The King told Mussolini bluntly, 'My dear Duce... my soldiers don't want to fight any more... at this moment, you are the most hated man in Italy.'

On 13 October Marshal Pietro Badoglio, the first premier of the new post-Fascist Italy, declared war on Germany and announced the formation of an Italian Army to fight alongside Allied forces in Italy. In his Order of the Day, he told the men of this new army: 'You represent the true Italy. It is your destiny to liberate our country and drive the aggressor from our homeland. Show yourselves worthy of the great task that lies before you. We are proud of you.' In a letter to General Eisenhower he wrote, 'By this act, all ties with the dreadful past are broken, and my government will be proud to be able to march with you on to the inevitable victory.'

The Italian Co-Belligerent Army had actually been in existence since 28 September, when in accordance with Royal Army Order 70/V, the Italian First Motorised Combat Group (*1 Raggruppamento Motorizzato*) was formed at tented reorganisation camps near Lecce. It had a strength of 295 officers and 5,387 men. The unit included elements of two divisions of the old Italian *Regio Esercito* - Royal Army, the 18th Infantry Division '*Messina*' and the 58th Infantry Division '*Legnano*.'

It first saw action at Monte Lungo in the Cassino sector where it fought hard but suffered heavy casualties and this determination convinced Allied commanders that the Co-Belligerent Army was a reliable and effective force. Following operations with the US Fifth Army it was reorganised and transferred to the Polish II Corps part of the British Eighth Army.

By April 1944 the flood of volunteers to the Combat Group had brought its strength to 22,000 and it was renamed the *Corpo Italiano di Liberazione*, or CIL – the Italian Liberation Corps – and organised into two new divisions, the *'Nembo'* and the *'Utili.'* *Utili* was formed around the First Motorized Combat Group and was named after its commander, General Umberto Utili and *Nembo* around the old Royal Army's parachute division of the same name.

The Italians had pioneered airborne forces, the first Italian paratroop units being formed in 1938, and the first Military Parachute school was established at Castel Benito, near Tripoli in what was then the Italian colony of Libya.

The first troops trained were part of the Royal Colonial Corps, the Libyan Parachute Bn and the 1st National Libyan Parachute Bn. To these were added the first battalions from the Italian Army and the first of three Carabinieri Parachute Battalions was formed.

Later, in mainland Italy, staff from Castel Benito set up the Parachute training school at Tarquina which formed the core of the future *Folgore* – Lightning Bolt Division. A second school was opened at Viterbo and a new division, the *Nembo* – Nimbus or Thunder Cloud – was formed. A third, the 183rd Parachute Division *Ciclone* – Cyclone – was planned but cancelled following the Armistice in 1943.

The 185th *Folgore* Parachute Division had been raised and trained in 1941 for Operation HERCULES, the assault on the strategic British-held island of Malta. When HERCULES was cancelled it was sent to North Africa to fight as conventional infantry. As an airborne formation it was ill-equipped for this role, with limited transport and heavy support weapons and crucially, only light 47/32 anti-tank guns. As part of the X Corps, commanded by General

Gioda, it fought with distinction at the Second Battle of El Alamein against the 44th Division and the veteran 7th Armoured Division. Low on water and under heavy fire the men of *Folgore* withdrew from the El Alamein front at 02.00 hours on 3 November 1942, carrying their anti-tank weapons. Three days later at 14.35 hours what was left of the division was captured by the British. The Italian paratroops had exhausted their ammunition and destroyed their weapons, but refused to raise their hands in surrender or show the white flag. Many felt that they had been abandoned by their German allies who were intent on saving themselves and withdrawing westwards.

General Hughes, commanding the 44th Division, paid tribute to the courage and stamina of the Italian paratroops. 'I wish to say that in all my life I have never encountered soldiers like those of the *Folgore*.' Today the fight put up at El Alamein is celebrated by the officers and men of the modern *Folgore* in a ceremony on 23 October.

The 184th *Nembo* Parachute Division was formed in 1942. It was first employed in the Spring of 1943 against Yugoslav partisans operating near Gorizia. In June 1943, the 184th and 183rd Regiments were sent to Sardinia where the main Allied landing was expected while the 185th was deployed to Calabria.

When the Allies landed in Sicily in July 1943, the 185th was dispatched to fight the invaders; however, the Allies had gained a secure lodgement and so *Folgore* now fought to protect the withdrawal of the Italo-German forces to the mainland. But once in Calabria there was no rest for the weary; they continued to engage in furious fighting in the Aspromonte mountains, delaying the Eighth Army's advance.

Following the Armistice, battalions of the *Nembo* chose

sides according to the personal loyalty of the commanding officer and/or the leadership the men recognised, which was either the King or Mussolini. Conventional units in the Italian Army that lacked clear leadership and suffered from low morale simply disintegrated – officers and men packed their bags and headed for home. However, the airborne forces were an élite; morale remained intact as did unit cohesion – even if loyalties were divided. Most of 3rd Bn *Nembo* decided to keep fighting with the Germans, as did the 12th, both eventually joining with the I *Fallschirm Korps* deployed around Rome. Other Parachute units of the *Regio Esercito* such as *Ciclone* and X *Arditi*, and parachute units of the *Regia Marina* and *Aeronautica* - Royal Navy and Air Force such as San Marco's NPs (*Nuotatori Paracadutisti*) and ADRA also sided with the Germans in their words '*per l'onore d'Italia*' – for the honour of Italy. Interestingly, however, even within these units there were divisions; as an officer with *X Arditi* Carlo Bonciani was part of a resistance cell in Rome before the city was liberated and he joined 'F' Recce Squadron.

Two weeks after the Anzio landings in January 1944 a battalion of the *Nembo* Parachute Group in training at Spoleto was rushed to help seal the beachhead, fighting alongside the *4th Fallschirmjäger*. Between January and June *Nembo* earned the admiration of their German comrades at Anzio and later in the fighting around Rome. At the end of the war in Italy on 4 May, 1945, *Nembo* was one of the last Italo-German units to surrender. 'To us, however,' remarked Bonciani, who would later become the Second-in-Command of 'F' Recce Squadron, writing about the Italian fighters whom some called lunatics, 'it seemed that these lunatics and those others, fighting alongside either the

English or the Germans, who were the only Italians who were a credit to their country. Any man who risks his life in fighting for his genuine convictions must be a man of some character. If he makes a miscalculation, he pays the price.'[18]

However, it is a reflection of the way that the war divided Italy that the *Nembo* 12/183rd joined the Allies and fought on the Allied side at Filottranto, Cazza Grizzano and finally provided volunteers for Operation HERRING.

Bonciani summed up the character of the Italian airborne soldier in World War 2, whether he fought for or against the Allies. 'Living, as he does at the age of twenty, in the society of men 'dedicated to death' among whom life is lived at exceptional speed and intensity, he does become a trifle eccentric, slightly different, and he revels in the feeling that that is so.'[19] Many soldiers would say that what was true for the men of *Nembo* and *Folgore* in World War 2 remains true for paratroops in the 21st Century.

By early 1945, though there were still Italians fighting on the side of the Germans, the CIL had grown to a formidable force that formed the nucleus for six separate divisional-strength *Gruppi di Combattimento* (Combat Groups), each with 432 officers, 8,578 other ranks, 116 field guns, 170 mortars, 502 light machine guns, and 1,277 motor vehicles.

The Combat Groups were given the names of old Royal Army divisions, '*Cremona*,' '*Legnano*,' '*Friuli*,' '*Mantova*,' '*Piceno*' and '*Folgore*' and were identified by a rectangular, tricolour arm patch on their left sleeve with a central figure. '*Cremona*' had a ear of wheat, '*Mantova*' an eagle, '*Legnano*' a knight, '*Piceno*' a Roman arch, '*Friuli*' a city gate and '*Folgore*', the formation that would provide some of the men for No 1 Italian SAS, a lightning bolt. On the collars of their uniforms the men had the star of the *Regio Esercito* – Royal Army. It was Allied policy that these groups were not to be formed into a separate wholly Italian force – an Italian Army, so they were attached to formations of the Fifth and Eighth Armies fighting on the Gothic Line.

Pack Transport Units composed of Italian volunteers led vital mule trains through mountain trails to supply the Allied troops with food, ammunition and supplies. This was very dangerous work as there were few trails and their location had been plotted by the German artillery observers. The volunteers were dressed in British battledress dyed dark green and wore an arm badge of a red circle with green letters 'TN'. Since many had been ex-Alpini troops, they often wore the distinctive Alpine hats.

Months before the CIL had been formed, a unique Italian formation that would make up a significant part of No 1 ISAS had already taken up arms against the Germans. In fact they had done so almost as soon as the Allies had landed in mainland Italy. That the force, 'F' Recce Squadron, came into existence and served as a valuable part of the Eighth Army in the campaign in Italy is down to two remarkable men, an Italian paratroop officer from *Folgore*, Captain Carlo Francesco Gay, and an Anglo-Italian officer, Casimir Peter Hugh Tomasi Isolani – known to his brother officers as Kym. Isolani was given the *nom de guerre* of 'Arnold' by the Allies because he had been an Italian subject until 1938, and therefore risked being shot if he was captured.

Isolani was the son of an Italian aristocrat who, while serving in the Italian Army in World War 1, had been wounded and evacuated to hospital where he met and married a British nurse serving in Italy. Kym, their son, had been educated in Britain and at the time of the invasion of mainland Italy in 1943 was an intelligence officer attached to 1st Canadian Division. In October 1943 he discovered a group of men from 9/3, 185 *Nembo* Rgt, *Folgore* Division who had been living in the hills of Calabria near Lucera, not far from Foggia. They had two trucks and their personal weapons, and following the chaos of the Italian Armistice had effectively been abandoned. They were free spirits who resented their treatment by the Germans, despised the corrupt Fascist authorities and were disgusted at the poor leadership in their own army. Meeting Isolani, they said that they were ready to join the British to fight the Germans.

In his words Isolani found the staff at HQ Eighth Army 'cheerfully and refreshingly unconcerned with the political implications of co-belligerence', and they were easily persuaded that the group should be integrated into XIII Corps. Initially known as 1st Special Autonomous Unit on 9 December 1943, the group was formalised as 'F' Recce Squadron under the command of Captain Gay but answerable to Isolani. The two officers were, therefore, following a well-established tradition. The Eighth Army had after all had several Private Armies in North Africa – the Long Range Desert Group (LRDG), SAS and Popski's Private Army.

In British battledress uniform and sporting a thick moustache Gay looked very much like any other young officer in the Eighth Army. The moustache may also have helped to disguise his boyish features and give him a look of greater maturity. The Squadron vehicles had the insignia of XIII Corps on the left mudguard, a bounding red gazelle inside a white circle on a red diamond background, and on the other a large parachute with a blue 'F' under it. The men wore the XIII Corps gazelle flash on their battledress with the title 'F Recce Squadron' above it; however, they retained their Italian rank insignia. As a flexible self-contained unit capable of mounting both conventional and covert operations, they were an invaluable asset to XIII Corps, which guarded them jealously. The men carried an identity card stamped, dated and signed by a Brigadier on the XIII Corps' staff with instructions in English that read:

The bearer is a member of the Italian 'F' Recce Squadron under command H.Q. 13 Corps. He should not be interfered with in any way and it is requested that he be given every assistance in the execution of his duties.

Of Gay, Lt General Sir Sidney Kirkman, who commanded XIII Corps until January 25, 1945, would say. 'Capt. Gay, the commander of 'F' Recce, was a capable and determined leader who had the complete confidence of his men. For an Italian he was unusually reserved and free from those excitable traits in the Latin character which are apt to be regarded with suspicion by British officers'.

Interestingly, in the early correspondence about the structure, training and role of No 1 Italian SAS, a staff officer at the Main HQ Eighth Army wrote of Gay and 'F' Recce Squadron, 'Their Commanding Officer would be a very suitable Commander for the whole ITALIAN SAS force. I further suggest that the whole force be built up round F Recce, thus avoiding a considerable organisational problem.' However, as the project developed, it was deemed more politically wise to have 'F' Recce and *Nembo* as separate formations with the joint force commanded by a British officer.

By 15 January 1944, 'F' Recce Squadron consisted of 116 men and nine officers, two of whom were not parachute trained and would later be posted out of the Squadron. There were also non-parachute-trained support troops. By March of that year its strength stood at 11 officers, 15 NCOs and 117 men. The fact that 'F' Recce Squadron was a formed unit with its own administrative staff meant that it was able to send in full after-action reports following Operation HERRING. The men from *Nembo* who had been formed into an *ad hoc* unit lacked this logistic and administrative back-up.

'F' Recce Squadron's operations began in the Majella mountains north of the River Sangro in February and March 1944. It was high-risk work, in which Isolani worked with small patrols dressed in civilian clothes who passed through the Allied front line into enemy territory to collect intelligence on German positions and equipment. In *'F' Squadron*, Bonciani, a World War 1 veteran who joined the squadron after it was established and became its unofficial chronicler, describes the build-up to a patrol.

'Really to understand what war means, a soldier must have done two things – a night patrol behind enemy lines and a withdrawal. The men of the 'F' Squadron earned their laurels with hundreds of night patrols deep into German-held territory. Up to the moment of setting out, nothing special happens. The men get ready, check over their weapons, and don't think or talk about anything in particular. Their comrades watch their preparations and often pull their legs. 'If your girl's a blonde you can leave her to me,' or, 'Wear your oldest boots, otherwise the Germans will take them off you before you're buried...' Five minutes later they had all vanished into the darkness. Those who remained behind used to look at their watches and calculate when they would be due back.'[20]

On one occasion, in the morning returning from an operation, Isolani's Jeep was mistaken for an enemy vehicle and strafed by USAAF Mustang fighters. 'We played hide and seek around a prickly pear bush,' he recalled afterwards, 'until they eventually got bored and flew away.' Tragically he would be badly injured soon afterwards when a Canadian carrier, a light tracked vehicle, crushed his legs.[21] However, 'F' Recce Squadron was established, conducting armed reconnaissance patrols, and suffering their first casualties. An officer and an NCO were captured and died under interrogation; the Squadron suffered heavily in the final battle for Ferrara. While Isolani was with the Squadron he was joined by two liaison officers, Captains Joe Liebmann, a South African, and Irishman Micky Birch. The big, red-headed Liebmann, who 'had the strength of an ox', was an excellent shot with his .45 Colt M19A1 pistol and would take every opportunity to practise with the weapon. However, he was also a man who had a great sympathy and affection for Italy and the Italians.

If a request was made of Birch it seemed to the Italians that his reply was almost always 'No', and then Gay or Bonciani would find that the young Irishman had answered their request and the problem had been solved or stores supplied. When they started to thank him, he would smile and slip away. It was, to Birch, 'a friend at court' in the Eighth Army that Bonciani credited with the last and most significant operation in 'F' Recce Squadron's short life – Operation HERRING. In fact, the decision to use the squadron in an airborne role had been taken at much higher levels.

However, HERRING was a year away when 'F' Recce Squadron was moved from the east coast to the west to

Cassino where between April and May 1944 it was involved in the hard fighting for the monastery stronghold. They would not enjoy the US Fifth Army victory parades in Rome and General Mark Clarke's short-lived triumph but were on their way north to see action near the ancient battleground of Lake Trasimene.

The Squadron would play a significant role in the battle for Florence and, assisted by local partisan groups, would prevent the destruction of two bridges over the Arno. Casualties had been heavy and the squadron received an intake of volunteers from the recently liberated city of Rome – many of them youngsters still in their teens.

18 'F' *Squadron*, Carlo Bonciani, J. M. Dent & Sons, 1947. I am grateful to Daniel Battistella, who has pointed out that 'F' Squadron veterans see Bonciani's book as a colourful and not entirely accurate account of the unit. I have therefore been careful and used quotes from it only to give colour to the history of Operation HERRING.

19 Ibid.

20 Bonciani.

21 After a spell in hospital Isolani returned to Italy and in June 1944 entered Rome with S Force, a group formed to take over and run the media. He worked for the Psychological Warfare Branch and was put in charge of *Italia Combatte*, which broadcast to the partisans in northern Italy. He transmitted instructions for sabotage operations and the targeted killing of notorious SS officers. It was said that these assassinations were carried out within a few days of the broadcasts. In 1945, after moving to Florence, he had the happy task of making the radio announcement of the capitulation of the German forces in Italy. On demobilisation in 1946, he was appointed MBE (military) and made an 'Honorary Partisan'. He subsequently enjoyed a long and valuable career in the diplomatic service, doing much to foster Anglo-Italian relations..

Chapter 4

Achtung Partisanen!

Know the enemy, know yourself: your victory will never be endangered. Know the ground, know the weather; your victory will then be total.

The Art of War, Sun Tzu, 400-320 BC

In their lifetime, many of the young volunteers from Rome who joined 'F' Recce Squadron had only known Italy as a Fascist state, since it had been in existence for over 20 years following Mussolini's 'March on Rome' on 28 October 1922. The march, intended to imitate that of the Italian national hero Garibaldi, had established Mussolini as *Duce* (Leader) and the primary power in the Italian Republic. Though he took control of the country and put an end to riots and unrest, there were those at both ends of the political spectrum who thought the Fascists were undemocratic and too powerful. Long before Mussolini was overthrown there was political resistance in Italy.

When they were detained, the opposition were usually sent to internment camps or held in prisons like San Vittore in Milan, Marassi in Genova, and Rome's Regina Coeli. In the latter years of the war several other buildings served as temporary unofficial prisons and interrogation centres. In Rome an apartment building in Via Tasso was taken over. Five cells were constructed by bricking up the windows and modifying rooms to produce cells about 15 by 20 feet, in each of which held 15 or more prisoners. They received one meal per day and prisoners left the cell only once a day for the lavatory or for interrogation.

The intellectual Sandro Pertini was among one of the first to mobilise public opinion against the Fascists. Mussolini's militia, the Black Shirts, beat him up and he was eventually sentenced to 15 years solitary confinement. Many members of the Italian aristocracy who were cultured Anglophiles were unhappy that Britain had become the 'enemy'. On 24 September 1943 this would prove to be life-saving for Captain Anthony Greville-Bell and his group, part of the SAS Operation SPEEDWELL.

The men were exhausted and short of food. At Fiesole, the town near Florence that about a year later would become the base for 'F' Recce Squadron, Greville-Bell realised that they were close to the home of an aristocratic critic of Mussolini who had been gaoled because of his outspoken views. The men were desperately hungry but as the officer remembered when they reached the villa:

'There was no way to creep in, just a big door, so I put the men in the bushes and rang the bell. It was opened and I said in my best Italian, 'I would like to see the owner please.' This butler looked at me and said in perfect English, 'Yes sir, and who may I say is calling?'. Then down the stairs came bouncing this chap about my own age, Count Blaise Fogliette. It turned out that he was married to an Englishwoman I had known as a boy in Devon. In fact I used to go to Pony Club meetings with her and her sisters. I'd fancied one of them, I seem to remember.

When the introductions were over, Greville-Bell went to fetch his men.

'They were already in the servants' hall – the cook was also English – having cups of strong tea. We stayed there for about three days.'[22]

While Italian aristocrats might be anti-Fascist, in the Vatican Pope Pius XI would remain an ambiguous leader who saw in Mussolini an ally against the godless forces of international Bolshevism. The church in Italy, like that in Germany in 1933, had signed a concordance giving up political influence in exchange for recognition as the state religion. Catholic youth clubs were disbanded and their members incorporated into Fascist organisations.

In 1935 Mussolini broke his promise to the people that he would give them 'peace and order' when, in what was later to be seen the first move of World War 2, Italian forces invaded the East African country of Ethiopia. In 1939 Mussolini signed the Axis Pact with Germany; however, many Italians were appalled when Italy declared war on France and Britain in 1940. By 1942, Italy had suffered heavily in fighting in North Africa, Greece and Russia. Conditions at home in Italy deteriorated and there were food riots. A bitter joke that circulated amongst the naturally anti-authoritarian Italians was that everyone was a Fascist – but no one was. Many university intellectuals and lecturers paid lip service to the Fascist government diktats but continued to teach democratic principles. Underground newspapers sprang up around the country.

As the Fascists reorganised in the north following Mussolini's release from captivity, they established the Italian Social Republic under the protection of the German Army. However, this acted as a spur to the formation of more resistance groups in different regions of the country. Some were composed of Italian soldiers whose homes were in the south and so, rather than face internment by the Germans, they had taken to the hills. Later, as Germany combed northern Italy for fit men as workers in the munitions factories or the huge *Organisation Todt* construction projects, more Italians joined the partisans. As their numbers grew the partisans were organised into committees.

This was fertile ground for agents of the Special Operations Executive (SOE), the British covert-operations service formed in July 1940 by the amalgamation of three bodies which had been created shortly before the outbreak of World War 2. They were Section D of the Secret Intelligence Service (SIS), which focussed on sabotage and already had some resources in the field in Eastern Europe; EH (named after its HQ, Electra House, on the Embankment), a semi-secret propaganda section of the Foreign Office set up in 1938 which was later to form the nucleus of the Political Warfare Executive; and Military Intelligence, Research (MIR), which had developed out of the research section of the War Office's general staff and which made a study of guerilla warfare.

In order to maintain SOE's independence from any of the orthodox services, it was made answerable to the Ministry of Economic Warfare, based in Berkeley Square, and not as might have been expected the Foreign Office (FO) or War Office. It was located away from Whitehall, with its HQ at 64 Baker Street, with its first Chief Executive Officer H. M. Gladwyn Jebb (later Lord Gladwyn), a member of the Diplomatic Service. When Jebb returned to the FO in 1942, he was succeeded by Sir Frank Nelson, then by Sir Charles Hambro and finally by Major General (Sir) Colin Gubbins as head of SOE. Gubbins would establish an SOE HQ at Bari in Italy for operations in Italy and the Balkans with its own training schools, radio stations and ammunition dumps.

SOE's mission, memorably and succinctly expressed by Churchill to the Minister of Economic Warfare, Hugh Dalton, was to 'set Europe ablaze'. It was to co-ordinate action against the enemy by means of subversion and sabotage, including propaganda, on behalf of the Allied war effort. It had first to identify, train, supply and co-ordinate the efforts of Resistance groups in Occupied Europe. It thus had a twofold purpose: ultimately, to raise secret armies to rise in concert with the eventual Allied invasion; in the meantime, to carry out a programme of sabotage detrimental to the enemy's fighting potential.

The SOE was divided into three branches: SO1 (propaganda), SO2 (active operations) and SO3 (planning). Its focus of activity was not only Europe, but also Africa, the Middle East and the Far East, including Burma and Malaya. The character of SOE operations reflected the conditions of the German occupation. In France, for example, there was a complex web of classic underground networks and armed Maquis groups; in Yugoslavia and Greece, the partisans waged open guerilla warfare. SOE officers were selected as far as possible for their linguistic skills and possible contacts in the area in which they might be operating. Like many other Allied special forces or covert organisations, it was disbanded in 1946.

Working alongside the SOE was the United States Office of Strategic Services (OSS). Like the SOE, it was a war child. Its origins could be traced back to the months before Pearl Harbor when the United States' President Franklin Roosevelt had become increasingly concerned about American intelligence deficiencies. It was the Canadian William Stephenson, the senior representative of British intelligence in the western hemisphere, who suggested that World War 1 veteran and Medal of Honor recipient General William 'Wild Bill' Donovan, now an attorney and Republican politician, would be the ideal man to plan an intelligence service. Donovan's brief was to look outside the narrow remits of US Naval and Army intelligence and address the global intelligence needs of the USA. In July 1941, after submitting his paper, 'Memorandum of Establishment of Service of Strategic Information,' Donovan was put in charge of the new organisation with the title of the Co-ordinator of Information.

The OSS was formally established by a Presidential military order on 13 June 1942. It was to collect and analyse strategic information required by the Joint Chiefs of Staff and to conduct special operations not assigned to other agencies. During the War, the OSS supplied policymakers with facts and estimates, conducted propaganda, espionage and subversion operations and undertook planning for the postwar period. At the height of its operations during World War 2, the OSS employed almost 24,000 people. In Italy, it had an advantage of being able to draw on the large US Italian community to work with the partisans.

Officers of the SOE and OSS were parachuted or landed

from submarine in partisan-controlled areas in Italy to help co-ordinate and direct attacks and sabotage operations, and to bring in supplies and munitions. Among the major formations with whom the SOE and OSS worked were, according to their political loyalties and affiliations: the Garibaldi (Communist Party), People's or Catholic Brigades (Catholic), Matteotti Brigades (Socialist Party), Mazzini Brigades (Republican), Red Flag Units (Anarchist) and the Justice and Freedom Brigades (Actionist Party).

In Northern Italy the mountainous terrain assisted the partisans since German and Fascist troops were often road bound in the valleys; this meant that there was always early warning of their approach. The main drawback to operations in the mountains was that the winters could be bitter.

The Allies realised that there was a need for an umbrella organisation to co-ordinate the diverse partisan groups, and so the *Comitato di Liberazione Nazionale* (CLN) or *Corpo Voluntari della Liberta* (CVL) was formed. It was headed by the moderate Italian General Raffaele Cadorna, who at the age of 55 had parachuted in behind the German lines. The son of the World War 1 Field Marshal, he was highly respected in Italy and in 1945 was named Chief of Staff of the Italian Army. As joint deputies in the CLN he had Luigi Longo, a Communist, and Ferrucio Parri of the Actionist Party. The Italian partisan movement would eventually become the largest in Western Europe; larger than the much-publicised French Resistance. In 1944 the SOE had delivered 513 tons of weapons and equipment to the partisans and the OSS a further 290 tons. In the first four months of 1945 the SOE and OSS dropped 1,229 tons including 666 tons of arms and ammunition, 292 tons of explosives and 271 of stores.

The leaders of the Communist Partisan groups saw the war as an opportunity to overthrow the old establishment and set up a Communist state after the war. In the Spring of 1944 the partisan groups in the northern Alpine and Apennine mountains had grown as large as 100,000 men and had established 'republics'. These were areas under control of the CLN. However, when the Allied operations came to a halt in the bitter weather at the end of 1944, a radio announcement broadcast in clear by General Alexander ordering the suspension of operations for the winter gave the Germans and their RSI allies the opportunity to launch a series of aggressive anti-partisan drives that recaptured areas held by the CLN and led to brutal reprisals against the population.

It was on 23 March 1944 that a partisan attack in Rome would trigger one of the most brutal and notorious reprisals of the war in Italy. A column of policemen from the 11th Coy 3rd Police Bn Bozen – composed of German-speaking Italians from the border provinces of Bolzano-Bozen were attacked in a narrow street with an 18kg improvised explosive device. The charge, which contained a mix of TNT and shrapnel, killed 28 men immediately while others later died of their wounds. The 16 partisans from the Communist *Gruppi d'Azione Patriotica*, who had launched the attack, escaped in the confusion.

The demand for reprisals for these deaths came from the highest quarters – when Hitler heard of the attack he agreed that ten Italians should be killed for every man who had died and ordered that the executions should be carried out in 24 hours. The ghastly arithmetic of reprisal actually led to the deaths of 335 Italians – some of whom were partisans held in prison, some Jews and some simply Roman citizens taken off the streets at random. On the night of 24 March they were taken to caves that had been formed by quarrying pozzolana near the Via Ardeatina. The victims were led in in batches of five and shot at close range in the back of the head – the bodies were eventually stacked a metre high. When the killing was over, German military engineers blew up the entrance to the caves to seal them. When Rome was liberated, the bodies were exhumed from the caves and given a proper burial.

Between 8 June and 4 July, following the liberation of Rome the Germans and their Fascist RSI allies began to regroup and pull back from the city towards the Gothic Line. Troops and equipment were moved between the east and west coast fronts and reinforcements came south to delay the advance by the Fifteenth Army Group.

The bombers of Mediterranean Allied Air Forces (MAAF) attacked road and rail links from the front line north of Rome as far as Bologna. At the request of Fifteenth Army Group about 50 teams with names (in Italian) such as 'SOUP', 'APPLE', 'POTATO', made up of between two and eight volunteers from *Folgore*, trained to parachute into the Apennines to attack inaccessible road and rail links that could not be hit effectively by MAAF bombers.

Targets were chosen in consultation with the Army and Air Force Intelligence Branches and blind DZs were selected as near as possible to the target area. The primary objective for the teams would be to cut railway track in one or several vital places such as junctions, culverts, small bridges, embankments and level crossings. Main and secondary roads and enemy transport being used for the movement of personnel and material was a subsidiary target. On completion of their mission the groups were instructed to join the local partisans. The operation that would be known as POTATO was an interesting pointer to HERRING launched about a year later.

For the Germans and their Italian Fascist allies the impact of the partisan operations varied in effectiveness. However on 21 August 1944 Field Marshal Kesselring wrote to the head of the SS in Italy, the chief of the Italian police and the general director of transport in the Italian Socialist Republic:

> *'Destruction of railway bridges by the partisans has mounted to such an extent that their reconstruction, indespensable for our operations, will shortly be impossible. These acts of sabotage are the work of powerful groups following minutely detailed plans. For example, to blow up a bridge between Turin and Milan, the Partisan engineers detonated charges of several hundred kilograms. As a result, important bridges must be guarded in force by the supreme chief of the SS and the police, with the latter required to supply all necessary personnel to the director of transportation.'*

As in France, the Germans employed brutal tactics that had first been crafted in the moral void of the Eastern Front. Collective punishments with villages being burned and hostages rounded up and shot or publicly hanged were a way of separating the partisans from the population that offered them support. In their sweeps through the mountains the Germans were more diligent in cordon and search operations, and in the Italian *Brigata Nere* they had a dedicated anti-partisan formation that had local knowledge and by 1945 little to lose.

Formation of the *Brigata Nere* had been sanctioned by a Fascist Republican Party law of 30 June 1944. Though they fought the Allies and partisans, they were also lethal enforcers who fought against political opponents and other Black Brigade members whose commitment to Fascism was seen as less than total. The driving force behind this organisation was 41-year-old Alessandro Pavolini, a highly intelligent but brutal man who as a journalist and essayist had made the intellectual case for Fascism with cultural and literary essays, such as *Disperata* – The Desperate – in 1937 and *Scomparsa d'Angela* – Angela's Disappearance – in 1940. In 1939, he had been appointed Minister of Popular Culture, and served in this capacity until January 1943.

In 1944 he explained to Mussolini that Italian soldiers were not suited to anti-Partisan operations. 'Wherever the army exists on national soil, it is directly represented by a nucleus of officers and men ready to desert and pass to the other side.'[23] What was needed was a dedicated Fascist force loyal to Mussolini.

Despite the grand title, the Black Brigades were actually formations of between 200 to 300 men. There were 41 territorial brigades, seven 'independent' and eight 'mobile' brigades, plus the 2nd Arditi Brigade. Although members of Black Brigades were issued standard Italian army uniforms, they favoured a black shirt or jersey. Over this they sometimes wore a drab or camouflage smock and grey-green military trousers. As headgear, the majority of Black Brigade members wore Italian army ski caps or berets dyed black. The badge or insignia of the Black Brigades was the death's head. The neatly moustachioed

Pavolini, who had previously appeared in public in well-cut suits, now wore the black uniform of the *Brigata Nere*. As James Holland observes, 'Considering the vast majority of civilians in northern Italy were no longer interested in fascism, and that the squadristi had hardly been loved by the Italian people, this intimidating look was not altogether sensible. In fact, the formation of the Black Brigades and the militarisation of the Party was a high-risk strategy indeed'.[24]

Another take on the final years of the war in Italy comes from the author of *The Tiger Triumphs – the story of three great divisions in Italy*, the history of the British Indian Army Divisions who fought in Italy. 'The picture of the German occupation in Central Italy was quite un-Prussian and nowhere more so than in the case of the 278th Berlin-Brandenburg Infantry Division. Its commander, Major-General Harry Hoppe, who in person resembled the caricature of Colonel Blimp, was an eccentric and irascible man. He welcomed a new draft peculiarly. 'You have come here to die,' he said, 'and to be quick about it.' But he eased the rigours of training with instructions that 'three times in each week, men will rest for one and a half hours after lunch'. His men sang ironically, 'Do you know the Hoppe step - one pace forward, then two back?' He fostered morale by broadcasting clichés: 'They Shall Not Pass' and 'Better Death than Captivity'.

The Italian partisan movement had begun to contribute to the deterioration of German morale. Better armed, better organised, and with the best imaginable terrain in which to operate, they were a constant drain and a danger to enemy detachments in the high mountains and sparsely-settled areas. (General Hoppe was obliged to describe

Easter, 1944, as a 'sombre festival', for on Good Friday partisans blew up a considerable number of his young men at a cinema performance). Death lurked for unwary Germans in the shadow of the woods, in dark alleys and on lonely roads. An even more serious aspect of the Italian revolt emerged during the construction of the Gothic Line. These fortifications had been planned at the time of the Allied invasion of Italy. Until the breakthrough at Cassino the work had proceeded slowly and spasmodically. Thereafter the *Organization Todt* hurriedly conscripted many thousands of Italians and rushed the defences to completion. The German press-gangs netted many partisans who supplemented the natural lethargy of forced labour with clever and effective sabotage. A poor quality of cement was supplied from Italian mills. Emplacements were built with blind traverses; pill-boxes unaccountably did not command all approaches. When battle was joined on the Gothic Line many of the gaps in the defences and 'soft spots' exploited by the Eighth Army owed their origin to bold and dangerous intervention by the patriot forces.'[25]

If Hoppe, a career soldier, veteran of World War 1 and the Freikorps, seemed like a Colonel Blimp figure to the British, to his fellow officers he was known as 'Stan Laurel' because his lugubrious appearance resembled that of the British-born Hollywood actor and comedian. Curiously, Hoppe had changed his birth name of 'Arthur' to 'Harry' in February 1943.

In 1945, as it became clear that Nazi Germany was doomed, many Italians in the north who had kept their heads down and not declared loyalty to any cause now became partisans, grabbing weapons that littered the battlefields and fighting to eject the Germans. It was these men who would provide muscle to the small groups of paratroops from No 1 Italian SAS, helping to liberate and hold villages and other key points and thus speed the advance of the Fifth and Eighth Armies.

At the close of the war in Italy, SOE liaison officer Captain John Orr-Ewing found himself asked to plead the cause of a German soldier who had been captured by the partisans. 'He was a young chap, about eighteen or nineteen. He'd been a member of the Hitler Youth. They said, 'We see he did one or two years' training for the Lutheran ministry, perhaps he's different. We thought we'll bring him to you and if you plead on his behalf we might spare his life.' But he was utterly aggressive. There was nothing penitent about him or anything, he was aggressive and absolutely a Nazi. So I'm afraid I said to him,. 'They brought you to me to try and save your life, but honestly, the attitude you've taken, what can I do?' And the partisans decided they couldn't keep him and they shot him. We weren't in charge, thank goodness, and I haven't got any guilt about it.'[26]

While many Germans were exhausted and war-weary in 1945, the attitude of this young soldier indicates that the final offensive planned for the spring of that year would not be a push-over. Some Germans would put up a fanatical resistance while others simply joked grimly, 'Enjoy the war. The peace will be terrible', and soldiered on.

As they pushed north the Allies encountered the partisans; Brigadier Pat Scott of the 78th 'Battleaxe' Division, Eighth Army, characterised them as one of two types. 'Those who put on their arm bands and slung their muskets round their shoulders after the Boche had pulled out, and those who did fight genuinely, many of whom still had fresh wounds. The second variety were extremely helpful and had detailed maps and drawings showing enemy positions and minefields which later proved to be very accurate. They all, however, had one big failing, common throughout Italy. Once having allowed them to start talking, nothing would induce them to stop. They held non-stop meetings throughout the day, which we soon referred to as 'Partisan O Groups' [Orders Groups]. These meetings resembled mobile arsenals, for all the men and also the women carried at least four weapons and were festooned with bandoleers, grenades, knives and every sort of 'what have you.'[27]

With the end of the war approaching fast, the Allies realised that once an area had been liberated by conventional forces of the Fifteenth Army Group it would be essential that the partisans should be disarmed, but that this should be done in an honourable and dignified way. In an Appendix 1 to 15th Army Group Operations Instruction No.5 dated 12 April 1945, the potential problems were addressed by a British staff officer:

'These Partisans have in large measure loyally obeyed the orders of the Allies and have caused very concrete losses and embarrassment to the enemy; they have thus earned as good treatment as can reasonably be afforded them. In addition, in the absence of fair yet firm treatment and, in the absence of positive and constructive employment, they might form a disillusioned and dangerous element under the disorganised conditions likely to exist during the period immediately following the withdrawal of the Germans and the arrival of the Allies.'

He identified the key role of men of the SOE and OSS in the disarmament arrangements.

'There exists in Northern ITALY a considerable number of Allied Missions, British, US, and Italian, working in close liaison with the larger Partisan bands. Upon the withdrawal of the enemy forces and the arrival of the Allies these missions should be able to provide valuable assistance to local AMG officers and Military Commanders ... information about local conditions, numbers of Partisans, numbers of arms etc.'

The officer proposed a simple but honourable way of taking the guns out of the community. There should be a parade that should not be seen as sponsored by the Allies but laid on for and by the partisans. Flags, bands, loudspeakers and advanced publicity would turn it into a major event and the Commanding Officer of the nearest Allied unit should be present to take the salute.

The partisans would then march to a point where they would hand over their weapons. This would however be presented as a fair exchange that started with the man or woman being awarded a Patriot Certificate. Food would be made available but crucially the men and women would receive clothing from US or British Army stocks that included underclothes, boots, socks, shirts, combat jackets or battledress and blankets. To prevent abuse of this clothing issue a large yellow 'V' would be stencilled on the items. Clothing was a very acceptable exchange – particularly boots in the rugged mountainous areas.

Wounded or sick partisans, the annexe explained, would be evacuated and treated in civilian or Italian military hospitals.

Finally, he proposed that partisans should be found work either through the Allied Military Government (AMG) or civilian labour organisations. They could be encouraged to enlist in the Italian Army, but most importantly as far as possible they should be returned to their homes and to civilian status. It was a dignified and honourable way of ensuring that the partisans and their weapons would not be a threat to the newly liberated Italy. It is a study that stands the test of time as a way of handling what today would be called a 'post-conflict situation.'

By the end of the war 224,000 partisans had been in action behind German lines. But not all of them would enjoy the Allied largesse proposed in this paper. Some 63,000 men and women had been killed and more than 33,000 wounded. In addition between 15,000 to 20,000 civilians who had been in areas under partisan control or who were thought to have assisted them, had been murdered.

22 *Stirling's Men*
23 *The Brutal Friendship: Mussolini, Hitler and the fall of Italian Fascism*, F. W. Deakin, Pelican, London, 1966
24 At the end of the war Pavolini attempted to escape, but was seen as he tried to swim across Lake Como. Trapped behind a half-submerged rock, he kept his pursuers at bay until he ran out of ammunition and was finally apprehended and executed by the partisans on 28 April 1945 in Dongo.
25 *The Tiger triumphs – The Story of Three Great Divisions in Italy* AAVV. HMSO India, 1946
26 *Forgotten Voices of the Secret War*, Roderick Bailey, Ebury Press, 2008
27 *Battleaxe Division*, Ken Ford, Sutton Publishing, 1999

Chapter 5

Behind the Lines

*One well-known Brigadier phrases his requirements of the ideal
infantryman as 'athlete, stalker, marksman'. I put it on a lower
plane and say that the qualities of a successful poacher, cat burglar,
and gunman would content me.*

Sir Archibald Wavell, *The Training of the Army for War*,
1933

Operation HERRING was the climax of SAS, SOE and
OSS operations in Italy in the winter of 1944 and the early
months of 1945. The SOE and OSS had enhanced the
capabilities of the partisans with parachuted supplies of
weapons, ammunition, clothing and rations and had then
directed their sabotage and ambush operations. The SAS
sometimes collaborated with the partisans but also
launched their own self-contained attacks against the vital
road and rail links.

Operation CANUCK was conducted by a small SAS
team in January 1945 and was so named because it was
commanded by a Canadian, Captain Buck McDonald.
One of the team, Jock Mackinnon-Patterson, remembered
that as he rolled up his parachute on the DZ he was
confronted by a startling vision - a pretty 20-year-old
Italian girl armed with a Sten gun, in a print dress, leather
waistcoat, leather bootees and short cotton socks. The lady

had a sister who was just as pretty, but they had a father and he was the local partisan leader, who told the young SAS men that the girls were strictly off limits. Sergeant 'Robbo' Robinson recalled that one of them was exceptionally brave, carrying an explosive charge hidden under vegetables and fitted with a time fuse; she then left it at a German checkpoint, explaining that she would be back once she had run home to collect her identity card.

The men of CANUCK disrupted German communications between the Italian Riviera and northern Italy. They were also able to equip and organise partisans. On 15 April at 05.00 hours the partisans, with the CANUCK team in support with two 3-inch mortars and a Browning .50 HMG, attacked the garrison of Alba, a small but strategically important town near Turin.

The mortar fire controller was Lt Philip Fell, and on the mortar line 'Robbo' Robinson recalled, 'We had a lot of bombs and there was one bloke sitting on a large heap of them giving us whatever we wanted, smoke or ordinary bombs, cap on or cap off ... if you left the metal cap on the bomb, it didn't explode straight away, it went through two or three floors and then exploded. It wasn't long before the barrels were red hot'. [28]

The town fell two days later in a second attack and Jack Paley, who had served in the Royal Artillery and Parachute Regiment before he joined the SAS, recalled that they let the partisans enter the town ahead of them as its liberators. When the British soldiers entered the town he recalled that there was blood running in the streets. 'The Partisans were taking revenge on some of their own people, shaving the heads of women ... shooting men and women in the streets.'[29]

Most of the SAS operations in occupied Europe were in territory with a friendly or, at worst, neutral population. Writing in *The Science of Guerilla Warfare*, T. E. Lawrence drew on his experience of the Arab Revolt against the Ottoman Empire in World War 1 when he explained, 'Guerilla war must have a friendly population, not actively friendly, but sympathetic to the point of not betraying rebel movements to the enemy. Rebellions can be made by two per cent active in a striking force, and 98 per cent passively sympathetic.'

The need for a civilian population that was prepared to offer active, or at the least passive, support was brutally demonstrated in Operation COLD COMFORT (later renamed ZOMBIE), an SAS raid that began with a parachute drop north of Verona in mid-February 1945.

The ski-mounted group was led by Captain Ross Littlejohn, a 23-year-old Scot who while serving with No 4 Commando had been awarded the MC during fighting in Normandy. Their mission was to to create landslides to block the main rail lines through the Brenner Pass, thus dramatically reducing the flow of German reinforcements moving south. Littlejohn, along with two Corporals, jumped on 15 February and linked up with local partisans. Once the young captain had assured himself that everything was in place for the main party, he signalled that they should parachute in on 17 February. However, within the partisan group there was a traitor who betrayed them. The Germans attacked the reception party as it made its way to the DZ. Fortunately some of the pilots in the B-24 Liberators, having failed to see any lights on the DZ, aborted the mission and returned to base but two aircraft dropped their men, happily, as it turned out, very inaccurately, nearly 20 miles away from the DZ where, had they landed, they would probably have been killed or captured.

The men from the two parachute-dropped patrols or 'sticks' spent most of their time in hiding and attempts to supply and reinforce by air were unsuccessful. With the spring thaw, the survivors split into two patrols and set out to attack German communications. Eventually by 31 March the situation had worsened to the point where exfiltration was ordered. On 25 April signals between Major Eric Barkworth and Christopher Sykes, the 2 SAS Intelligence officers tasked with tracking the location of SAS troops missing behind enemy lines included the good news 'Littlejohn and Crowley of COLD COMFORT officially reported PW'. Tragically the news that they were prisoners-of-war could not have been further from the truth. Both men had been captured, and Littlejohn was subjected to what captured SD officers later interrogated by Barkworth called a 'thorough interrogation' followed by a 'stricter interrogation'. The officer remained silent and it was only after he had been tied to an iron bar, hung from a step-ladder and beaten that he agreed to make a statement. Littlejohn released Crowley from his oath of secrecy. On 19 March the two men, along with a US Army Air Force pilot, Charles Parker, were driven to a remote location where the vehicle halted because it had a 'puncture' and they were ordered out of the car. As they walked away, the SD officers opened fire with their sub-machine guns. Like earlier captured SAS soldiers, they had been murdered under Hitler's Commando Order.

Operation GALIA, under Captain Bob Walker-Brown, was launched on 27 December 1944. It would prove to be not only a military success but also an epic of survival in some of the grimmest weather the area had seen in many years.

With 33 men of A Troop 3 Squadron 2 SAS he parachuted into an area between Genoa and La Spezia with orders to support the forthcoming offensive by the 92nd Infantry Division, Fifth Army and harass communications on the axes La Spezia-Parma, Spezia-Genoa and Aulla-Reggio and link up with local partisan groups. The daylight jump into the area north of La Spezia was deliberate, since it was hoped that it would be observed by the Germans, being intended to simulate the deployment of a large formation of the British 2nd Independent Parachute Brigade, who were actually in action in Greece against a Communist-inspired insurgency. The men landed near the mountain village of Rossano about 14 miles north of La Spezia on a far from ideal DZ – a terraced vineyard. The group was scattered and containers stolen by the local partisans.

Walker-Brown broke the GALIA operation down into an HQ of eight men and five patrols of four to six, each commanded by an officer or sergeant. A day after landing, three of the patrols moved out to take up positions in the area of the main roads whilst the remainder set about hiding the stores and linking up with the partisans. The screening effect of the mountains made radio communication impossible.

Walker-Brown shared similar misgivings as did many SOE and SAS officers about many of the partisan groups. 'The mountains were dominated by two different groups of partisans... one being the so-called Justice and Liberty Brigades who were anti-fascist and pro-Allies; the other being the communist brigades whose aim was to receive all the weapons dropped for the other Partisans and store them for the post-war revolution. They were a tricky lot...on one occasion I had a run-in with the commies.'[30] However, he had an excellent SOE officer already in place. Remarkably Walker-Brown and Major Gordon Lett of the SOE had already met in a PoW camp in Italy. Lett warned Walker-Brown that the Communists were unreliable and that news of his arrival would soon reach the Germans via informers – it took about two weeks.

On 30 December Walker-Brown's group with the 3-inch mortar and 35 HE bombs teamed up with the partisans and set up an ambush on the Spezia-Genoa road. They hit a convoy, destroying three vehicles and setting a fourth on fire. This attracted heavy fire from a 20mm cannon mounted on an escorting armoured vehicle and the party withdrew, leaving behind four enemy dead and a number of wounded. On New Year's Day 1945 they attacked the enemy garrison in Borgeto di Vara. The attack had three objectives; first, to make the presence of the SAS known to the enemy in the shortest possible time; second, to create uneasiness among the garrison troops on the Spezia-Genoa road and cause them to be reinforced, and finally to stop enemy movement on that road. In the attack 34 mortar bombs were fired from a range of 1100 yards, with direct hits on a number of houses occupied by enemy troops.

Two trucks approaching Borgeto stopped when the drivers heard the mortar fire but they were destroyed at close range by Bren gunners of the ambush cutoff group.[See Appendix 3]. During this attack a party of 14 partisans, under the command of the SAS, were instructed to stop any enemy leaving Borgeto to the south. No contact was made as the entire garrison withdrew and did not return for a day.

On 3 January one of Walker-Brown's patrols moved to the area of Valeriano and radio contact was finally established and a resupply request transmitted. News came through that a patrol of five men had been been captured in Montebello by a group of *Brigata Nere* who had been mistaken for partisans because they were dressed in civilian clothes. The Fascists interrogated, tortured and finally shot the patrol's Italian guide. Walker-Brown remarked that the patrol had 'made the classic mistake of moving into an empty building while waiting to ford a river... it was spotted by Fascisti and surrounded'. It was fortunate for the SAS men that however savage the *Brigata Nere* might be to their fellow Italians, they treated the British soldiers according to the Geneva Convention and consequently they survived the war in a PoW camp.

Meanwhile, in increasingly bad weather (the winter of 1944-45 was one of the most severe on record throughout Europe) the Troop HQ awaited resupply. They received a radio message saying that the aircraft could not fly to the original DZ[31] near Rossano code-named 'Huntsville'. Walker-Brown replied that this was the only viable DZ on two counts. First, because it was the easiest DZ for getting supplies to detached patrols as it was located in the centre of the Troop's operational area. Second, there would be plenty of warning of any enemy attacks against the SAS since they would have to come through country under partisan observation.

By 4 January, the weather had deteriorated further. It was extremely cold and there was deep snow on the ground. Icing conditions and the snow on the mountain goat tracks made movement very difficult and tiring. When the operation had been launched no-one had anticipated how severe the winter would be and as Walker-Brown recalled, 'When we landed all we were wearing was a silk vest, battledress and a camouflage jumping smock. We had no snow clothes, although I did send a signal asking for some snow clothing. I received a drop of khaki drill tops.

The greatest problem, however, was boots. The army-issue boot was useless because it wore out in no time. In the end Walker-Brown used operational money to have boots made by the local shoemaker.'[32]

Major Thomas 'Tommy' Macpherson, a veteran SOE officer who was operating in Italy at the same time concurred. 'Unlike France, it was not car banditry. You were on your feet, so things took much longer to do. You couldn't say, 'I'll reconnoitre this tonight, and I'll do it tomorrow.' Each task was an expedition.'

Whilst waiting for the resupply drop one of Walker-Brown's patrols mined the road near Valeriano and that night a German truck was destroyed, killing 12 and wounding eight. Another patrol was in position on the Spezia-Genoa road and here it attacked a staff car, killing four officers.

Despite the many requests for the drop to be made at 'Huntsville', the reply kept coming back that the drop would take place on 'Halifax'. For the men on the ground this meant an extra five hours' march through deep snow. Markers were put out on 'Huntsville' and two patrols then set off on the arduous march to 'Halifax'.

On 9 January at 15.30 hours the drop was made on

'Halifax' and the remainder of the Troop made their way from 'Huntsville'. The drop was scattered over four square miles and it was impossible to prevent pilfering with the small number of men available; consequently 40% was stolen by the partisans of the Communist Liberty and Justice Brigade from Pieve. The following day was spent trying to recover the stolen equipment from the partisans.

That night Walker-Brown with his party abandoned the attempt to cross the mountains to ambush the Spezia-Genoa road and spent the night at Sero. The mountain tracks had become solid ice and any movement was impossible without making too much noise. Next day Walker-Brown took a reconnaissance patrol to check the road bridge at Lago as a possible demolition target. It was decided to use 300 lbs of PE for the task. Some of the Troop returned to 'Halifax' to prepare the necessary charges whilst the remainder moved into an ambush position about 300 yards from the Fascist HQ in Borgeto di Vara. They heard vehicles moving down the road towards the bridge but the party at the bridge held their fire as they only had one Bren and the vehicles were allowed to approach the main ambush position. There were three, one of them a captured British staff car, with a trailer, a 10-ton truck with a large trailer and a third vehicle which turned off in Borgeto. As the remaining two vehicles left Borgeto the Bren gun crews opened fire. They fired 32 magazines – a total of nearly 1,000 rounds, and both vehicles and trailers were destroyed with 26 enemy killed.

The following day *Brigata Nere* were reported to be burning houses in the village of Brugnato in reprisal for the ambush; word had reached the Germans and their Fascist allies that the SAS party had halted in this village the

previous day on their way to the ambush. They were not to know that Walker-Brown and his party with the 3-inch mortar and Brens, had returned and taken up positions on the mountain covering the road bridge. By attacking Borgeto twice it was anticipated that the enemy would be forced either to reinforce the garrison or employ a larger forces to clear up the area controlled by the SAS. The intention was to prolong the attack as long as possible and so to prevent transport from using the Spezia-Genoa road.

Fortuitously, before the first mortar bomb had been fired at Borgeto, a lone Republic P-47 Thunderbolt fighter-bomber attacked the town, but its bomb failed to explode. The SAS party then fired three mortar bombs, making the enemy withdraw towards the bridge and the river. This group was engaged with further fire and went to ground on the far side of the river, returning fire with heavy machine guns. Under mortar fire the enemy platoon withdrew in disorder along with small groups as they tried to ford the river.

At 16.00 hours, with all their ammunition expended except the reserve, the troop prepared to move. At this point four Thunderbolts roared over the mountains and attacked Brugnato and Borgeto and strafed the road. To the already shaken enemy it appeared that the SAS had ground-attack aircraft on call. The enemy then brought up a 105mm gun and shelled the hillside heavily. However, the gunners were firing 'blind' and so with no observer to spot targets no rounds fell on the mortar position. The SAS party then withdrew up the mountain with no casualties.

On 14 January there was no resupply as the weather was bad, but on the 15th a drop arrived that included two

Vickers MMGs [See Appendix 3]. The SAS moved back to Rossano, leaving three men guarding the remainder of the supplies that could not be moved as no mules were available.

The group rested on 16 and 17 January but a day later Walker-Brown led them to Colodo with a plan to launch a machine-gun attack on the 300-strong German garrison in Vignola, using the recently-delivered Vickers. They were obliged to abandon the plan because the the approaches were under enemy observation. They moved on to Arzelato and were joined by 20 partisans who, wishing to team up with the SAS for an attack, placed themselves under Walker-Brown's command.

At first light on 19 January the combined group set up an ambush on the Pontremoli-Aulla road. Rumours had circulated in the area that Mussolini would be travelling along this route so there was a prime target to be had. The two Vickers were sited to fire on fixed lines to a point where the road took a drop of 50 feet to the west and a steep cutting to the east. The road was silent until the ambushers heard the sound of motor vehicles coming from Pontremoli and then they picked up the clatter of horses' hooves that indicated that a battery of horse-drawn 10.5cm Howitzers was approaching the town. They waited until both groups were in the ambush 'killing ground' and opened fire. Casualties were unconfirmed but the Germans told the local civilians that there were many dead on the road. The enemy returned ineffective fire but sufficient to make the partisans withdraw hastily.

Just after midnight the party withdrew to Corvette, arriving there, extremely tired, at 07.00 hours. Fifteen minutes later, as dawn was breaking, about 800 German

Gebirgstruppen, specialised mountain troops almost invisible against the snow in their white camouflaged smocks were spotted 250 yards away advancing in extended order. The alarm was raised and incredibly the SAS party pulled back, under mortar and small arms fire but suffered no casualties. A lot of equipment, including sleeping bags, rations, mules and unfortunately the two Vickers MMGs had to be abandoned.

This dawn attack was part of a wider operation in which many towns and villages were hit simultaneously in a bid to eliminate the partisans and SAS. As Walker-Brown and his men moved on to Rio they came under fire from 7.5 cm GebG 36 mountain artillery and pressed on to Monte Gottero and spent the night climbing up the mountain.

At dawn on the 21st they crossed the 5,500-foot summit and halfway up picked up two men of another patrol and some partisans. At 21.00 hours that night they crossed Monte Groppo. A force of 1,200 partisans from varying bands were holding Monte Groppo but vanished on hearing that 400 Germans were one hour's march away. The SAS party continued on to Boschetto and learned that the Germans were still pursuing them and were only one hour away.

On 22 January at 07.00 hours they left Boschetto, which proved to be fortuitous for an hour later 2,000 Germans attacked the town, capturing one of the partisan leaders. At 13.00 hours the party reached Buzzo, joining up with two other patrols. By this time Walker-Brown's group had completed a gruelling 59 hours of continuous marching without rations or rest. They moved into the mountains one hour's march away from Buzzo, cooked up rations and rested for 12 hours. Over the next two days German patrols were everywhere and the party marched for two hours to Nola where they remained on the alert at 'Stand To' positions.

On the 27th the area was reported to be clear and the whole troop linked up in Rossano. The next two days were spent digging up rations, ammunition, a radio set and taking some well-earned rest. Radio communications were very bad with the mountains screening transmission and a blind message was sent requesting a resupply drop. The weather was very bad with low cloud and mist, so they were delighted and very impressed when on 2 February at 08.30 hours a lone USAAF Dakota ran in over the DZ. There was a heart-stopping moment when they realised that the pilot had failed to see the the markers laid out on the ground. For 90 frustrating minutes Walker-Brown's men could hear the aircraft circling the area as the pilot searched for the markers. The pilot finally spotted the DZ signals and with cloud and mist covering the mountains made six very accurate run-ins, allowing himself little or no safety margin. The pilot then made a farewell pass over the DZ and was gone. Remarkably, two hours later he returned and repeated the virtuoso performance. Along with stores and ammunition he dropped a doctor, Captain Milne RAMC, the 2 SAS Regimental Medical Officer (RMO), from the extremely low altitude of about 350 feet. Tragically, it was reported that the pilot crashed soon afterwards in the appalling conditions.

Between 3 and 4 February they awaited the arrival of mules for a move to Borseda and Milne checked the condition of the men, one of whom was now very sick and unable to move. Milne said that once he had recovered he should make his own way back through the lines. On the

5th the troop moved out of Borseda. Walker-Brown decided to ambush the Aulla-Spezia road and mortar the town of Padivarma.

On the night of 7-8 February during the ambush on the Aulla-Spezia road, they destroyed eight enemy vehicles and inflicted heavy casualties on a party of German troops and mules bivouacked by the road. Meanwhile the remainder of the troop attacked the Genoa-Spezia road, destroying two trucks and immobilising a third. Partisans later reported that many enemy had been killed and wounded.

After being hit by SAS mortar barrages the Germans had now taken to requisitioning houses and using the civilian occupants as a type of 'human shield', so to avoid causing civilian casualties the mortar attack on Padivarma was cancelled. In the past the Germans had ejected the owners and so the houses presented a simple target.

On 10 February Walker-Brown decided it was time to begin a slow withdrawal towards the Allied lines. The troop was split into two parties, the first moving off at 15.00 hours and the second two hours later. It was later decided to make a complete withdrawal on Milne's advice that the men were exhausted. It had not been possible to get the mules across the River Magra and as a result the men carried only two days of emergency rations – consisting of one tin of bully beef.

Two days later they reached Vicchette, picking up guides, and the next day continued south. It was a long and tiring trek over very rough country. Rucksacks were dumped and the Bren guns left with the partisans. Only carbines and reserve ammunition were carried in the final slog over Monte Altissimo, which would prove arduous and extremely tiring. It was a dark night and they could not use the normal track since it was known to be mined. This meant that they had to make a 2,000-foot climb on a slope of 1 in 4. They reached the pass at the top of the mountain at about 23.30 hours and at the same time an enemy mortar carried out a heavy shoot on several points along the track. An enemy patrol was avoided and about 03.00 hours a trip flare was set off by one of the party. Fortunately it was not covered by fire and the men pressed on to the Allied lines. They reached safety on 15 February, slipping between two German regiments holding positions on the Gothic Line. Walker-Brown, who led his men back to Allied forces at Livorno was awarded a well-deserved DSO.

The small group had more than achieved their mission. They had destroyed 23 enemy vehicles and killed between 100 and 150 Germans. Goaded by their operations, the Germans, who had been led to believe that the SAS group was much larger than its actual size, had launched an anti-partisan drive and sent 6,000 troops, including a battalion of *Gebirgstruppen* to sweep the area. Crucially the SAS had helped to take the pressure off the battered US 92nd Infantry Division.

Walker-Brown had enjoyed a final triumph as they were close to the German front line, 'Having forded a river at night they came across an isolated cottage in which they found a German Captain 'cementing international relations with an Italian girl'. Walker-Brown's scornful gaze fell on the lovers. 'You're coming with us,' he told the German.'[33]

On 4 March 1945 Operation TOMBOLA was launched. It would prove to be one of the most successful SAS operations in Italy. It showed that the SAS could operate for sustained periods behind enemy lines, assisting the local resistance forces. It had been thought that the desert was the only environment in which special forces could set up a base and attack enemy communications and logistics. For the partisans, the SAS would put extra strength into forces which had previously sometimes avoided contact with the Germans. In the TOMBOLA operational area, Captain Mike Lees of the SOE had already built up the confidence of the local partisans, and they had provided the Allies with a steady supply of valuable low-level intelligence. However, his coup came when he located the position of a German Corps HQ at Albinea, a village in the Po valley.

Lees had collected detailed intelligence about the garrison and HQ through various sources, including a partisan girl courier. Her Italian partisan commander, a man with the unlikely code name of 'Kiss', explained how the intelligence had been gathered.

> *'Well, one of the couriers whom we employ is a very beautiful young lady.' He smiled and, true Italian that he was, a dreamy look came into his eyes. 'She is not averse to love. Last night she returned from Castelnovo where she was visiting the officer in charge of the garrison troops there. She obtained this information. He handed over a slip of paper. There is an important German headquarters at Villa Rossi in Botteghe. It is the HQ of 273 Corps and serves as forward headquarters of the XIV Army. General Feuerstein is living in the villa. Last week Marshal Graziani visited him there.'* [34]

When Major Roy Farran from 3 Squadron 2 SAS parachuted into the area on 4 March, Lees knew that Farran and the six other soldiers were the advance party of a force that could launch an effective attack on the German HQ. Farran had been told by HQ Fifteenth Army Group that he could not be part of the TOMBOLA team. Faced with the prospect of a staff job at HQ, the energetic young Major had contrived to accompany the SAS mission as the dispatcher, and as the men jumped he contrived to 'trip and fall' out of the door of the Dakota, happily whilst wearing a parachute. It was fortuitous, because Lt Easton, who would have commanded the operation, was injured when he landed.

Chatting to Lees, Farran explained with mock innocence,

'Well, a man on a parachute can't go upwards, so here I am ... Of course, there's no way I could get out of here again, is there? I'm supposed to be doing a base job – chairborne!'

I gave him the lead he wanted...

'There's a courier service of course and we've never lost a man on it yet – but it's very dangerous, very dangerous indeed.'

'And we'll be liberated soon?'

'Oh yes, very soon I expect.'

We both burst out laughing. Roy shook my hand.

'In that case I think I ought to stay. Now tell me all about this place you want to beat up. I'm itching to get at it.'[35]

In his after-action report it is clear that Farran

thoroughly enjoyed Operation TOMBOLA. The final paragraph of the summary page reads:

'The details of this story might well be from a book by Forrester. The artillery piece named 'Molto Stanco', the two women staffetas sent to reconnoitre, Barba Nere surrounded by his Q staff of swindlers, Victor Modena the swashbuckling Russian, and finally Major McGinty [Farran] *who by threats and persuasion was able to to achieve cohesion and efficiency from so heterogeneous a force.'*

The bulk of the force, 25 officers and men, that would make up Operation TOMBOLA arrived by parachute on 9 March but in his next equipment request Farran asked for a piper, and on 24 March, Piper D. Kirkpatrick of the 2nd Bn Highland Light Infantry dropped in 'kilt and all, with his pipes under his arm'. Farran admitted that the request gratified his own vanity and 'a piper (would) stir the romantic Italian mind'. It was also a piece of psychological warfare, Farran thought, that for the Germans the sound of a piper leading an attack deep inside enemy lines would be deeply demoralising. By 1944-45 unusual requests were becoming quite common. In France Paddy Mayne had requested that his service dress, complete with Sam Browne, be parachuted in after he had discovered that a Highland officer had arrived behind enemy lines sporting a kilt. At this period SAS troops wore the maroon beret of airborne forces and as a cover for the arrival of these British troops it was explained to the partisans that they were in fact a delegation of the British Labour Party on a liaison visit to the Italian Communist Partisans. The cover worked so well that Lees was asked if the man dressed as a British officer was Sir Stafford Cripps. Stafford Cripps had served as the British Ambassador in

Moscow from 1940-42 and then returned to Britain to become Lord Privy Seal. Farran, who would later stand in an election as a Conservative candidate, would have been amused to have been turned into Sir Stafford Cripps, notorious as a cold, austere dogmatic Socialist.

Farran, who a year earlier had worked with the French Maquis in occupied France, made a telling assessment of the Italian partisans under his direction in his report in 1945.

> *'The partisan forces consisted of three Communist Garibaldini Brigades and one Right Wing Green Flame Brigade, each about three hundred strong and united under the command of a weak but non-political Italian Army Colonel called 'Monti'. Each of these Brigades had good detachments of old partisans, about fifty strong, who carried out offensive action perhaps once a month, but the remainder were absolutely useless and no menace to the enemy. They would fire with Stens at ranges of over two thousand yards but if the Germans came any closer they would run away. Against Italian Fascist troops, however, they would fight.'*

The attack on the German HQ on the night of 26-27 March would be a twenty-minute operation, the aim of which would be kill as many of the 300 Germans at the HQ as possible, ideally the Corps commander and to burn down the two villas that housed the HQ. The Russians would secure the road leading to the villas, while the SAS, partisans and some Russians assaulted the two buildings that made up the HQ: Villa Calvi – the Corps HQ and operations room – and the soldiers' billets and the Corps Commander's accommodation in the elegant red-stucco Villa Rossi.

Farran contacted HQ Fifteenth Army Group for clearance to launch the operation and was given the go-ahead. However, with the planned major offensive in the Po valley in the offing in April the HQ staff realised that if an attack were launched a few days later it would cause added confusion. If the attack was launched earlier it might give the Germans some indication that larger operations were in the offing. They signalled the TOMBOLA force to delay the attack, but it was too late; Farran and his force had started the long march from the mountains down to their objective. His radio remained back in his mountain hideout and so the cancellation order never reached him. He added in his after-action report 'In any case, having once committed a Partisan force to such an attack an alteration in plan would have been disastrous to guerilla morale in the whole area.'

Farran divided the force into three columns and an HQ. The HQ was composed of himself with two SAS soldiers and two Italian guides. The Left Column, under Lt Ken Harvey, a young Rhodesian officer was made up of nine SAS and 20 Garibaldini. They would attack Villa Calvi. The Centre Column under Lt J. Riccomini with nine SAS, Lees and a mixed force of Russians and Italian partisans would attack Villa Rossi. The Right Column under Major Victor Modena would block the road to the south leading to Botteghe d'Albine, the most likely route that a German quick-reaction force would take.

The 70 Russians who were part of the partisan group were in Lees' view rather suspect. Some, starving in PoW camps, had been recruited by the Germans for service in the Wehrmacht as anti-partisan troops and in this role they had proved to be particularly brutal. Now, as the war swung against the Germans, they had escaped to join the partisans. However some were genuine escaped PoWs including Modena, one of two officers.

Lees remembered the final briefing before the attack. 'I looked at the ring of faces around the fire. Italian-Russians-German-British; features so different but in expression all the same. Quiet, determined and unafraid, thinking not of the morrow but only that we must succeed tonight...It was black as pitch in the yard outside. A last minute inspection was completed, to ensure that all hands and faces had been liberally blackened with soot, a word of command whispered and the column moved off into the night.'[36]

The plan called for the crew of a 2.36-inch M1 Rocket Launcher, a lightweight anti-tank weapon commonly known as a Bazooka, to fire at the back door of Villa Calvi, but in the event at the critical moment there were two misfires and Harvey realised that German sentries were approaching. 'I could see the sentries now only a few feet away, four of them marching up the road.' He stood up and opened fire; 'It was essential this was all done at point-blank range to ensure they were killed immediately because the shots would set off the whole area.'[37] Farran noted in his report that 'All four sentries were killed before they knew that they were being attacked. The door was locked but was eventually forced after weakening by Bren fire. There was furious fighting...The ground floor was taken but its was not possible to ascend the spiral staircase. More casualties were inflicted on the defenders on the upper floors, however, by Bren and Bazooka fire from the lawn.'

The attack went in, with Piper Kirkpatrick playing 'Highland Laddie'. In the darkness now shattered by gunfire, a German MG42 machine-gunner ripped off bursts of fire in Kirkpatrick's direction. Besides the effect on British and Partisan morale of the sound of the piper, Farran reasoned that this unique warlike music would confirm to the Germans that this was a British-led attack and so hopefully reduce the risk of German reprisals against the local population.

At Villa Calvi the SAS force drove the Germans upstairs and in Farran's words, 'a fire was carefully started in the registry and the map room. As the party was withdrawing Villa Calvi was burning furiously'.

At Villa Rossi the attackers suffered casualties because the Germans had had a few seconds' warning. The alarm was given by an air-raid klaxon and all the lights went on, illuminating the courtyard. Fortunately the elaborate iron gates were open and the SAS force stormed through under machine-gun fire. The front door was open and after fierce fighting on the ground floor the Germans withdrew upstairs but fought hard, rolling grenades down the elegant curving staircase. Two attempts to storm the staircase were repulsed and Lt Jim Riccomini was killed.

Riccomini, a veteran of Operation GALIA, had volunteered for TOMBOLA but yearned for the end of the war so that he could join the girl he had married back in 1939, just weeks after the outbreak of war. In a letter home to his young wife before the operation he anticipated the problems of adjustment that would plague – and still plagues – Special Forces soldiers who have lived on the edge: '...the real thing that worries me is that I might never be able to settle down after all this ... however, darling, remember that I do think of you very often, and that one day I will be home again.'

In the darkness and cacophony of Villa Rossi six Germans attempted a counterattack down the stairs but died in a hail of gunfire. The SAS soldiers shot out the lights on the ground floor and an attempt was made to start a fire in the kitchen. After twenty minutes, when Farran fired a signal flare, the party withdrew, carrying its wounded through heavy fire.

South of the two villas, Farran reported that the Russian troops returned fire very accurately 'and their ring was never broken during the attack. Several enemy machine-guns were silenced and heavy casualties were inflicted, especially in the area of the Telephone Exchange. Towards the end of the attack the anti-aircraft guns at Puannello were firing at Villa Rossi and star shells were fired from Botteghe, Modena and Reggio.'

It was a spectacular action at a critical time in the war in Northern Italy. Though they had failed to kill General Hauck, the Corps commander, who was absent, the SAS and partisans had killed 60 Germans, including the Chief of Staff, and destroyed maps, orders and reports in the Corps HQ which would have disrupted the whole of the enemy front from Bologna to the sea. Total casualties were three killed (all British), three British, three Italian and two Russians wounded and six Russians captured.

Among the wounded was Mike Lees. In the attack on the Villa Rossi he had been hit by a grenade fragment that had paralysed his left leg from the knee downwards. Over 22 hours the partisans carried the wounded SOE officer back into friendly territory and then smuggled him deeper into safety in a captured German ambulance. An Italian doctor warned him that if he did not receive proper medical attention he was in danger of losing his leg. Eventually a captured German Fieseler *Storch*, now in RAF markings and flown by an Italian pilot escorted by P-51 Mustangs, landed in a remote mountain airstrip. It was a tribute to the pilot and aircraft that he landed and took off on a field only 100 yards long and 30 wide, and Lees was evacuated to safety. The nerve damage to his leg was repaired and he regained full use of the limb, returning after the war to join his partisan comrades in unveiling a plaque on the wall of Villa Rossi to those killed in the attack.

Goaded by the attack, the Germans quickly launched an aggressive sweep of the mountains in the area. The partisans under Farran's direction employed the local civilians to dig three defensive positions which were permanently manned and intended to protect the valley in which the force had set up its base. Two were sited on high ground – Mt Penna Ridge and Mt Torricella and the third covered Cias Pass. The pass was well protected with a 75mm M1A1 Pack Howitzer, 3-inch mortar, Vickers MMG and ten Bren guns and garrisoned by a mixed British and Garibaldini force. On Mt Penna the Russian Coy had a 3-inch mortar, a .50-in Browning, an Italian Cannone da 47/32 47mm gun and ten Bren guns. Finally Mt Torricella, held by an Italian Coy, had a 47mm gun, 3-inch mortar and ten Bren guns. The three positions had sufficient rations for a week, with a reserve buried in the snow behind Mt Cusna that would last for another week. In addition, a mobile force of ten British and ten Italians was held in reserve at Santonia to fight a rearguard action if the valley came under sustained and heavy attack. Farran's orders to all the detachments reflected the reality of this type of operation. They were 'to hold on to the outer positions as long as possible after the partisans had run away, then to withdraw to the main positions which would be held for at least a week.' All companies would then withdraw into a position at Cisa, higher up the mountains.

They were still in action at the end of April when the Allied spring offensive was launched. Their operations would in many ways mirror those of No 1 ISAS, albeit launched from a secure base and with with greater resources. Under Farran the motley group of partisans, Russians and SAS had built up an impressive armoury which included Jeeps, a 75mm Pack Howitzer {See Appendix 3], mortars, heavy and medium machine guns.

In his after-action report Farran would note under 'Lessons Learnt' – 'The gun and the mortar are essential adjuncts to an S.A.S. Operation and it is surprising that we have never before realised their value. The overall effect of shelling an enemy-occupied town, I am quite certain, is much greater than killing a few Germans with small-arms fire on a road, even if the shell-fire produces no casualties whatsoever.' Between 28 March and 23 April his force would shell 19 enemy-held towns and villages.

In a memorable account Farran describes how the SAS team with their howitzer spotted a German column withdrawing over a bridge across the Sécchia south of Modena on 22 April. The troops were from the 114th, 232nd and 334th Divisions, elements of which would later have tangled with men of No1 Italian SAS as they struggled to escape to the illusory security of the River Po. To Farran, the cavalryman, it was 'a wonderful sight - the sort of target the gunners dream about at Larkhill [the British Army school of artillery]....'[38] He writes in his report:

'This was the biggest day of the whole operation... at 14.30 hours we opened fire on the ford at Magreta, which was crammed full of trucks and carts. Aircraft overhead had obviously taken no notice, presumably supposing it to be an Allied column. Many shells were fired into the target and two trucks were set on fire. Horses and carts bolted or turned over. The aircraft noticed the smoke and dive-machine-gunned the column until twelve trucks were on fire, of which we claim three. We supposed then that the column would abandon the attempt to cross until nightfall, but within two hours they were crossing again and also crossing over the bridge at Sassuolo, obviously in an awful hurry. We opened fire again at the Sassuolo Bridge over open sights. The shooting was very good and five more trucks were destroyed. Many shells fell on the bridge but the column continued to cross.

We switched to the Magreta ford again and the enemy vehicles spread out in the river bed. Some ambulances drew off and formed a circle, lighting fires to show that they were ambulances and did not expect to be fired on. Horses and carts bolted again. One big truck towing a gun got stuck in the river and did not move again.

I put the Vickers MG in position to fire at the road running from the Sassuolo bridge. It destroyed three large trucks for certain and an unknown number of horses and carts.'

Given the rather grandiloquent title of *Battaglione Alleata* by its partisan leader, at the end of the war Farran's force had inflicted 600 casualties on the enemy and captured over 400. Like the men of No 1 ISAS they found that the Fifth and Eighth Army offensives had swept over the area and now, with the enemy gone, Farran could bring his men down from the mountains into Modena.

As his group, consisting of four Jeeps, two civilian cars, two captured trucks and a German ambulance towing the 75 mm howitzer bowled past the tanks and trucks of the US Fifth Army, he was aware that 'we were all covered with grime of months in the mountains, and our shabbiness was in sharp contrast to the huge armoured columns we passed on the road. They must have wondered who on earth we could be.

'We were 'Battaglione Alleato' (SAS), otherwise known as the 'Battaglione McGinty', whose motto was '*Chi osera ci vincere*', which being translated means 'Who dares wins.'[39]

At the close of Operation TOMBOLA Farran would say of the Italians and Russians, 'The Russians were only good in mass fighting in defensive actions and I was very disappointed in the reduction of their offensive spirit after they had had a few casualties. The Italians were only just worth feeding when they had a little British stiffening. Consequently, all the burden of this operation fell on the British component of the battalion, who were first class but very tired towards the end.'

There was a bitter end of the operation for Roy Farran; he received orders from remote SO (M) headquarters in Florence to disarm his Russian troops. 'I am afraid to say that I had not the moral courage for what seemed to us at the time to be such a cruel, unfair and premature act...I left orders with a rear party to disarm them in Reggio, after the victory parade in four days' time.'[40]

28 *Stirling's Men*, Gavin Mortimer
29 Ibid.
30 *Stirling's Men*
31 The Drop Zone (DZ). For parachutists and containers in a covert operation, this was normally open ground (870 by 220 yds) at the edge of a wood where, once they had been recovered, containers could be opened and contents distributed. Agricultural carts provided by local farmers were positioned to recover the containers quickly. In open ground a Eureka radar homing beacon was positioned and a man with a signalling torch gave the pilot a visual and electronic fix on the DZ. Aircraft were fitted with an answering device codenamed *Rebecca*, which showed range and orientation to port or starboard on a vertical scale. For the final run-in and visual fix for the pilot on the DZ, three bonfires spaced at 100-yard intervals were ignited by partisans and the parachute containers were dropped from a height of 100 to 200 yards.
32 *Stirling's Men*
33 *Stirling's Men*
34 *Special Operations Executed*, Michael Lees
35 Ibid.
36 *Special Operations Executed*
37 Ibid.
38 *Operation Tombola*, Roy Farran, Collins, London, 1960
39 Ibid.
40 Ibid.

Chapter 6

The Last Offensive

Snow melts in the sun and liberty descends from the mountains with our Partisan brigades. A superb dawn breaks on our 25th of April.

La Resistenza Italia, 21 April 1945

Nineteen months after the Allied landings in Sicily, and after hard fighting up the rugged mountainous spine of the Italian peninsula, the goal of a quick victory and knock-out blow had eluded the Anglo-American commanders in the Mediterranean Theatre. However, there were some clear successes Rome had been liberated and Fascist Italy had become a shadow state based in the German-occupied north. Elsewhere in Europe, France and most of Belgium had also been liberated, and in the east the Soviet Union had reclaimed almost all of the territory previously conquered by the Germans in 1941-2.

However, in the larger strategic arena, by spring 1944 Italy had become a sideshow, a secondary theatre as the western Allies shifted their military resources north to support the build-up and execution of Operation OVERLORD, the invasion of Normandy. After that, there had been no turning back on the Anglo-American side, with its main effort directed east through the northern

European plains. By April 1945 Germany was besieged on three sides, although the Allied forces in the south, strung out along the northern Apennines overlooking the Po Valley, were now the farthest away from the tottering Third Reich. Churchill continued to strongly support an advance from northern Italy into the Balkans and southern Germany. However, the ability of the Italian-based Allied armies to sustain such an effort with minimal support in men and materiel seemed problematic.

The aim of the Fifteenth Army Group offensive in Italy in April 1945 was to break through the German defensive line along the Apennines and the River Po plain to the Adriatic Sea. They would then swiftly push north to occupy northern Italy and drive for the Austrian and Yugoslav borders. However, German fortifications, demolished bridges, mined roads, irrigation and drainage canals and localised resistance over the Po Valley plain would make this a tough challenge. The fear was that German forces might be able to fight a phased withdrawal using the river lines, delay the Allies and then fight a sustained campaign secure in the mountains of the *Alpenfestung* – Alpine Fortress – of Austria and southern Germany. There were even intelligence reports that Nazi leaders had secure bases already constructed for a final defence of this Alpine Valhalla. The possibility of having to fight in the Alps and that Nazi leaders might evacuate Berlin and go to ground in the mountains haunted Allied planners and would be one of the drivers for launching the offensive in Italy in 1945.

As the year opened, the Allies still faced an organised and determined foe in Italy, consisting of twenty-four German and five Italian Fascist divisions. The Axis units were divided among the Tenth, Fourteenth and Ligurian Armies, all under Army Group C, Lt General Heinrich von Vietinghoff's command. Lt General Joachim von Lemelson commanded the Fourteenth Army, consisting of the LI Mountain and XVI Panzer Korps, which opposed Truscott's Fifth Army in the west. Opposite the Eighth Army to the east was the German Tenth Army, commanded by Lt. General Traugott Herr, with the I *Fallschirm* and LXXVI *Panzer Korps*. The main road through the city of Bologna, still in Axis hands, constituted the boundary line for both sides.

The majority of Axis troops in Italy were experienced veterans in relatively intact units. Although fairly well led and supplied in 1944, they lacked vehicles, firepower and air support, and by early 1945 were experiencing increasingly troublesome fuel and equipment shortages. Yet the winter had allowed them some respite and time to build a line of defences that made maximum use of the rugged Italian terrain, rivers and waterways.

Their first line, along the northern Apennines, protected Bologna and blocked entry into the east-west Po Valley, about 50 miles further north. The German Fourteenth Army had built fortifications on steep mountain fingers anchored on higher ridge lines and consisting of mutually supporting positions providing good observation and fields of fire. Although the mountain fingers widened as they neared the flat valley floors, here the terrain was intersected by tree lines, hedgerows, and drainage ditches that restricted cross-country mobility and provided excellent cover. In addition, the Po's southern tributaries emerged from the mountains to cross the valley floors, intersecting possible routes of advance and serving as potential defensive positions.

However, this terrain would work against the Germans when the full weight of the Fifteenth Army Group spring offensive broke over northern Italy, and Army Group C was forced out of its defensive positions and began to retreat northwards to the Po. The Germans would find themselves restricted to a limited network of roads and tracks and unable to travel cross-country. It was this inability to manoeuvre that would play into the hands of the roving patrols from No 1 Italian SAS.

The German generals planned to anchor their second defensive line along the Po. From its source in north-western Italy, the river meanders east to the Adriatic Sea. It varies in width from 130 to 500 yards and is often bordered by steep embankments serving as natural fortifications that could be made stronger with fieldworks, mines and barbed wire. As in northern Europe, the towns and villages along the river would provide natural fortifications, while the more developed east-west road system would ease the resupply for the defenders.

The third line of fortifications in the Alpine foothills, named the Adige or Venetian Line, after the river around which they were built, extended east and west of Lake Garda; it would be held to cover a last-ditch Axis withdrawal into north-east Italy and Austria. The Adige Line, with its intricate system of trenches, bunkers and machine-gun emplacements, was reminiscent of World War 1. If stoutly defended it could be the toughest line yet encountered in Italy. Before he was posted to the battered Western Front Kesselring had prepared Operation AUTUMN MIST, the withdrawal to Adige.

In 1944 the Fifteenth Army Group, under Field Marshal Alexander, consisted of General Clark's Fifth Army and

General Oliver Leese's Eighth Army. By the summer of 1944 they had become a formidable team that had ended the stalemate on the Gustav Line, advanced up the Liri valley, captured Rome, and pursued retreating Axis forces north across the River Arno into the northern Apennines, to the very edge of the Po Valley and the heart of northern Italy.

In December 1944 General Truscott replaced General Clark following the latter's departure to command the Fifteenth Army Group. Before Truscott took command, however, the Allied offensive in the northern Apennines had ground to a halt. Both Allied armies were exhausted; men, equipment, and supplies had been siphoned off to support operations in north-western Europe and elsewhere. This lack of resources, combined with the harsh winter weather, rugged terrain and stiff resistance, had left the Allies short of their immediate goal, the heavily fortified communications centre of Bologna, a few miles to the north in central Italy.

However, the Axis were also operating under severe handicaps. The most significant were the 'no retreat' orders imposed on commanders in the field by Hitler and the OKW, and by Germany's growing shortages in manpower and equipment. Senior commanders in Italy had made repeated requests to withdraw from the Apennines to the stronger positions along the Po before the expected Allied offensive. Permission was always flatly denied and Hitler's subsequent directives compelled local commanders to hold their positions until enemy action forced their retreat. Rigid adherence to this policy posed many risks for the defenders and made it difficult, if not impossible, to conduct organised withdrawals in the face of overwhelming Allied air and ground superiority.

As the Axis forces dug in, the Fifth and Eighth Armies prepared for the coming battle. In the first four months of 1945 intensive efforts were made to rebuild strength and morale. Front-line units were rotated to the rear for rest, relaxation and training. Replacements were worked into tired units and damaged or worn equipment was replaced or rebuilt. Staff officers and quartermasters requisitioned, hoarded and stockpiled equipment and supplies, especially artillery ammunition. Fuel pipelines were built, supply dumps planned and bridging equipment collected. However, due to the shortages caused by the equipment and manpower demands of other theatres, this process took time. In the end, however, Allied manpower and artillery superiority, critical in the rugged Italian terrain, outnumbered the Axis by two or three to one. By now the Eighth Army – like the Fourteenth Army in Burma – was beginning to receive equipment that had been developed for the D-Day invasion and other amphibious operations. Among the vehicles were Kangaroo armoured personnel carriers – actually turretless M4 Shermans and amphibious Buffalo LVTs – Landing Vehicles Tracked. Equipped with the LVTs, which the British called Fantails, on the right flank, Lake Comacchio would no longer be an obstacle for the Eighth Army but a way to outflank their German opponents. Terrifying flame-throwing Churchill Crocodile tanks would prove brutally effective against bunkers and field fortifications and Ark bridge-laying tanks would allow armour to cross the ditches that would have normally slowed them down. The armour included Sherman tanks fitted with spoon-shaped extensions to their tracks that allowed the armour to operate on soft ground – they were called Platypus Grousers. Grouped in the 9th Armoured Bde commanded by Brigadier R. B. B. Cooke, the tank crews had honed their skills in a training centre on Lake Trasimeno.

By early 1945 the Fifth Army had about 270,000 men (with over 30,000 reserves in replacement depots), over 2,000 artillery pieces and mortars and thousands of vehicles, all positioned along a 120-mile front extending east from the Ligurian coast, across the crest of the Apennines, to a point south-east of Bologna. The commander's major combat units included five US infantry divisions (the 34th, 7th, 88th, 91st, and 92nd), the US 10th Mountain, a specialist division made up of volunteers who before the war had been climbers or skiers and consequently were often college educated, and 1st Armored Division, the Japanese-American 442nd Regiment, as well as the 1st Brazilian Infantry Division, the Italian CIL *Legnano* Combat Group, and the 6th South African Armoured Division. The South African division would have the distinction of serving in both the Fifth and Eighth Armies and having within its order of battle the British 24th Guards Infantry Brigade. The US IV Corps in the west, under Major-General Willis D. Crittenberger, and the US II Corps in the east, under Major-General Geoffrey Keyes, shared control of the ten division equivalents.

On the Fifth Army's right flank was the Eighth Army, commanded by General McCreery. Containing the Polish II Corps and the British V, X, and XIII Corps, the Eighth Army was composed of eight divisions from four different nations, as well as four co-belligerent Italian battle groups and a Jewish brigade recruited from Palestine. By April 1945 their line extended from the Bologna area east to the Adriatic, ten miles north of Ravenna. The Poles, desperately under strength in the autumn of 1944, had received 11,000 reinforcements during the early months of 1945, mainly from their fellow nationals conscripted into the German Army and taken prisoner in Normandy the previous year. However, though the Poles were superb soldiers, they required careful handling, since they felt that the British and Americans had betrayed their country at the 'Big Three' Yalta Conference. Poland had passed into the Soviet sphere of influence and the homeland for which they had fought was still not free. Poles would say that under the Nazis they risked losing their lives, but under the Soviet Union they risked losing their souls. Despite these tensions, Clark, writing in his autobiography *Calculated Risk* said, 'In all our plans for the offensive, the Polish corps figured prominently – I had high confidence in their fighting spirit, and they were moved into a vital spot along the north side of the road to Bologna.'

This move was part of a new general offensive that Clark planned to launch in early April 1945. Unlike earlier campaigns in Italy he clearly assigned the major role to American forces. Prior to the main offensive, D-Day–5, the US 92nd Infantry Division was to launch a diversionary attack, Operation SECOND WIND, along the Ligurian coast, to capture Massa and push towards La Spezia. Then, on 9 April the Eighth Army was to penetrate enemy defences east of Bologna, drawing enemy reserves from the vital communications hub.

Four days before the offensive, McCreery assembled all the officers under his command down to the rank of Lt

Colonel at a cinema in Cesena. 'In his quiet, almost apologetic, voice,' recalled Colonel R. L. V. ffrench-Blake, who was present at the briefing, 'he said that the theatre had been stripped of troops for France; that the army was like an old steeplechaser, full of running, but rather careful; that it was his intention to destroy the Germans south of the Po, rather than to allow them to withdraw to further defence lines in the north. The plan was then outlined.'

That evening Colonel ffrench-Blake returned to the cinema to see the new colour film of the Shakespeare play *Henry V* starring Laurence Olivier. 'Suitable entertainment for the occasion' he recalled 'though the scene where the king goes round the camp at night and talks to the young soldier was rather too poignant. The boy says: 'We see yonder the beginning of the day, but I think we shall never see the end.'

Following these diversionary attacks, the Fifteenth Army Group's main effort, Operation CRAFTSMAN, would be launched by the Fifth Army around 11 April. Initially, Fifth Army units were to penetrate the enemy's defences west of Bologna, move into the southern Po Valley and then capture the city itself. Rather than destroying the German forces, the initial phase of CRAFTSMAN was intended to penetrate the Axis front and seize key ground as a base for further operations in the Po Valley. Truscott intended to attack with forces from both corps advancing on two parallel axes, staggering the assaults to allow the maximum concentration of air and artillery support for each. Crittenberger's IV Corps would attack first, west of Routes 64 and 65 that led north to Bologna. One day later, Keyes' II Corps would attack north along Route 65 and take Bologna. During Phase II, both Allied armies would continue north towards the Bondeno-Ferrara area, 30 miles north of Bologna, trapping Axis forces south of the Po. Finally, Phase III would see the combined Allied armies cross the Po and advance to Verona, 50 miles further north, before fanning out into northern Italy, Austria, and Yugoslavia, completing the destruction of the Axis forces in southern Europe.

On 5 April 1945 the US 92nd Infantry Division began its diversionary attack on the Ligurian coast. The division had been rebuilt after it had been bloodied in Operation WINTERGEWITTER – Winter Thunderstorm, an Axis counter-offensive in December 1944 – and had suffered again during a stalled offensive in the River Serchio valley in February 1945. The SAS Operation GALIA had been launched in December in part to draw German forces away from the front line and take the pressure off the battered and demoralised division. The 92nd, designated in the Fifth Army order of battle 92nd (Negro) Division was in the words of Dominick Graham and Shelford Bidwell, 'in effect the American equivalent of a 'colonial' division, with black NCOs and rank and file, some black officers, but the command and staff mainly white. Such a unit can only be effective if pride of race is actually encouraged and only the best of white officers employed, and it was precisely these two essentials that were ignored.'

The division was restructured and reinforced with one black regiment made up of the best of the original infantry, one Nisei regiment of US-born Japanese and a regiment of men from the anti-aircraft artillery retrained as infantry. The new 92nd Division, preceded by air and artillery bombardments, attacked before dawn with the 370th Infantry and the attached 442nd Regimental Combat

Team. As troops of the 370th advanced through the foothills along the coastal road towards Massa, they were halted by heavy enemy fire.

Further inland, however, Nisei soldiers of the 442nd scaled the Apuan Alps to outflank Massa from the east. After several days of such savage fighting, they captured Massa, and by 11 April pushed north to the famed marble quarries of Carrara. Here, determined enemy resistance held up the American drive for over a week.

It was during this fighting that Los Angeles-born Sadao S. Munemori, whose parents had emigrated to the United States from Japan, would win the Medal of Honor. In fighting for a hilltop position near Seravazza, Munemori, of Coy A, 100th Infantry Bn, 442nd Regiment took command of his squad when the squad leader was killed. He then led them through a minefield, grenaded two machine gun positions and then, when a German grenade landed amongst his men, he threw himself on it, taking the full blast, but saving the lives of his comrades. In the fighting in Italy the Nisei would win 47 DSCs, 354 Silver Stars and more than 3,600 Purple Hearts – their loyalty to the United States and courage in battle had been proved beyond question.

Corporal Bill Pickering, an SOE radio operator with the partisans, recalled the surprise of the population of the small Italian town of Superga to see that the liberating US soldiers were Nisei troops of the 442nd.

To the east, on the Adriatic coast, Polish, Indian, New Zealand, and British soldiers of the Eighth Army surged forward on 9 April, after a massive air and artillery barrage that began with strikes by 234 USAAF medium bombers, which dropped 24,000 20lb incendiary bombs. They were followed by ground attacks by 740 fighter-bombers and finally raids by 825 heavy bombers, which dropped 1,692 tons of bombs on targets around the city of Lugo. The artillery fire plan that followed began with a 42-minute barrage by 1,500 guns; when it stopped and the dazed defenders braced themselves for the armour and infantry assault – it did not come. What did come, after an interval, was another barrage, followed by two more 'false alarms'. General McCreery had the advantage of being able to deploy the heavy bombers of MATAF, which had previously been tasked with attacks on strategic targets in southern Germany. While the artillery hit the lightly-manned front-line positions, the bombers were able to destroy the German depth positions that had been sited out of range of heavy artillery.

On the coast, on the strip of land that divided Lake Comacchio from the Adriatic, men of the Royal Marines were tasked with launching attacks in a deception plan codenamed Operation ROAST. It was designed to keep the Germans distracted and take their focus off where the main weight of the Allied offensive would fall. Deception operations were also launched to suggest that a landing might be made on the Adriatic coast and this led to General von Schwering and the LXXVI *Panzer Korps* being positioned north of Lake Comacchio – a position where they would have little influence on the upcoming battle. (There is an interesting parallel with the deception plan employed by Coalition forces in the First Gulf War in 1991 when Iraqi commanders were convinced that an amphibious assault might be made on Kuwait and consequently deployed men and equipment along the coast).

It was during the fighting around Lake Comacchio that

Anders Lassen, a 24-year-old Danish officer commanding a squadron of the Special Boat Service – formed from No 1 SAS - would win the first SAS Victoria Cross. Lassen had already won the MC with two bars in earlier operations. The citation for his VC published in the *London Gazette* of September 4, 1945 read:

In Italy, on the night of 8/9 April, 1945, Major Lassen was ordered to take out a patrol and raid the north shore of Lake Comacchio. His task was to cause casualties, capture prisoners and give the impression of a major landing. The patrol was challenged and came under machine-gun fire. Major Lassen himself attacked with grenades and silenced two enemy posts, capturing two prisoners and killing several Germans. The patrol had suffered casualties and was still under fire. Major Lassen moved forward and flung more grenades into a third enemy position, calling upon the enemy to surrender. He was then hit and mortally wounded, but whilst falling he flung a grenade, wounding more of the enemy and enabling his patrol to capture this last position. Finally, he refused to be evacuated lest he should impede the withdrawal and endanger further lives. His high sense of devotion to duty and the esteem in which he was held by the men he led, added to his own magnificent courage, enabled Major Lassen to carry out with complete success all the tasks he had been given.

Lassen was in many ways like his fellow SAS officer Paddy Mayne – a violent man who thrived on the adrenaline fix of war. Many years later, an SBS veteran who served under him said of Lassen that he had two drives – bedding women and killing Germans. Peacetime Denmark would have been an impossible place for him and perhaps his death weeks before the end of the war should not be seen as a tragedy. Three years earlier, on the night of 3/4 October 1942, it was Lassen's raid on the Channel Island of Sark, leading a small party from the Small Scale Raiding Force (SSRF) in Operation BASALT that led to Hitler's promulgation of the Commando Order (See Appendix 1).

On 2 April 1945, 21-year-old Corporal Thomas Peck Hunter, serving in 43 Commando Royal Marines, would win the first Royal Marine Commando VC. When his section was pinned down by enemy machine guns, Hunter picked up the section Bren gun and charged alone across 200 yards of open ground under most intense fire towards a group of houses where three MG42 machine gun were sited. So determined was his charge that the enemy soldiers were demoralised and six of the crew surrendered. The remainder fled. Hunter cleared the house, changing magazines as he ran and continued to draw enemy fire until most of the troop had reached cover. Hunter was killed, firing accurately to the last.

During the following days the Eighth Army took on the 26th Panzer, 98th Infantry, 362nd Infantry, 4th Parachute, and 42nd Jäger Divisions across the entire front, gradually pushing them north toward the vital Argenta Gap, just west of the muddy waters of Lake Comacchio. To the south of Argenta the marshy ground and the rivers Sillaro and Idice made movement by vehicles difficult. In spite of the stubborn resistance of the German Tenth Army, the British 78th Division, assisted by the amphibious operations launched from Lake

Comacchio, seized the Argenta gap on 18 April, threatening to turn the entire left flank of Army Group C. To the men of the Eighth Army the Argenta Gap was more than a tactical feature – a breakthrough would ensure that the war in Italy was brought to a speedy conclusion and this in turn meant that their chances of survival were greatly increased.

Above them, General McCreery, flying in an Auster Aerial Observation Post (AOP) aircraft, watched the battle develop. 'In the evening dusk, the spectacle was most impressive', he recalled, 'the usual huge artillery and fighter bomber support being supplemented by the flame-throwing tanks.'

On 10 April V Corps, under General Keightley, had launched the first of two amphibious hooks on the muddy water of Lake Comacchio, outflanking the German Tenth Army. The first, Operation IMPACT PLAIN, put men of the 56th Division ashore at Menate; they turned the flank of the forces covering the critical Argenta Gap. A second amphibious operation, IMPACT ROYAL, followed on 18 April.

The Eighth Army's successes had set the stage for the Fifth Army's main effort. The American attack was planned for 12 April, but was postponed when dense fog covered most Allied airfields. It was on that day that American and Allied morale dipped when they heard the news of the death of President Franklin D. Roosevelt. He had been a firm ally of Britain, even when the United States was not at war, and a President, who even though he was suffering from increasing ill health, had been an inspirational national leader.

A day later, conditions in fog-bound northern Italy had

not improved and forecasts for the following day were equally grim. On 14 April, General Crittenberger, commanding IV Corps, was still waiting and the first weather forecasts that morning remained gloomy. However, as the sun rose it began to burn the fog away, and fighter-bombers of the XXII Tactical Air Command took off to attack Axis positions and communications. The navigators now had detailed target folders with photographs and marked maps but despite this, 21-year-old Nardina Donnatini, living in the Appenine village of Marradi, would see the grim results of what today would be called collateral damage.

On market day, walking into town, she heard the sound of approaching USAAF medium bombers:

'I immediately knew, something told me, the Americans were coming to bomb the bridges...The bombs started to fall, and I heard the scream as they fell. I threw myself flat on the ground and the bombs burst. I could feel the air beat over me and debris all over my head. When the bombers had finished there wasn't much left of Marradi...A terrible sound came from the town below – screams and moans and the injured and trapped, men's voices and animals in pain. Those sounds have stayed with me to this day. Many people were killed and injured – my aunt and cousin were among the dead. The railway bridge and road bridge were untouched.'

Knowing that the bridges would be a target for a subsequent attack, the family left Marradi, returning after the Allied offensive had swept over the area. 'There were Indian soldiers living in our house,' she remembered and added, 'and the bridges were still standing'.

Shortly after the air attacks by the XXII Tactical Air Command, at about 09.00 hours on 14 April Truscott ordered the Fifth Army to attack. Crittenberger initially planned to push IV Corps north against the Fourteenth Army, with the 10th Mountain and 1st Armored Division moving abreast between the valleys of the Rivers Panaro and Reno. They would stagger their attacks to allow concentrated fire support for each unit and to help the 10th Mountain Division seize the Rocca Rofferno massif, north of the Pra del Bianco basin, a small bowl-shaped valley marking the division's starting position. Control of these and successive heights would ease the 1st Armored Division's attack to the east and pave the way for the seizure of the village of Ponte Samoggia, 20 miles further north, midway on the Modena-Bologna road on the southern edge of the Po Valley.

The crossing of the Pra del Bianco was a critical first step in breaking through the Axis defences. Guarded by minefields and numerous strongpoints, the heights provided enemy soldiers of the 334th, 94th Infantry, and 90th Panzer Grenadier Divisions of the LI Mountain and XIV Panzer Korps with excellent defensive positions and fields of observation. Nonetheless, after 40 minutes of air attacks and a 35-minute artillery bombardment, the 10th Mountain Division began its advance. Although the Americans quickly discovered that the Axis defences were still largely intact, they doggedly pushed forward.

To the east, the 1st Armored Division had launched a two-pronged attack in the valley of the River Reno along Route 64 and the adjacent heights. At 17.50 hours the 81st Cavalry Reconnaissance Squadron began the offensive by storming the heavily-defended town of Vergato just west of the river. Within two hours the Americans controlled half of the town, but were halted by fierce enemy mortar and machine-gun fire and costly street fighting before they resumed their drive north.

West of the two attacking American divisions, men of the 25,000-strong Brazilian Expeditionary Force went into action. Patrols had entered the town of Montese, west of the Pra del Bianco, in the early morning without making contact with the 334th Division, but a larger force moving into the area later in the day encountered strong resistance from an alerted enemy, and a sharp firefight followed. After lengthy and bitter fighting the Brazilians forced the enemy to withdraw.

Between 15-18 April, the IV Corps area was the scene of intense ground action as the 10th Mountain and 1st Armored Division slowly pushed northward, expelling Axis forces from Monte Pigna, Monte Mantino, Monte Mosca, Monte Pero and the valley of the Reno. As elsewhere during the Italian campaign, the fighting consisted of fierce small-unit actions between ridge lines and valley towns, accounting for heavy casualties on both sides. Yet superior American firepower and aggressive infantry attacks slowly pushed back troops of the 94th Infantry and 90th Panzer Grenadier Division, XIV Panzer Korps, who fought stubbornly but futilely to halt the Americans. Although the IV Corps had advanced only six miles by 19 April, US Army soldiers were beginning to detect signs that the first Axis defensive line in the northern Apennines was about to give way.

To the immediate east, Keyes' II Corps pursued its own offensive. During the afternoon of 15 April over 760

MATAF heavy bombers, concentrating on the rectangular area between Routes 64 and 65 and the defences around Bologna, pounded the 15 miles of lines facing the II Corps held by the 65th Division and 8th Mountain Division of the XIV Panzer Korps and the 1st Parachute and 305th Infantry Division of the I Parachute Corps. An additional 200 medium bombers and 120 fighter-bombers of the XXII Tactical Air Command then hammered targets immediately opposite II Corps in the Monte Sole area and in the Reno valley north to the town of Praduro, about half-way to Bologna. They dropped 1,500 tons of bombs on the German positions – a tonnage that James Holland notes was three times that dropped by the Luftwaffe on Coventry in November 1940. A massive artillery barrage followed and then the 6th South African Armoured Division and the US 88th Infantry Division opened the ground offensive just after midnight, moving towards objectives between Routes 64 and 65. By the end of the first day, the South Africans had gained control of the much-fought-over Monte Sole feature, so opening the way north up Route 64 and into the valley of the Reno.

South African Corporal 'Dick' Frost of the Royal Natal Carbineers had witnessed the awesome air bombardment by what seemed to him to be 'hundreds' of bombers dropping ordnance that included the newly-developed napalm – known to the men on the ground as petrol bombs. These attacks were followed by ground-attack fighters armed with rockets and bombs. 'Really a terrific sight. The rockets must be terrifying and petrol bombs almost as bad.'

Meanwhile, the 88th Infantry Division attacked enemy positions on the Monterumici hill mass and Monte Adone, the dominant terrain features west of Route 65 and the key to Axis resistance in the area. Throughout the night and into the next day the 88th Division battered at the Axis defences in small-unit battles reminiscent of the struggles for the Gustav and Gothic Lines the year before. By nightfall, however, both features were still in enemy hands.

Further east, the US 91st and 34th Infantry Division attacked north along Route 65 in the valley of the River Savena with similar results. The defending 65th Division had heavily fortified the ridge lines on both sides of the valley, and stiff resistance immediately stopped the American drive.

On the morning of 17 April the Americans renewed their attacks across the II Corps front against a wavering but still determined enemy. Building on its previous gains, the 88th Infantry Division succeeded in taking most of the Monterumici massif, raising hopes of an imminent breakthrough in the II Corps area. To exploit a possible breach in the Axis line, Truscott released the US 85th Infantry Division, from the Fifth Army reserve, to assist Keyes in what he hoped would be the final northward push by the 6th South African Armoured and the 88th Infantry Division. But simultaneously he redeployed the 1st Armored Division from the IV Corps' eastern flank to the west so that it could exploit any break in the Axis line toward Modena and northward.

By nightfall on the 17th, the 10th Mountain Division had succeeded in punching through what remained of the enemy's first defensive line, and other successes soon followed. Only a rapidly disintegrating Axis force and then about 30 miles of relatively flat terrain stood between the IV Corps and the Po itself. To the east, aware of the threat to their flank from IV Corps advances, Axis units facing the

II Corps also began to withdraw as rapidly as possible towards the Po. In the face of superior Allied air and ground forces, and with negligible reserves, the Germans had little chance of containing the emerging American breakthrough.

The character and pace of the battle began to change on 18-19 April as five armoured infantry columns of the repositioned US 1st Armored Division began to drive up the valley of the River Samoggia west of the 10th Mountain Division. The 90th Panzer Grenadier Division resisted with its few remaining tanks in a series of sharp, one-on-one armoured engagements that were very rare for the Italian campaign, but ultimately gave way after sustaining heavy losses. With the Brazilians and the 1st Armored Division dealing with the bulk of Axis forces in the Samoggia valley, the 10th Mountain Division advanced six miles due north, taking some 2,900 Axis prisoners and capturing Monte San Michele, just 12 miles short of Ponte Samoggia. Pushing forward a further three miles, the leading troops then halted for the night to allow reserves and support elements to catch up. To the east, the 85th Infantry Division advanced against light opposition, keeping pace with the 10th Mountain Division.

Further east and closer to Bologna, the II Corps hammered away at the enemy. By dawn on 18 April, Keyes' units had accelerated their advance, pursuing the rapidly withdrawing German forces. As Axis defences cracked, the bulk of the Fifth Army passed west of Bologna and Generals Keyes and Crittenberger repositioned their units for the final push out of the Apennines.

The turning point in the spring offensive came on April 20, with both the Fifth and Eighth Armies in position to launch high-speed armoured advances from the Apennines foothills toward the Po crossings. Given the flat terrain and excellent road network in the Po Valley, unlike anything yet encountered during the Italian campaign, Fifteenth Army Group orders now emphasised a faster-paced offensive where speed and mobility could be exploited to destroy surviving enemy forces before they escaped. The Italian campaign would now become a race between Allied and Axis forces to see who could reach the Po first and the Alpine foothills beyond. Truscott ordered II Corps units to capture or isolate Bologna and to encircle Axis forces south of the river by linking with the Eighth Army at Bondeno, about 20 miles north of Bologna. To the west, along the coast, the 92nd Infantry Division prepared to advance to La Spezia and then on to Genoa. In between he wanted the 1st Armored Division to mop up the remaining Axis forces in the foothills southwest of Ponte Samoggia, capture Modena, and drive for the Po. Meanwhile, the 10th Mountain Division, now pouring from the foothills, cut Route 9 between Bologna and Modena, took Ponte Samoggi, and swung north.

To increase the impetus of his northward advance, on 20 April Truscott ordered the 6th South African Armoured Division and 85th Infantry Division to join the all-out drive for the Po as soon as they had cleared the foothills of the Apennines. Elsewhere on the II Corps front, the 91st Division continued its operations west of Bologna, while the 34th Infantry Division advanced on both sides of Route 65 to the southern outskirts of the city. It was on the night of 19-20 April that the men of No1 Italian SAS jumped behind German lines to further destabilise the enemy defence that was rapidly collapsing and to hasten their withdrawal.

By 21 April the Allies had broken through the German defences and the advance had taken on the character of a *Blitzkrieg*; a fast-moving armoured and mechanised pursuit. The final units of Crittenberger's IV Corps emerged from the Apennines foothills with the 1st Armored Division on the left, the 10th Mountain Division in the centre, and the 85th Infantry Division on the right. Truscott's first priority was to have Crittenberger expand his base in the Po Valley and cross the River Panaro north of Bologna before the enemy could reorganise there. On the left, the 1st Armored Division turned northwest along Route 9, heading for Modena. In the centre and on the right, a motorised task force of the 10th Mountain Division passed through Ponte Samoggia and advanced a further 15 miles, seizing intact a bridge across the Panaro. The rest of the division followed, while a steady stream of prisoners flowed to the rear. On IV Corps' right, the 85th Infantry Division relieved 10th Mountain Division rear detachments before crossing the Panaro further east.

It was on 21 April that ULTRA intercepts recorded the last message from Hitler to the commander of Army Group C and his troops in Italy. Von Vietinghoff had informed Hitler that only by adopting a 'mobile strategy' could the Army Group avoid being split in half and destroyed. With characteristic obduracy the Führer replied to von Vietinghoff that defending his position with fanatical grimness was the only way of breaking the Allied offensive.

At Poggio Renatico the 17th/21st Lancers leading the 6th Armoured Division had arrived at the walls of the town. Incredibly the HQ V Corps signals intercept units picked up a radio message from the German commander of the detention centre in the town: 'There are tanks here at Poggio Renatico,' he said desperately before another voice came on the air and told him to be quiet.

The commander of Bologna's German garrison was attempting to cut a deal with the Archbishop of Bologna and the Fascist mayor that if he withdrew his forces without demolishing the public utilities the partisans would not attack his troops. In the city the partisans were handicapped by the loss of their secret radio, the execution of their top commander, and the capture of the liaison officer who had attempted to cross Allied lines to alert them. The partisans had, however, heard the cryptic BBC Italian Service message, 'There will be racing at the Hippodrome tomorrow.' So, confident that the Allies were approaching, they rose on 19 April and in the fighting that followed accounted for 1,300 Germans dead or captured and salvaged the city's electric, gas, and water works. Two days later two divisions of the Fifth Army had reached the city gates from the west as Polish forces of the Eighth Army entered from the east.

Fittingly, Truscott left Bologna to be cleared by Italian troops who, with their helmets decked with flowers, were welcomed by cheering crowds. The 34th Division was sent west towards Modena. By reinforcing the IV Corps' left flank, Truscott hoped to isolate enemy divisions still retreating from the northern Apennines and to deny them Po crossings west of the 1st Armored Division. Attaching the 34th Division to the IV Corps, he instructed Crittenberger to put it astride Route 9 between the 1st Armored Division and the Brazilian Expeditionary Force. Subsequently, the 34th Division reached Modena on 23 April and continued its attack northwest ten miles further along Route 9 towards Reggio. Meanwhile, the 6th

South African Armoured Division led the II Corps' advance to the Panaro and on to the Po, with the US 88th Infantry Division mopping up the rear areas of Axis stragglers. On their right, the 91st Division skirted the western outskirts of Bologna, captured the airport, and continued north, rapidly approaching the Panaro.

By dawn on 22 April the entire Fifth Army was well into the Po Valley. On the right flank, Axis forces attempted in vain to prevent the juncture of the Fifth and Eighth Armies, desperately trying to buy time for small detachments of their comrades to escape. But the Allied onslaught, now moving at full speed, quickly swept aside the hasty defences erected by the 1st and 4th *Fallschirm* Divisions, overwhelming and annihilating numerous Axis rearguard detachments in the process.

In the west, the 10th Mountain Division's spearhead reached the Po at San Benedetto, 30 miles north of Ponte Samoggia, on the evening of 22 April. By midnight the rest of the division had arrived and river-crossing equipment followed. Masses of wrecked enemy vehicles and guns littered the south bank of the Po, showing the devastating effects of Allied air power. Not one bridge remained standing. As the 10th Mountain Division waited to cross, the 1st Armored Division skirted Modena over a bridge that had been captured across the Panaro four miles north of Route 9, then moved west, reaching a southwestern loop of the Po on April 23. The units' armoured vehicles then spread out along several miles of the river's southern bank to block crossings by any remaining enemy soldiers bypassed in the headlong race for the river. The rapid American advance along the 40-mile wide front had left many pockets of Axis soldiers, and special task forces were now created to mop up rear areas as the main Allied units pressed further northward. Ultimately, over 100,000 Axis troops were forced to surrender in the areas south of the river.

Although the majority of the Po bridges were destroyed, the US 85th Infantry Division, like other fast-moving Fifth Army units, had been able to take many spans south of the Po intact, including the Panaro bridge at Camposanto, 11 miles north of Ponte Samoggia. Early on 22 April, fearing efforts by German rearguard units to destroy the span, a sergeant from the 310th Engineer Bn quickly plunged into the river, and as rifle and machine-gun fire churned that water he cut the demolition cables and saved the structure from destruction. Once across, the 310th repelled an enemy counterattack and managed to hold the town. As one regiment cleared Camposanto and secured the bridge, another swung to the left, crossed the bridge seven miles south at Bomporto, and quickly covered the intervening 24 miles to reach the Po just before noon on 23 April. The division then cleared the south bank, capturing hundreds of prisoners and huge stocks of weapons and equipment.

By 24 April the entire Fifth Army front had reached the Po. Two days earlier the German rocket artillery battery commanded by *Oberleutnant* Hans Golda had reached the river and been confronted by a sight that was like some modern version of Goya's 'Horrors of War'. The south bank was littered with smashed and burning vehicles, horses hung dead in harness of the limbers and wagons and men tried desperately to cross the river, its waters swollen with the spring thaw. Golda was faced by the grim prospect that he would not be able to get his men across the river unless they abandoned the vehicles and towed multiple-rocket launchers. The drivers who had nursed their vehicles through the Italian campaign 'cried like children' as they drove them into the Po to render them unusable. He managed to find a ferry but when the men of 8 Battery looked back he recalled that 'Our spirits were zero when we looked back at the other bank. The long, burning columns of tanks blown up, the many plumes of smoke – each of which was the grave of a valuable vehicle. With a last, painful look, we said goodbye.'

In the west, IV Corps' units advanced west, northwest and north, pushing forward bridging equipment for the assault river crossing. The 10th Division, using 50 M-2 assault boats, began ferrying troops across at noon. Air bursts from German artillery caused some casualties, but enemy actions failed to significantly delay the crossings here or elsewhere. Once on the far bank, the 10th Mountain quickly secured its bridgehead. By 1800 hours two regiments were across, with the division's third regiment crossing during the night.

To the east, by nightfall on 23 April the Eighth Army was closing with the Po with 6th Armoured Division at Bondeno, the 8th Indian Infantry Division ten miles further east, moving through Ferrara, and the British 56th Infantry Division nearing Polesella, another ten miles to the east. The Italian *Garibaldi* Combat Group, soon to be joined by the Italian *Cremona* Battle Group, was closing on the Po delta and would cross it to join the drive to liberate Venice.

In the centre of the Allied line, the II Corps reorganised its units before crossing the Po. Keyes wanted the 88th and 91st Infantry and the 6th South African Armoured Division to establish independent bridgeheads. On the right, the South Africans became responsible for maintaining contact with the Eighth Army left flank, while the 91st Division moved to the centre and the 88th Division concentrated on the left. At noon on 24 April, the 88th crossed the Po at two locations against patchy resistance, followed the next day by the 91st in the centre and the South Africans on the corps' right wing.

Meanwhile, as the 10th Mountain Division awaited the completion of construction of heavier spans across the Po, other IV Corps' units drove due west. On the IV Corps' left, the Brazilian Expeditionary Force protected the flank of the 34th Infantry Division, which reached Reggio, about 15 miles west of Modena, early on 24 April. North of Modena and Reggio, 1st Armored Division task forces along the Po's southern bank blocked all remaining escape routes. The division now prepared to put armoured elements across the Po in the 10th Mountain Division's zone to protect the flank of its projected advance north into the Alpine foothills.

To take advantage of the deteriorating enemy situation and the feeble resistance along the river, Truscott discarded plans for a slow, deliberate river crossing, and instead issued instructions to jump the river as quickly as possible and press the attack. He wanted the Fifth Army to shift its advance northwest towards Verona, about 60 miles above Bologna in the Alpine foothills. Its capture would deepen the rupture between the German Fourteenth and Tenth Armies, block escape routes to the Brenner Pass, and breach the Adige Line before it could be fully manned.

However, lack of bridging equipment threatened to delay his plans. With no permanent spans surviving the MATAF air bombardments, a variety of amphibious craft, rubber rafts, wooden boats and ferries were pressed into service to carry men and light equipment across the Po. But heavy equipment had to wait on the south bank until pontoon bridges had been built. Since Fifteenth Army Group plans had assumed that II Corps would be first to reach the river, the Fifth Army now had to push additional bridging for the IV Corps forward on already overcrowded roads. Nevertheless, through the efforts of Army engineers, pontoon and treadway bridges spanned the river within two days of the first crossings.

Over the next three days, 24-26 April, Fifth Army forces erupted from their Po bridgeheads and split the Axis forces in Italy. In the centre, Fifth Army divisions raced for Verona. The 10th Mountain Division started north after midnight on 24 April, and by 09.45 hours had advanced 20 miles to the airport at Villafranca, just southwest of Verona. On its right, the 85th Division moved from the Po shortly before noon on 25 April, stopping within ten miles of Verona by nightfall. Only slightly further east, the 88th Division also started north early on 25 April, moving by foot, Jeeps, captured vehicles, and bicycles, and covering the 40 miles to the outskirts of Verona in just one day.

Operations on the Fifth Army's flanks continued apace. On the left, the Brazilians and the 34th Infantry and 1st Armored Division pushed west and northwest along Route 9 towards Piacenza on the Po, 50 miles west of Reggio. On the right the US 91st Infantry Division also began its advance north from the Po, with the South African armour on its right, heading towards the town of Legnago on the River Adige ten miles further. Verona fell on 26 April as three American divisions converged on the city. The 88th Division secured the town at daybreak after a vicious night battle. Just after dawn the forward elements of the 10th

A pre-war picture postcard showing Italian paratroops as heroes of the new Fascist Italy. Within the armed forces the paratroops would remain an élite formation, fighting with distinction against the 8th Army in North Africa. *WF*

A photograph taken around 1944 shows an Italian paratrooper in a camouflage shirt with a German stick grenade tucked into his belt and armed with a Moschetto automatico modello 38/42 sub-machine gun. *WF*

The impassive gaze of Lt Colonel 'Paddy' Blair Mayne, wearing his battered beige beret and with SAS wings above his medal ribbon bar, conceals his explosive and at times unpredictable nature. *IWM AP 6069*

A No 2 SAS 3-inch mortar crew in action in the Alba area of northern Italy. The men may be from Operation CANUCK. As they duck away from the muzzle blast, one man braces the mortar baseplate with his foot. *IWM NA 25411*

A No 2 SAS Vickers MMG crew in April 1945. Between them they carry the gun, tripod, water for cooling the barrel and belts of .303in ammunition. Their mixture of kit and clothing reflects the practical approach adopted by the SAS. *IWM NA 25407*

An Italian Partisan strikes a heroic pose with a captured German MG 34 machine gun. He wears civilian clothes but has a military cap – British battledress uniform delivered to the Partisans became popular and gave them a greater semblance of being a military force. *IWM NA 14561*

The grave of the Danish SAS officer Major Anders Lassen at the Argenta Gap Commonwealth War Graves cemetery in Northern Italy. Corporal Tom Hunter VC of 43 Commando RM is buried in the same cemetery. *WF*

The memorial on the wall of Villa Rossi that commemorates the men who died in the attack on the German Corps HQ at Botteghe during Operation TOMBOLA. The plaque was unveiled by Mike Lees in a ceremony after the war. *WF*

Dressed in winter white camouflage smocks, men of F Recce Squadron on patrol in the bitter winter of 1944/45. While much of the equipment might be British, the men have retained their Italian sub machine guns. *IWM NA 22159*

An informal group portrait of several of the key players in F Recce Squadron. From the left, Lt Aldo Temellini, Captain Joe Liebmann (liaison officer), Captain Carlo Gay and Captain Carlo Bonciani. *Daniel Battistella*

Men of F Recce Squadron prepare PE 808 plastic explosives and prime No 36 Grenades. The close proximity of this mixture of high explosives is a perhaps a reflection that war had made these young men hardened or blasé about the risks of working like this. *Daniel Battistella*

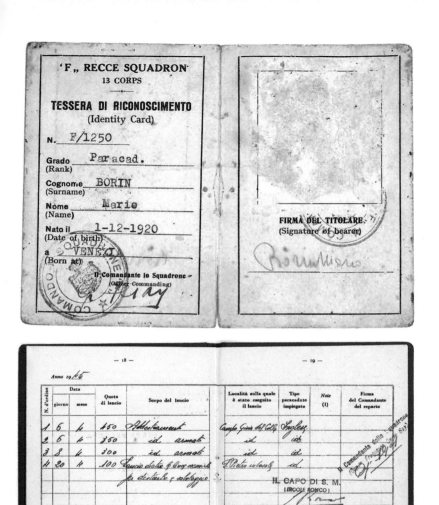

The Operation HERRING identification card issued to Parachutist Mario Borin who jumped over DZ 18. *Daniel Battistella*

- SENIOR ALLIED OFFICERS CONVEYING THE B[ ]
WISHES OF GENERAL MARK CLARK, 15 ARMY GRO[ ]
COMMANDER, TO THE "F. RECCE SQUADRON, IMM[ ]
IATELY PRIOR TO THEIR DROPPING BEHIND T[ ]
ENEMY LINES.-

Just prior to boarding the Dakotas, men of No 1 Italian SAS hear messages of good luck and encouragement from General Mark Clark, commanding 15th Army Group, and General McCreery, commanding 8th Army. *Daniel Battistella*

The awkward final steps up into a Dakota for men of No 1 Italian SAS, burdened with weapons, equipment and parachutes, as they begin the first stage of Operation HERRING. *Daniel Battistella*

The interior of the USAAF Dakota with the men of patrols V and W from F Recce Squadron moments before they took off on Operation HERRING. The confident smiles show the high morale of the formation. *Daniel Battistella*

The Douglas C-47 Skytrain – better known as the Dakota, the transport workhorse of World War II, and the aircraft that would carry the men of No 1 Italian SAS into action in Operation HERRING. *WF*

A 'Rupert' parachute dummy dropped to the east of the HERRING DZs to confuse the Germans. Made from strong hessian material and resembling the shape of a man, these dummies were sometimes fitted with explosives or incendiary devices that were triggered on impact when the 'Ruperts' hit the ground. *WF*

Parachutist Amelio De Juliis (left), killed in action in Operation HERRING, who would become the youngest Italian soldier to win the Gold Medal for Military Valour (MOVM), talking to Corporal Luigi Fregoni. *Daniel Battistella*

The elegant parachute canopy-shaped memorial to the men of Operation HERRING, the *Dragoncello di Poggio Rusco*. It lists the men of F Recce Squadron and *Nembo* who participated and those who were killed in action. *Daniel Battistella*

Benito Mussolini, *Duce* of Fascist Italy, strikes a heroic pose at the apogee of his glory. Initially admired by Hitler, Mussolini and Italy would become a liability and when the *Duce* was arrested it was the Germans who rescued him. *WF*

PER IL NUOVO ORDINE SOCIALE, PER LA CIVILTÀ

An Italian Fascist propaganda poster declares 'Victory for the new social order for civilisation' as a grim-faced Japanese, Italian and a German Waffen-SS soldier lunge forward. By late 1943 the prospect of victory was fading fast and the Germans and Italians had in some cases become enemies. *WF*

SS-*Sturmbannführer* Otto Skorzeny, who led the spectacular glider-borne *coup de main* operation at Gran Sasso d'Italia to rescue the *Duce* on 12 September 1943. Though the Nazi propaganda machine made much of the Waffen-SS role, it was a joint operation with German paratroops. *WF*

General Mark Clark with a WAAC Sergeant in a field HQ in Italy. Clark was ambitious and – though he attempted to conceal it – an Anglophobe. He felt sidelined in the Italian theatre and his moment of glory in Rome was eclipsed by D-Day. *US Army Signal Corps*

Refugees make their way across the Ponte alle Grazie, Florence in August 1944. F Squadron played a significant part in the fighting for the city that summer. *US Army Signal Corps*

Field Marshal Sir Harold Alexander confers with General Lucien Truscott Jr – one had the nickname 'Alex', the other 'Old Gravel Guts'. Truscott the cavalryman would be a dynamic commander of the Fifth Army in 1945. *US Army Signal Corps*

Emblazoned with the Allied recognition star, a US Army M24 Chaffee light tank enters the battered suburbs of Bologna in April 1945. The city was liberated by Italian troops in the Allied spring offensive that year. *US Army Signal Corps*

A DC-3 Dakota drops supply containers over typical Italian farmland. For speedy recognition, the colour of the parachutes was used to indicate the contents of the container. *US Army Air Force*

Mountain Division roared into town, followed two hours later by the 85th Division. The seizure of Verona now brought the Fifth Army up to the final Axis defensive line in Italy, fully prepared to implement Phase III of Operation CRAFTSMAN. It was on 26 April that the partisan station Milan Radio Liberty began broadcasting.

The intricate system of trenches, dugouts, and machine-gun positions in the Alpine foothills that made up the Adige Line varied in depth from 1,000 to 5,000 yards. It was a formidable obstacle; however, the rapid advance of the Fifth Army had not allowed the enemy to fully man these defences. Even if the time had been available, by now the Axis lacked the materiel and manpower to organise a cohesive defence.

Fifth Army orders for the final phase of operations emphasised blocking the retreat of enemy troops south of the Alps. From this point the Allied advance more closely resembled a tactical march than a combat operation as most Axis units had disintegrated into small groups of harried soldiers retreating as best they could. Therefore, after the IV Corps had secured Verona, Truscott decided to send the II Corps northeast to help the Eighth Army in its drive to capture Padua, Venice, and Treviso.

The II Corps' 88th Division crossed the River Adige at Verona on 26 April and prepared to move northeast about 25 miles to Vicenza. About 20 miles to the southeast, the 91st Division crossed the Adige at Legnago, securing the 88th Division's right flank. Generals Truscott and Keyes personally observed the 91st Division's passage over the Adige, concerned with the level of resistance encountered. If the crossing went uncontested, both men reasoned, it would show that the enemy was more interested in surviving than in making a stand from their prepared positions on the Adige Line. The American generals soon had their answer. Although the soldiers of the 91st were harassed by sporadic German artillery fire, the division crossed largely unopposed by any organised, coherent force. Meanwhile, to the right of the 91st Division, the 6th South African Armoured Division advanced in the area between the Adige and the Po, stretching out to Eighth Army units further east and encountering equally weak opposition.

Truscott now directed units of IV Corps to seal the Brenner Pass in the north and destroy the Ligurian Army in the west. Moving quickly, the 10th Mountain Division's lead element, Task Force Darby, commanded by Col. William O. Darby, the officer who can justly be called the father of the US Army Rangers, left Verona on 26 April for nearby Lake Garda, where it soon worked its way up the eastern shore. On the 10th Mountain Division's right flank the 85th Division moved uncontested through the Adige Line north of Verona and went into Fifth Army reserve on 27 April.

To the west, the 1st Armored Division began sealing all possible escape routes into Austria and Switzerland along the Po Valley's northern rim from Lake Garda, 50 miles west to Lake Como. On the 1st Armored Division's left, the 34th Infantry Division drove west, taking the towns of Parma, Fidenza and Piacenza in quick succession and gathering large numbers of prisoners. In the far west, along the Italian Riviera, north of La Spezia, the soldiers of the US 92nd Infantry Division encountered only slight opposition as they swept up the coastal road towards the port city of Genoa. As the lead elements of the division entered the city without opposition on the morning of 27

April, they discovered that the 4,000-strong Axis garrison had already surrendered to Italian partisans the day before.

Even as Fifth and Eighth Army units spread across northern Italy, the secret negotiations to end the fighting between the Germans and Allies had begun to produce results. Negotiations had opened in March in Lugano, Switzerland between Swiss military intelligence officers, a prominent Milan industrialist and SS-*Standartenführer* Eugen Dollmann, adjutant to *SS-Obergruppenführer und Generalleutnant* Karl Wolff, the most senior SS officer in Italy. As a gesture of good faith Dollmann was asked to arrange for the release of two Italian Partisan leaders. It was when this had been done that Allen Dulles, the senior OSS officer in Switzerland, received permission from Allied HQ Mediterranean to begin more formal negotiations.

Code-named Operation CROSSWORD or SUNRISE by the Allies for the Germans these contacts were aimed at gaining either the co-operation or the acquiescence of the western Allies. This would then allow Germany to continue the war in the East against the Soviet Union, using Axis forces redeployed from Italy. Although neither Dulles nor Allied military leaders shared or even seriously considered Wolff's goals, they were interested in any possibility of ending the fighting in Italy without further bloodshed and destruction to the infrastructure. Hitler had given orders that a 'scorched earth' campaign be conducted to destroy as much of Italy's communications, utilities and cultural heritage as possible.

On 8 March Dulles met Wolff in Zurich where the OSS officer emphasised that the German surrender would have to be unconditional and to the three major powers. Wolff said that he would try to bring the German Ambassador in

Italy into the negotiations and Field Marshal Kesselring commander of Army Group C. When Kesselring was posted out of Italy and replaced by General von Vietinghoff, Wolff had to approach the new commander. In the next meeting on 19 March at Ascona on Lake Maggiore in Italy, two officers from Alexander's HQ US General Lyman Lemnitzer (a future head of NATO forces in Europe) and British General Terence Airey were present.

The Soviet Union, although officially an ally, had not been privy to these initial contacts but they learned of them through their secret agents operating in the West, notably the British traitor Kim Philby. On 22 March the Soviet Foreign Minister Vyacheslav Molotov sent an angry letter to the US Ambassador in Moscow. He wrote; 'for two weeks, in Bern, behind the back of the Soviet Union, negotiations between representatives of the German Military Command on one side and representatives of American and British Command on the other side are conducted. The Soviet government considers this absolutely inadmissible.' Moscow demanded that a representative from STAVKA, the Soviet High Command, should be present, but were refused.

On 1 April *Reichsführer*-SS Heinrich Himmler, sensing that something was afoot and now not wanting to be upstaged in any peace feelers to the West, forbade Wolff from leaving Italy – but by then it was too late. The overwhelming success of the Allied offensive in Italy in 1945 robbed the German negotiators of any remaining bargaining power and on 28 April German emissaries led by Lt Colonel von Schweinitz, Chief of Staff Army Group C, arrived at the Fifteenth Army Group HQ in Caserta, to arrange a cease-fire and the unconditional surrender of the remaining Axis forces south of the Alps. At a subsequent ceremony Generals Truscott and McCreery were present when Lt General Fridolin von Senger und Etterlin, Vietinghoff's representative, formally surrendered the remaining Axis forces in Italy to General Clark, ending World War 2 in the Mediterranean.

General von Vietinghoff told his soldiers 'Hitherto, you have obeyed your Führer. Today, you must obey your orders.' The devastating impact of the Allied offensive in April, however, had so shattered Axis communications and unit cohesion that the Fifteenth Army Group agreed to withhold announcement of the cease-fire for three days, until late on 2 May, to provide enemy commanders the opportunity to notify their scattered units. So, in the meantime, though the war was officially over, the fighting continued and men died.

By 28 April Truscott's Fifth Army front stretched from the French border in the west to Verona in the east, curving in and out of the Alpine foothills. Between 28 April and 2 May there were firefights and small actions, but for the most part Allied troops rolled across northern and northwestern Italy without encountering serious opposition. The stream of prisoners taken since mid-April turned into a deluge during the last days of the campaign, and several combat units left the front lines to guard the tens of thousands of Axis soldiers swelling makeshift PoW camps in northern Italy.

At midday on 2 May, Corporal Günther Drossinger, a 20-year-old veteran of 1st Coy *Fallschirmjäger Sturm Bataillon*, and his men, dug in on a hillside near Lake Caldonazzo, received news of the capitulation. 'We felt like 14-year-old boys again. We were delighted. Of course we were delighted.' However, there was a sense of unreality; the German soldiers did not surrender all their weapons until the beginning of June, their American captors viewing the partisan groups in the area with almost as much suspicion as the Germans, and men who had been enemies only days before took turns mounting guard. 'The Partisans were a common enemy', said Drossinger, 'You didn't know at this stage what side they were on. There were groups who were against us, groups who were against the Allies, and then groups who fought against both. Then there were Communist groups, Christian groups etc. The Partisans could not believe that the Americans were no longer shooting at us.'

To the north, as the 10th Mountain Division pushed along the eastern shore of Lake Garda, in the Alpine valleys leading to the Brenner Pass they found the narrow defiles often blocked by last-ditch enemy rear guards. On 30 April, in response to reports that Mussolini and other senior Fascist officials were in a villa on the western shore, elements of the division crossed the lake only to discover that their intelligence was false. Indeed the Americans soon learned that Communist Partisans had executed Mussolini near Lake Como on 28 April.

For a man who had courted drama and the cult of personality, and who had boasted after an attempt on his life on 6 April 1926, 'If I advance, follow me. If I retreat, kill me. If I die, avenge me', – the death of the Duce would be squalid and banal. He was captured by partisans of the Communist 52nd Garibaldi Brigade at Dongo on Lake Como, in a German convoy in which he was attempting to escape into neutral Switzerland. Here Mussolini and his entourage, that included his mistress Clara Petacci, hoped to take a flight to neutral but pro-Fascist Spain. The man who before the war had strutted through Italy in exotic Fascist uniforms was found in a truck hunched in a Luftwaffe greatcoat, wearing dark glasses and a German steel helmet. For the partisans his chance capture posed the problem – what were they to do with the powerless and disgraced *Duce*. He was kept overnight in the village of Mezzegra, where orders were given to execute him, probably by the National Liberation Committee (CLN), and the following day a former metalworker, Walter Audisio, whose *nom de guerre* was Colonel Valerio, was given the task. The prisoners were driven away from Mezzegra and under the pretext of a breakdown they were ordered from the car near the gateway of the Villa Belmonte in Mezzegra.

'Stand at the corner of that wall', shouted Audisio. Sensing this was the end, Petacci hugged Mussolini, shouting 'You can't do that', and refused to move away. In the ragged volley of automatic fire Petacci was the first to fall. Mussolini opened his jacket and shouted 'Shoot me in the chest'. Audisio shouted 'I execute the will of the Italian people', and fired – Mussolini fell, but as he lay on the ground it was clear that he was still alive and in pain, breathing heavily. Audisio fired another round into his chest and Italy's *Duce* was dead.

On 29 April Mussolini's body was strung up by its heels from a garage forecourt on the Piazzale Loreto in nearby Milan, the city in which Mussolini had established his first Fascist movement. Only days before, captured partisans had been shot at the same location by men of the *Brigata Nere*. Alongside the *Duce* and the body of his mistress were those of Roberto Farinacci, the General Secretary of the Fascist party and Carlo Scorza, the Party Secretary. The bodies had been shot – one woman firing five rounds into the *Duce*'s body, shouting 'This is for my five dead sons' – others had stamped and urinated on them – yet despite all this, as Petacci was strung up, her skirt was secured in place, giving her body some slight dignity. It was a brutal and obscene image that, it was reported, would haunt Hitler and determine his decision that when he took his life in Berlin, his body was to be burned beyond recognition.

Men of the US 10th Mountain Division reached the northern end of Lake Garda on 30 April and it was here that Colonel Darby was killed by a random enemy artillery shell, just days before the end of hostilities. By the time of the final surrender on 2 May, the division had taken the towns of Riva, Torbole, and Nago, and was ready to advance into the Alps.

Immediately south of the Alps, the 1st Armored Division continued to drive westward on 27 April, meeting Italian partisans from Milan who reported that they had already liberated the city, a fact US troops confirmed two days later. On the afternoon of 30 April, General Crittenberger and a composite command representing the entire IV Corps entered Milan, the largest city in northern Italy. In the meantime, the 1st Armored Division had moved west and southwest of the city, clearing small pockets of resistance and reaching out 20 miles further west to the River Ticino by 2 May. Behind it, the 34th Division continued its clearing operations until it relieved the 1st Armored Division north of Milan, sealing off any Axis elements still attempting to withdraw north. On 28 April, south of Milan, the Brazilian Expeditionary Force bottled up the 148th Grenadier and Italian *Bersaglieri* Division. On the following day the German commander surrendered; during the next twenty-four hours the Brazilians collected over 13,500 prisoners.

By 1 May clearing operations had ended, and a Brazilian task force joined the 92nd Division at Alessandria, 45 miles southwest of Milan, while the Japanese-American soldiers of the 442nd Regimental Combat Team entered Turin, about 50 miles further west, later that day. By 30 April the last organised Axis force in northwest Italy, the Ligurian Army, composed of the German LXXV Corps and the Italian Corps *Lombardia*, capitulated. For the next forty-eight hours, as the appropriate orders trickled down from the headquarters of what remained of Army Group C, the Ligurian Army's subordinate units surrendered piecemeal to IV Corps troops.

In north-eastern Italy the 88th Division left the Adige for Vicenza, arriving on 28 April, and cleared the city in bitter house-to-house fighting before moving further north, stretching out along Route 11 between Verona and Vicenza. There they captured thousands of retreating enemy soldiers before sealing the last escape route north. On the last day of April, Truscott transferred the 85th Infantry Division from IV to II Corps, and on the following day both the 85th and 88th Infantry Divisions drove north, moving along the River Piave towards the US Seventh Army moving south from Germany, linking up on 4 May. Elsewhere, the 91st Infantry and the 6th South African Armoured Division protected the flank of Eighth Army forces driving north and northeast, the latter reaching Trieste where they linked up with Marshal Tito's Yugoslavian Communist Partisans on May 2.

To the civilian population of the delightful port city, the arrival of the Eighth Army would be more than liberation – they had been under German domination from 1943 – but now in 1945 there was a new terror with the prospect of the arrival of the Yugoslav Partisans, who saw the Italians as the 'enemy' and their leader Marshal Josip Tito, who saw the city as his for the taking. In a bizarre twist it was German troops who defended Trieste and its population against the Yugoslavs until the Eighth Army arrived.

In London Field Marshal Lord Alanbrooke, the Chief of Staff of the Imperial General Staff (CIGS), recorded in his diary for 30 April the mood of the Cabinet meeting chaired by the British Prime Minister Winston Churchill; 'an unpleasant Cabinet with Winston in a bad mood. In spite of the fact that Alex [Field Marshal Alexander] had made the greatest advance he had yet brought off, he was abused for not having taken Trieste!'

To 22-year-old Clara Duse, an art student in Trieste, the hours before the Allied liberation were terrifying, with gunfire echoing through the city. It was the New Zealanders who had fought in Greece, Crete, North Africa and the Italian peninsula who had the honour of liberating the city. Clara Duse remembered their arrival. 'You should have seen the rejoicing. The New Zealanders were kissed and given flowers – we were all so relieved. It was incredible.'

41 *History of the Second World War*, Purnell & Sons, London 1966.
42 *Tug of War*, Dominick Graham and Shelford Bidwell, Hodder & Stoughton, London 1986.
43 *Images of War*, Marshall Cavendish Partworks.
44 Hans Golda memoir, Bundesarchiv-Militärarchiv, Freiburg-im-Breisgau, cited in *Italy's Sorrow*.
45 SS-*Obergruppenführer und Generalleutnant* Karl Wolff would prove to be a survivor. In May 1945 he was captured at his villa at Bolzano by men of the US 88th Infantry Division and then transferred to a British prison in Germany on General Alexander's orders. Wolff was allowed to retain his badges of rank. He appeared as a witness at the Nuremberg Trials but as a member of a proscribed organisation, the SS, was tried by a German court and sentenced to five years imprisonment and hard labour in November 1948. Seven months later his sentence was reduced to four years and he was released. A man of considerable charm, he became a successful Public Relations executive. However, in 1962, after he had given an interview in the previous year at the time of the trial of Adolf Eichmann, Wolff was again tried and convicted of deporting 300,000 Jews to the Treblinka extermination camp. He was found guilty and in 1964 sentenced to 15 years imprisonment. Wolff served only part of his sentence and was released in 1969 for good behaviour and the condition of his health – he lived on until 17 July 1984.
46 *Images of War.*
47 *War Diaries 1939-1945 Field Marshal Lord Alanbrooke*, edited by Alex Danchev and Daniel Todman.
48 *Italy's Sorrow.*

Chapter 7

A New Elite

You chaps will do more good for Italy
than all your politicians put together.
Major Alex Ramsay,
addressing the men of No 1 ISAS

'Defeat is an orphan, but', as the shrewd Italian proverb goes, 'Victory has many fathers'. So too did No 1 Italian SAS have many fathers, both British and Italian – men who believed in the idea, who organised the training and ordered the specialist stores and finally the soldiers from 'F' Recce Squadron and *Nembo*, who made Operation HERRING a reality.

The first of the fathers was Lt Colonel Sir John Marling, Bart GSO 1 Plans Eighth Army who in February 1945, as plans were being prepared for operation CRAFTSMAN, drafted a Top Secret paper proposing an unusual operation.

Special Forces had proved very effective operating behind enemy lines and these small numbers of men, working in conjunction with partisans, had in modern parlance become a 'Force Multiplier'. The Allies had tough veteran troops of the Italian CIL, some of whom were trained paratroops, fighting on their side. In 'F' Recce Squadron the British XIII Corps had Italian troops who were fully integrated into the Eighth Army and who were parachute trained. A staff officer at the Main HQ Eighth Army had noted in mid-March 1945, 'F Recce Squadron... has lately been doing some parachute training with SOE as a private enterprise. I am informed that they are all very keen to go back to parachuting and that they would welcome this sort of job.' These Italian formations were a unique resource that had not yet been employed in the Special Forces role that had been developed by the Special Air Service, initially in North Africa and later in Italy, France and Belgium.

It was in North Africa that a small group of French parachute trained soldiers had joined the SAS and in the years that followed the force had expanded so that by 1944 there were two French battalions 3 and 4 SAS. They were parachuted into France following the Allied landings in June 1944. The French battalions and the Belgian Independent Parachute Company 5 SAS, had given heroic and invaluable assistance with their command of the local language and hard-driving courage behind enemy lines in France and Belgium. There was obviously a place for Italian SAS troops on their home territory. Colonel Marling wrote;

Notes on Proposed Italian S.A.S. Troops

Tasks

1 To harass and delay all enemy withdrawal south of the R. PO or further north if the forces cannot be raised in sufficient time.

Method

2 The following is required to supplement Air Forces and Partisans.

3 Small parties of 3 or 4 uniformed paratroops armed with one LMG and personal weapons, and equipped with light mines, demolition gear will be dropped in large numbers in a deep belt South of the Po when the enemy has begun to withdraw under pressure.

4 Parties will blow culverts and small bridges, mine roads or with dummy mines and ambush columns by night. By day lie up in the vines and ditches or with local inhabitants, raiding Partisans. Night ops will provide targets for Air Forces by day.

Numbers Required

5 15 North and South roads between L. COMACCHIO and OSTIGLIA through a belt 20 miles deep. To make sure of harassing all roads sufficiently, parties are required on a scale of one per road mile = 300 parties = 500/1300 men. These will be effective for a minimum of 4-6 days. Desirable to have a second flight to re-inforce...

6 Recruitment

Job would appeal to the Italian temperament and Italians more likely to get help from Partisans and local inhabitants. If not sufficient available, any good type of basically trained soldier will do. Italians should be able to raise the small number of volunteers required.

British or US troops desirable to stiffen the Italians if necessary or in any event to rein them in the tactics to be employed once on the ground.

7 Training

> Para training a simple matter - 2 days synthetic sufficient for purpose using SOE methods.
>
> Training for the ground tasks is the major problem. British SAS, PPA and LRDG instructors would be required and might be available.

8 Consider 60 instructors, one clear month would be sufficient for training. 14 days would be required to brief and train the instructors and organising etc before beginning in earnest....'

In the first week of March the draft was passed up the chain of command and on 12 March General Richard McCreery, the man who had supported the original and risky operation to liberate Ravenna using 28th Garibaldi Brigade Partisans, Popski's Private Army and the Canadian 12th Royal Lancers, wrote

'I am in favour of the employment of 100-200 picked men to make attacks on enemy transport in the rear areas.' He added that volunteers should come from the *Folgore* Gruppo but that training should not interfere with the preparedness of the 2nd Para Brigade. It was assumed that this force would be big enough to cover both the frontages of the Fifth and Eighth Army attacks and therefore it was felt that training should be a Fifteenth Army Group responsibility. Without McCreery's backing the project would have ended up as just that – a paper submitted by a staff officer. The commander of the Eighth Army is without question another of the fathers of No 1 ISAS.

In March a Lieutenant Colonel at the Main HQ Eighth Army wrote rather tartly that since it appeared that the numbers of Italian paratroopers would be comparatively small, Fifteenth Army Group had passed the responsibility for recruiting and training back to the Eighth Army. The 2nd Parachute Brigade would not have time to train the 100 Italian soldiers, so he telephoned Lt Colonel Nigel Birch of G-3 Plans Allied Forces HQ (AFHQ) to see if the SOE, which had a parachute school and battle training school at Sienna, would be prepared to take on the task. 'The capacity of the training school is 100 men in four days, if additional tentage and transport is provided. The capacity of the battle school, which teaches sabotage and such like subjects, is 200 men.' he explained.

On 16 March Birch in turn contacted Lt Colonel Harcourt on the Special Operations Mediterranean SO (M) Liaison Staff at Allied Forces HQ to establish how many Italian soldiers could be trained. At this stage in the correspondence there is a sense that the staff officers are trying to pass the buck, or in modern military slang, trying to make the project become 'SEP' - 'Someone Else's Problem'.

However, on 20 March there was real movement, and it is in a letter from the Chief of Staff at HQ Eighth Army that the title of the unique formation first appears in print.

4 *Nigel said that SOE would be prepared to take on the training of our ITALIAN SAS at about a week's notice and would send an officer over to arrange details.*

5 *I do not think we should need to use these SAS bodies until D+10 at the very earliest. We have therefore one month in which to find them, organise them, train them and get them down to airfields from which they can be launched.*

I think that if tackled energetically, this would be just sufficient time if SOE undertakes the training.

The prospects for the operation being planned and launched were set fair following a conference at Fifteen Army Group four days later. Chaired by Colonel P. D. Miller, the G-3 Fifteenth Army Group, it brought together an impressive group of officers from the Eighth Army who covered Plans, Special Forces, Engineers and the Mediterranean Allied Tactical Air Force (MATAF).

The ever-versatile SOE confirmed to Colonel Birch that they would be able to train the paratroops in sabotage and demolition techniques. Colonel L. Franck at HQ SO (M) CMF wrote to Fifteenth Army G3 Support operations that four-day courses would be run at the Battle Training School at Palazza al Piano while No 4 Parachute Training School at Gioia would undertake the parachute training.

Within a day, requirements for transport – four three-ton trucks and one 15cwt vehicle – had been issued and the training and administrative staff requirement established. It would be a compact team of two liaison officers, two demolitions instructors from the Royal Engineers and cooks, general duty men and crucially, eight interpreters. The total strength of HQ 1 Italian SAS would be 16 British and 17 Italian officers and soldiers who would be found from SOMTO and the Eighth Army.

By now a syllabus had been devised for a four-day course for four batches of 50 students. It would cover British and German demolition stores, attacks on road and rail communications, attacks on ammunition and fuel dumps and ambushes.

The British Army instructors from the Royal Engineers and their Italian counterparts in the training team must have been delighted by the stores list – among the demolition equipment they would receive was 5,000 lbs of plastic explosive, six rolls of Primacord or Cordtex, 100 fire pots, 144 No 36 grenades and four 20lb tins of Ammonal. [See Appendix 3] There would also be booby trap switches, 1000 detonators, adhesive tape and waterproof fabric.

Now the dates, spread through April for the ground training, had been finalised. In addition to the demolition and sabotage the men would be taught field craft and how to operate by night. By 1944 the SOE Training Syllabus had distilled the experience of agents in the field into a useful series of Minor Tactics Appendices and 'General Movement by Night'. It had eight headings: Factors influencing the choice of route; Clothing for Night Work; Personal Equipment; Timing and Communication; All-round Defence at Night; Use of Field-glasses at Night; Techniques of Individual Movement and The Best use of the Senses at Night. For the Italian paratroopers who would attend the course, much of this would simply be revision or refreshing lessons learned the hard way on patrols in enemy-held territory. One telling observation in the syllabus noted that,

A loud explosion has the same effect on hearing as a flare or other bright light has upon sight. ..In the same way that the moment after a dazzling light has subsided is a good moment for moving (because the enemy is blinded) the moment after an explosion is a good one for noisy movement that has to be made, because the enemy is deafened.

In a few days after their courses had ended the students would have plenty of opportunity to test both theories in the lethal pyrotechnic violence of Operation HERRING.

Since the operation was not intended to last longer than a couple of days it was reckoned that they would not need to be taught specialised radio communications techniques and indeed, they would not carry radios as part of their equipment load.

At a planning conference a Royal Engineer representative from the Fifteenth Army raised the issue that demolitions by the paratroops might actually delay the Allied advance. After some discussion it was agreed that the chief role of the forces was to spread confusion and that actually, the destruction by the enemy and air strikes by the Mediterranean Allied Tactical Air Force would probably be greater. 'In consequence', wrote the minute-taker at the conference, 'it was agreed that the forces must be given a free hand to cause as much confusion as possible.'

At the conference it was also agreed that an overall commander for the force should be appointed.

On 25 March a cipher signal classified Secret from Lt Col J. G. Beevor of Special Operations Mediterranean SO (M) was transmitted to London. It was brief and concise. 'Code name is Operation HERRING.'

A day later it was confirmed that volunteers could be found from two parachute-trained formations; the '*Nembo*' Regiment, part of the *Folgore* Gruppo of the CIL, and 'F' Recce Squadron with XIII Corps. Three days later a brief was drafted for the OC of this formation and the Italian SAS came into existence.

'F' Recce Squadron had been operating in a grim salient at Vezzola in the Apennines when Captain Gay received a signal that they were to return to their base at Montegrande. They reached it after dark and here Gay opened an envelope containing a personal message from General McCreery.

To the C.O., 'F' Recce Squadron

A special operation is being planned, in which it is intended to use a body of Italian parachutists. In view of the excellent record of your unit while under command of 13th Corps during the last eleven months, I wish you to select five officers and one hundred other ranks for this task. I want all the personnel selected to be volunteers. I also consider it most important that all the men chosen should have had previous experience in operational jumping. I am sure that this opportunity, which will undoubtedly give your squadron the occasion to add further laurels to the one it has already earned for itself, will be welcomed by both officers and men alike. The personnel chosen for this operation will be put through a short preliminary course of training. Since time is short, I will be glad if you will arrange for the selection of volunteers as soon as possible.

McCreery, Lieut-Gen, G.O.C., 8th Army

HQ XIII Corps received a brief signal from the Chief of Staff HQ Eighth Army on the subject of the formation of HQ ISAS. An *ad hoc* HQ was to be formed to command the two Italian formations. It would initially be under XIII Corps but once formed would come under command of

Fifteenth Army Group. It was to be ready to move no later than 2 April and it was anticipated that this unique HQ would disperse about eight weeks later.

On 29 March Colonel Beevor confirmed to Fifteenth Army Group and the Eighth Army that Major Alex Ramsay of 2 Para Brigade had been recommended as Force Commander for Operation HERRING. In a letter on 25 March hand-delivered by Major Charles Villiers, the No 6 Special Force Staff Section liaison officer attached to 6th Armoured Division, to Lt Colonel Sir John Marling, GSO 1 Plans, Eighth Army, Beevor had written:

> *I confirm that we can and will provide the commander you require, to supervise the training, see that the training is properly tied up with the operational requirements, supervise the mounting of the operation when ordered by Army Group and finally centralize the collection and debriefing of the operational squads when they are over-run by the Allied advance...*
>
> *The problem of this operation, as I see it, is that it lies on the border line between a regular airborne operation and a SOE operation. If it were a normal airborne operation, resupply would be essential. If it were a SOE operation, we should regard its as essential to have:-*
>
> *(I)   W/T communications;*
>
> *(II)   Prolonged special training;*
>
> *(III) Either instructions for contacting and organising local Partisan organisations, or instructions for a planned attack on specific targets.*
>
> *I mention this point because if HERRING is to produce anything more than a haphazard diversionary effect we should*

be kept fully in the planning picture regarding targets suggested by 5th and 8th Armies.

In Ramsay, Beevor had made an ideal choice; not only was the young Major a paratrooper but he spoke Italian, though he assured the men under his temporary command that his Italian was poor. Ramsay must be counted as the third father of No 1 ISAS. He was personally briefed by Lt Col Marling on the intended scope of the operation. Contemporary photograps of Ramsay show him as a lean young officer with a spare and intelligent face with the corners of his eyes creased with laugh lines.

After the operation Bonciani would write of Ramsay, 'I liked this Englishman. He was human, extremely intelligent, an excellent parachutist [Bonciani noted that Ramsay had 26 jumps to his credit, six of which were operational] and had all the charm of a man of action. In the two months he spent with us, both before and after the operation, he never once made us feel what so many others had so often tried to make us feel – namely, that he was English but we were merely Italians.'

Ramsay received his detailed Top Secret brief for the new and challenging command.

Brief for Commander Italian Special Air Service

1. You have been nominated by HQ SOMTO to command a force of Italian parachute troops being raised by HQ 8th Army for Operation HERRING.

2 Outline of scheme: The force will consist of F RECCE SQN and volunteers from the *NEMBO* Regt. of the *FOLGORE* Gruppo organised as a company. All operational personnel will be volunteers and have already received parachute training. The number of volunteers likely to be available is not yet known.

3 For political reasons, these two sub-units will retain their identity and be self-supporting. A small BRITISH HQ, which you will command, is being formed for the equipment administration, training and planning of the force. This HQ is purely temporary and will exist for a period of not more than six weeks or two months. No establishment exists for it against which promotions or increases of pay could be authorised.

4 The force is being formed by Eighth Army, which has delegated responsibility to 13 Corps. When formed it will come under command 15 ARMY GROUP for all purposes, though a call may be made on Army for any special assistance.

5 **Operational Tasks:**
   Outline plans for alternative tasks for this force are being submitted to Army Group by Armies. A copy of the Eighth Army outline plan will be given to you as soon as possible.

6 In general, the proposals are that the forces shall be dropped in small parties of three or four men behind the enemy lines when he is withdrawing in disorder after a major defeat at the hands of 15 ARMY GROUP. Tasks of these parties will be to harass and delay the

enemy's withdrawal by all possible means. It is accepted that, once dropped, parties must exist and operate without any further assistance living on and fighting with the equipment they take with them, and whatever they can find in the country. Parties would not be dropped unless the battle is fluid and there would be a reasonable expectation of their being over-run by our own troops within a few days.'

7 **Target Date**

The target date for preparations is as soon as possible after 20 April.

Tactics

8   It is expected that these parties could carry out little in the way of operations by day, though targets of opportunity might well be attacked under favourable conditions. Operations will therefore be mostly by night directed against the enemy's road traffic, with the special object of creating traffic jams which might make favourable targets for the air forces next day. The actual tactics to be employed will be decided by you, but it is suggested that the mining and booby trapping of roads and the creation of road blocks together with ambushes would be the principal methods. Demolition of bridges and culverts will only be carried out with the permission of the Army on whose front they would be operating.

Training

9 Arrangements have been made for conversion parachute courses at No 4 Parachute Training School RAF GIOIA. Courses at the SOMTO battle School at SIENNA have

been arranged for the specialist ground training required. SOMTO are preparing a syllabus. In between these courses, you should arrange for training under unit arrangements at ROSIGNANO. It is hoped to arrange a rehearsal of the operation in the ROSIGNANO area when volunteers have completed training.

10 The specialist training will be carried out in batches of 50 at a time. Transport to GIOIA will be by air leaving MALIGNANO on the dates shown in the Training Programme, weather permitting.

11 You will be responsible for making the detailed arrangements for all training matters in conjunction with 15 ARMY GROUP, MATAF and HQ SOMTO.

Equipment

12 All special airborne equipment has been released by AFHQ and is being despatched to No 2 Special Stores Depot, OSS CECINA, addressed HERRING. Weapons and explosives of a special nature are being supplied by HQ SOMTO. Normal items of equipment required over and above the present scales of F RECCE SQN and an ITALIAN Coy will be provided by Army on application.

13 You will be responsible for collection, issue and return of training and operational equipment.

Movement

14 After formation of your HQ, you will take comd of F RECCE SQN and the Coy of the *NEMBO* Regt on 2

Apr. Thereafter, subject to agreement by 15 ARMY GROUP, the whole force (less volunteers on course) will move to ROSIGNANO, from which airfield the actual operation will be launched. One pl RASC (less two sections) will be attached to you to make the force self-supporting for movement to and from training courses and for drawing equipment, etc.

15 On launching the operation, you will set up collecting points in each of the FIFTH and EIGHTH ARMY areas for the reception and reorganisation of volunteers over-run by our forces. 15 ARMY GP will warn all troops likely to over-run volunteers, and arrange for their interrogation and immediate despatch to your collecting points.

16 GSI (E) EIGHTH ARMY is arranging for special identity cards to be issued to all volunteers prior to the operation to ensure their quick recognition by friendly troops when over-run.

Administration

17 Until moving to ROSIGNANO, the force will remain under the sqdn comd of HQ 13 CORPS, who have also been responsible for the production of all equipment including accommodation stores. On moving to ROSIGNANO, you will come under the adm cmd of 15 ARMY GROUP. At the moment F RECCE SQN is drawing the BRITISH scale of rations while the *NEMBO* Coy is drawing the somewhat lower ITALIAN scale of rations. This will continue in the 13 CORPS area. It is hoped, however, to be able to allow

the *NEMBO* Coy to draw BRITISH scale of rations while at Trossignano.

It was at an early planning conference at Fifteenth Army Group HQ at Cascine that Gay and Bonciani were able – speaking through Birch – to explain that 'F' Recce Squadron operated with ten-man patrols. The Fifteenth Army Group staff were looking at dropping four-man patrols – similar to many earlier SAS operations. While a large number of small patrols might cause confusion over a wide area and convince the Germans that a large force had landed behind their lines, the chances of survival for four-man groups were low. Four-man patrols, they explained, would also break up the cohesion of the squadron, and, as the Italian officers pointed out, ten-man patrols had a better chance of inflicting serious damage in their attacks.

At the beginning of April, the volunteers began arriving at the tented holding camp at Rosignano and the British training team put them through an intense specialist training programme under Ramsay at the Special Operations Executive training school at Malignano.

The first students, 55 men from 'F' Recce Squadron, arrived at Rosignano at 07.30 hours on 29 March. Through the interpreters they were given a brief explanation about the training programme and then it was straight into an introduction to demolitions. After the theory of preparing charges and initiation systems they moved on to firing small charges and the day ended with calculating charges. The skill of calculating how much explosive would destroy a target like a bridge or culvert was essential – if the charge was too small the damage would be negligible and the enemy could make quick repairs – too much and valuable explosives would be wasted. Firing small charges was a useful practical introduction to demolition stores; the SOE syllabus suggests that though detonators should be crimped to the safety fuse using the issued crimpers, they can be crimped with the teeth. This remains a quick and very hazardous method now no longer practised by combat engineers – the small explosive charge contained at the closed end of the soft aluminium tube of the detonator is very sensitive; bite too far up the detonator and the explosion that results can lead to the loss of a jaw and blinding – or at worst, death.

On the second day the paratroopers learned about detonating fuse and fuse chains. This would allow them to attack a target by placing several charges around it which would explode simultaneously – the cutting effect of two charges placed against steel girder would be almost like the blades of a pair of explosive shears. The second day included time delays and pressure and pull switches. These would allow them to booby-trap obstacles and construct improvised explosive devices. At the end of the day there was a switch from demolition to lectures on ambush tactics against road transport, followed by a practical exercise. Ramsay would note after Operation HERRING that the Italian paratroops were already in a high state of training when they arrived at Rosignano and consequently some subjects could be taken out of the course syllabus – this in turn meant that by 20 April a force of 240 men had been trained rather than 200 as had originally been anticipated.

Day three of the course covered attacks against railways and rolling stock. They would learn that the most effective way to cut a track was to place charges on a curve. This would not only increase the chances of a train being derailed but also that curved lengths of track were much harder to replace. A length of damaged railway track had been located in the vicinity for practical training. The Royal Engineers taught them how to construct and position incendiaries so that the intense heat from 2½ lb Thermite grenades or fire pots would create a greater fire among combustible stores. The ideal target for these attacks would be ammunition and fuel dumps, and this was also covered on the third day.

On the fourth day the students learned about German demolition stores, firing systems and mines and booby traps. This knowledge would allow them to neutralise or avoid the minefields and booby traps that the Germans might have emplaced as they withdrew. They would also be able to fire German demolitions prematurely or neutralise them. At the close of the day the instructors summed up the lessons that had been taught.

The next intake of 55 men, also from 'F' Recce, arrived on 3 April and then the 53 men from *Nembo* on 6 April and the last from *Nembo* on 8 April. It was an intensive course, with each intake moving on to parachute training at Gioia del Colle airfield; they also received a rapid but thorough training update with British parachute equipment and American aircraft and made three practice jumps. The first 'F' Recce Squadron intake made a jump at 07.30 on 1 April with only main and reserve parachutes. A day later at 11.00 they jumped with full equipment. There was casualties – though fortunately no deaths – on 6 April Sergeant Major De Giorgio broke a leg when he landed badly and Parachutist Lelio Pellegrini broke his shoulder when he was dragged by his parachute moments after landing. Despite these injuries, at the close of the training Ramsay was pleased by the high standard that the men had achieved. The men were jumping using the British X Type parachute. [See Appendix 3]

It was fortunate that 'F' Recce Squadron, which was a well established unit, had brought its own transport, since this could be used on the drop zone to collect paratroops after they had landed and consequently made this phase of the training speedier and more efficient. In the original plan No 1 ISAS would have received 13 three-ton trucks; in fact they ended up with only two 15cwt trucks, but fortunately were able to obtain two more trucks through HQ SO(M).

The British parachute instructors found that their Italian students had a different exit drill. As Bonciani explained to the Parachute Jump Instructor (PJI) Sgt James, 'Your jumping is cold and passive; a short pace up to the exit, a step out, and down, nothing more than that. Ours, on the other hand, is a flying jump, athletic and irresistible. The man isn't sucked out of the plane, but jumps out with all his might. He doesn't jump as if he'd made a mistake, but as if he really meant to. His movements are decisive and vigorous: he attacks the air!' The Italians, like the Germans, favoured a downward dive from the door of the aircraft with arms and legs spread wide to produce something like the 'Spread Stable' position favoured by modern sport parachutists. British and American paratroops jumped with their arms folded above their chest-mounted reserve chutes and their legs locked close together. To ensure as speedy an exit as possible the men were instructed to think that their boots should be landing on the helmet of the man who had just jumped. A fast exit ensured that the stick landed close together, which in turn made regrouping quicker.

Bonciani would recall that the PJIs were impressed when in the Dakota they saw the men lustily singing the Italian paratroopers' song *Like the Lightning from the Sky* right up to the moment when the first man exited. However the real triumph was at the end of the course when the British commandant addressed the Italian paratroopers.'Your conduct, your dash and determination, are remarkable. As a parachutist myself, I can say that you are the most outstanding of all the parachutists of many different nationalities whom I have had under my instruction. Good luck to you all'.

As part of the training at the battle school, the Italian paratroops had evaluated all the current Allied automatic weapons. The SO (M) planners had tried to acquire from the US Army the folding-stock M1A1 carbine for the operation. This elegant little .30in calibre self-loading carbine had been developed for airborne forces; it weighed only 6.19 lbs and the wire frame stock could be folded down to produce a weapon 25.4 inches long. In the end a heavy weight of automatic fire from a sub-machine gun would be more desirable. The Thompson was reliable but heavy and the Sten light but unreliable, so they selected the more reliable Italian M.A.B. 38/A, the 'mitra Beretta', a weapon with which they were thoroughly familiar [See Appendix 3]. For extra firepower, each stick of paratroops would have a Bren gun team.

In their leg bags the paratroops would have a formidable armoury: three 24-hour ration packs, 100 rounds of ammunition and two loaded magazines, morphine, four

No 36 grenades, clasp knife, maps and compass. Demolitions equipment included 9 lbs of explosives, 5½ lbs of incendiary charges, three pull switches and three pressure switches and the necessary demolitions stores like crimpers and adhesive tape.

Ramsay was assisted by two veteran SOE officers, Major George Seymour and Major John Forster. Both men had extensive operational experience in Yugoslavia, Albania and France. Seymour, who had been awarded the MC for his work assisting the Nationalist partisans in Albania, had endured the frustrating experience of seeing the Communists infiltrate and discredit the work of these men, eventually branding Seymour and the Nationalists as 'Fascists'.

As the pace of training quickened and the groups completed their courses at the 8th Army G (Plans) section a Lt Colonel identified the potential flaws in Operation HERRING. In Appendix E to the operational orders he concluded that the best teams should be given extra training and additional specialist equipment with which to attack priority targets. These he identified as pontoon bridges which were often concealed in daylight, pipelines that had been reported to exist across the Po, static transport and vehicle parks and known ammunition and POL (Petrol, Oil and Lubricants) dumps.

At this stage of the planning there was also some discussion about equipping the patrols with S-Phones, a UHF radio that could be used by a man on the ground to communicate with aircraft. A remarkable piece of electronics, the radio was a duplex receiver that did not require the operator to switch from 'Send' to 'transmit and receive' to hear the reply. It operated using ten miniature rechargeable nickel-cadmium batteries. The S-Phone was ideal in clandestine operations where aerial re-supply had been requested – the set was very directional so the operator had to face the aircraft as it started its run-in. This, however, meant that the signals could not be picked up by a hostile ground monitoring station that was more than a mile away. Given the time available for training, language problems and the fact that HERRING was intended to be a short-term operation, the idea of equipping the teams with S-Phones was discarded.

A great deal of thought had gone into the planning and training for the Italian paratroops but despite five years of war no-one seems to have made allowance for the old maxim 'No plan survives contact with the enemy'. HERRING would shape up into a successful but very different type of operation than the one envisioned by the staff at HQ Eighth Army.

At HQ Fifteenth Army Group, Operations Memorandum 2 by the Chief of Staff, Major General A. M. Gruenther, dated 11 April put Operation HERRING on a more formal footing and identified the structure of the organisation, its equipment and role.

'5 Organisation and Equipment

a. The basic unit will be the section of 8-10 men under a leader. The section may be sub-divided on the ground at the leader's discretion.
b. Two men of the section will man a Bren Gun, the remainder being sub-machine gunners and demolition numbers. A selection of grenades, incendiaries and a small quantity of explosives will be carried.

c. Containers with additional supplies will be dropped with sections. There will be no serial resupply.

6. Tasks

a. Night attacks on retreating enemy vehicle columns to create traffic blocks South of the River PO of sufficient size to produce good air targets by night or in the early morning.
b. Attacks on specific types of target, e.g. premature demolition of a bridge already prepared by the enemy, or else the neutralisation of demolitions on a bridge whose preservation is desirable.
c. Cutting of enemy wire communications.
d. To create general alarm and despondency by all means found possible...

10. Return after Completion of Operation

a. Each parachutists will carry a printed identification card as supplied by Headquarters, Eighth Army.
b. After completion of the operation, ISAS personnel will make contact with our troops by the best means available at the time, and will present their identity card.'

The card was a simple but effective form of identification. Printed in Italian on the front was the message 'Bearer is a member of a Parachute Force operating behind the Enemy Lines for the Allies. All Allied and co-Belligerent Troops are enjoined to give him every assistance and succour to pass him, by the quickest possible means, to the nearest Unit or Formation H.Q. for return to his Unit.' The soldier wrote his name and rank in block capitals plus personnel number, signed the card and printed it with his thumb print before it was signed and stamped by the issuing officer. On the reverse the same message was written in Polish and English. To ensure that the card was authentic an intelligence officer had only to check the front with the rank, name and number. At the end of each line was a full stop sized dot to the right and above the dotted line. The men of Operation HERRING would also have the added advantage that speedy identification would be helped by their being dressed in British uniforms and armed largely with British weapons.

The memorandum listed 34 drop zones for the sections; however, not all would be used. The weight of the operation would be in the square formed by the Po to the north and Route 9 to the south, with the western boundary the road between Modena and Ostiglia Revere (Route 12) and the eastern the road from Modena to Ferrara (Route 64). The area was flat, intersected by rivers and drainage canals, with villages built at crossroads and junctions. While some DZs in the area were suitable for two sections, others would accommodate four, but two were only big enough for a single group of 8 to 10 men. When the operation was launched those sections that were able to link up became a more effective force – capable of taking on German troops in fire fights and causing serious damage with ambushes and roadblocks.

A day after the memorandum had been issued General Brann Chief of Staff at HQ Fifteenth Army Group signalled Colonel Franck at SO (M).

Reference Operation HERRING. During training it has become clear that morale of Italian 1SAS troops which is now high is likely to deteriorate if British personnel do not accompany on operation. Originally ITAPD not envisaged Major Ramsay would take part in actual operation. In view of above however now consider it most desirable he should do so to bolster general morale and prevent Italians suspecting operation to be a suicide mission. This HQ would select mission for Major Ramsay involving minimum risk of his becoming casualty. Request your concurrence if at all possible.

Franck replied on 14 April, 'To maintain morale and ensure success agree RAMSAY should take part in actual operation. Am informing him accordingly'. So Major Alex Ramsay, who had put together a training programme, obtained stores and ensured there were no tensions between the two Italian airborne units, would now join them in Operation HERRING. In many ways the men were right – this parachute drop would not be onto a remote secure DZ like those selected for SOE or SAS operations. However, nor would it have the element of surprise. The DZs were dotted over territory that would be teeming with the enemy – angry and aggressive Germans who had been under attack from the air and on land. Almost within hours of landing the Italian troops would find almost the whole weight of the US II Corps of the Fifth Army crashing across the area, intent on reaching the River Po. Finally the British II Polish Corps and British V Corps would thunder in from the eastern flank.

For this high-risk operation the volunteers from *Nembo*

made up a company commanded by Lieutenant Guerrino Ceiner. The company was composed of four platoons, each of three sections of between eight and ten men. The first three platoons received the numbers of their original battalions while the fourth was formed from volunteers from the Artillery Coy, Mortar Coy, Engineers and Carabinieri. The overall strength was five officers, 13 NCOs and 93 paratroops.

As James Holland says in *Italy's Sorrow* the men of *Nembo* and all of the CIL were predominantly Royalist and right wing and this may in part have been one of the reasons why 'F' Recce and *Nembo* were not integrated for the mission. By Bonciani's account, politically the men of 'F' Recce Squadron were a mixed group ranging from Monarchist to Communists; they were also very close-knit and politics was not an issue within the squadron. Holland notes that behind the lines, the men of *Nembo* had encountered the often left-wing and undisciplined partisans. 'One of the *Nembo* officers caught a partisan raping the wife of a Fascist who was being held in prison. When the partisan fired at him, the officer smoked him out with a grenade. A handful of *Nembo* paratroops got into a brawl with some Partisans, and having got the upper hand, made the Partisans drop to their knees and kiss a Fascist identity card'. These were hard men who had already endured four years of war.

In the course of the training for Operation HERRING another possible subject for tensions between the two groups had been addressed. On 2 April Ramsay obtained permission to draw the more substantial British rations for the *Nembo* detachment who were on the lower Italian CIL rate. As part of XIII Corps 'F' Recce Squadron had been on British rations from its first formation. When the *Nembo* company arrived to begin the training for Operation HERRING they brought with them only a small amount of personal kit, two blankets and their weapons. Among the stores that Major Ramsay and his small staff had to track down were tentage, bedding and cooking equipment. 'This was only half successful', he noted, 'but the gaps were more than covered by imagination and the acceptance of the difficulties by the men concerned.'

However, as General Kirkman explains in the foreword to the English edition of *'F' Squadron*; since the unit was 'supplied with British transport, equipment, and uniform, and during the latter part of its existence when its reputation had been established, wearing the 13th Corps sign, the unit was outwardly indistinguishable from a British unit. Treated, I have always suspected, with some suspicion and even latent hostility by the Italian General Staff.'

A signal dated 21 March from XIII Corps to the main HQ of the Eighth Army reflected the way the staff of XIII Corps felt an almost paternalistic concern for 'F' Recce squadron.

Consider proposal to call for NEMBO volunteers from FOLGORE GRUPPO to join F RECC SQN would exacerbate existing difficulties and tension… Recommend NEMBO detachment retain identity based on existing Coy 111/BN with selected personnel.

Almost all of 'F' Recce Squadron made up a company formation under its veteran commander Captain Carlo F.

Gay. It had an overall strength of nine officers, 14 NCOs and 90 paratroops, formed into 12 patrols. That the record of Operation HERRING appears to be slanted towards 'F' Recce Squadron is a reflection of the fact that it had its own HQ and establishment whereas *Nembo* was an *ad hoc* formation brought together for the operation. 'F' Recce Squadron had the clerks and staff to produce detailed reports from the patrols.

At 10.00 hours on 19 April, Ramsay, whose rank and position in the 'F' Recce Squadron report reads as 'Il capo della I.S.A.S. Magiore RAMSEY', gave a full briefing to the 14 patrol commanders. Four days earlier he had given a background briefing to the OC and Second in Command of 'F' Recce and *Nembo*. The operation he explained was code-named HERRING, or to the Italian soldiers 'Harring'. It would be a 36-hour short-term operation. At the briefing the section commanders received 1:50,000 and 1:100,000 scale maps of the area and aerial photographs of the DZs and other key targets.

It was believed that there would be no partisan activity in the area; however, on landing, the men of No 1 Italian SAS would find that many of their compatriots had taken up arms against the retreating German forces.

At 14.00 hours Gay received the first of three good-luck messages – a telegram from General Ronco, the Chief of Staff of the Royal Army or SMRE. It was a morale-boosting tribute to the Squadron that listed its earlier operations from the Abruzzo to the Gothic Line and the part it would play in the upcoming operation that would complete the liberation of the Patria. The General signed off the telegram with the inspirational words 'il mio saluto piu affetuoso – VIVA L' ITALIA!'

The area into which 'F' Recce Squadron and *Nembo* would be jumping was held by men of the 278th Infantry Division commanded by Major-General Harry Hoppe. In the last months of the Third Reich the division had now been redesignated the 278th *Volksgrenadier* Division – as if this National Socialist title could somehow change its fortunes and raise the morale of the soldiers defending the southern borders of the Reich.

In the territory nominally under the control of the 278th *Volksgrenadier* Division the '*Nembo*' company had been assigned DZs 25 to 28 around Poggio Rusco (Mantova) and Revere-Ostiglia on the Po, while to the east 'F' Squadron DZs 13 to 19 inclusive and 23 were in an area to the south around Mirandola, Medolla, S. Felice Sul Panaro and Finale Emilia. Ramsay would jump on DZ 26, Ceiner on DZ 28, and Gay on DZ 23. Though in earlier discussions about the operation, bridges had been identified as possible targets for premature destruction, it was now emphasised that they were not to be destroyed.

The password challenge would be '*Folgore*' and the reply '*Nembo*'. Bonciani would be jumping on DZ23. What is remarkable about him was that at the time of HERRING he was a veteran of World War 1 and at 46 he was, compared to the young paratroops in 'F' Recce Squadron, an old man. He recalled the map showing the other DZs;

> '*it was dotted with coloured circles, each with a small number inside. At '23', exactly halfway between Cento and Finale dell' Emilia, I paused. If I shut my eyes the circle seemed to come to life and spread out at my feet, at first hazily and then more clearly, until every detail was visible.*

Then I could recognise the rows of vines on the Spada farm, the wide, greying walls of the Villa Bevilacqua, the haystacks at Santa Monica, and the cart track, half hidden among the mulberry trees, which led up to the railway bridge. I wondered if I should land up on one of the electric pylons which stood on the Sant' Anna property. I wondered if I should embrace one of the poplars on the bank of the Reno, or if I should smash the tiles on the Casa Rossa.'

On 19 April a short Message Form was sent to MATAF by the G-3 Air post at Fifteenth Army Group. It requested that in support of night-time attacks, the Allied searchlights that were being shone at the clouds to produce 'artificial moonlight' should be switched off along designated corridors between last light and 02.00 hours, in order that the Dakotas carrying the men of No1 ISAS should not be illuminated. The Message Form was signed by the staff officer tasked with coordinating Army and RAF and USAAF operations; his name was Lt Colonel John Profumo.

This highly intelligent and well-connected 30-year-old was at the time also the Member of Parliament (MP) for Kettering in Northamptonshire, a seat he had won in 1940, making him the youngest MP in the House of Commons. At the close of the war John, or more commonly Jack, Profumo would be awarded a military OBE for his work at Fifteenth Army Group. With a good war record his political career progressed well and it seemed appropriate when in July 1960 he was appointed Secretary of State for War in the Conservative Government. However, his name would forever be associated with the 'Profumo Affair'. In July 1961, at a party at the country house of Cliveden, home of Viscount Astor, Profumo met Christine Keeler, a strikingly attractive young model with whom he had a short sexual relationship. Since Keeler also had an affair with Yevgeny Ivanov, the senior Naval Attaché at the Soviet Embassy, the 'Profumo Affair' took on a national security dimension and this was pursued ruthlessly in Parliament by the Labour MP George Wigg. The Profumo Affair rocked the British establishment and would eventually bring down the Conservative government of Harold Macmillan. Profumo withdrew from public life and worked for a charity in the tough East End of London as a volunteer helper, starting, in an act of self-imposed penance, by cleaning the lavatories. When the Cold War ended in 1989 and Ivanov was free to speak he said that at no time did he learn anything from the pillow talk of their joint mistress.

However, back in 1945 on 20 April a Routine, Top Secret signal was transmitted from HQ 15 Army Group to 2 Parachute Bde, AFHQ and SO (M):

OPERATION HERRING WILL RPT WILL BE LAUNCHED TONIGHT 20/21 APRIL

The trucks picked up No 1 ISAS at Castigioncello and drove them to Rosignano-Solvay airfield south of Leghorn, arriving at 17.00 hours. Half an hour later the men moved to the dispersal area where they met the Air Liaison Officers from the 64th Troop Carrier Group USAAF [see Appendix 2] and the two units ate evening meals. The parachutes had been delivered from the training school when the men arrived and, assisted by the school OC and his staff, the men fitted and adjusted them. As many veterans of both operational and training jumps will testify, the minutes before a parachute is fitted are a critical, private moment – not necessarily for the soldier to delve into his reserves of courage, but to empty his bladder before the straps of the parachute harness make the exercise almost impossible. The three containers [See Appendix 3] that would be dropped that contained the explosives, 500 rounds of .303 ammunition and 500 rounds of 9mm ammunition arrived from SO (M) at 16.30 hours and the stick commanders sent parties to load them under the direction of the aircraft crew chief.

At 19.45 hours the men began the walk out to the waiting Dakotas. The bulky leg bags that contained weapons and equipment were delivered to the aircraft and strapped to the men's right legs just before they climbed the short steep ladder into the aircraft.

These buff canvas bags with their simple lace-up closure were also known as a Valise, and photographs show men of No 1 ISAS aboard a Dakota with the barrels of their Beretta SMGs protruding from the top of the leg bags as they sit facing one another in the aircraft. Once the men had exited from the aircraft the drill was to release the two pins that secured the leg bag inside its canvas sleeve and then, as veteran paratrooper John Weeks explains in *Airborne Equipment*, the skill was to allow the 20-foot rope attached to the leg bag to slide through the sleeve, like an angler playing a fish.

'To let the rope run was fatal, it ripped through the sleeve and in a second was going too fast to ever stop. In another second the sleeve became nearly red hot from the friction and there was nothing for it but to let go. Sometimes the rope broke... On reaching the end of the line, the valise swung gently until landing, when it was immediately available to its owner, who merely pulled in the suspension line. He could, therefore, recover it even when lying down in the pitch dark, in fact without ever seeing it.'

The leg bags contained three 24 Hour ration packs, a total of 160 rounds of 9mm ammunition and demolition charges, batteries, two thermite bombs, four fire pots, 40 metres of cordtex, 24 feet of safety fuse, three pull switches, three pressure switches and eight Fog Signals for attacks on rolling stock moving along railway tracks [See Appendix 3].

In addition each man had the tools of a demolitions specialist's trade. The complete load came to 36¾ lbs, and out of this total each man was allocated 4 lbs for personal kit that included two field dressings and three Morphine syrettes, of which Bonciani would comment 'so that any mortally wounded man can die painlessly, or any man whose wounds can be treated can wait without unnecessary suffering until he can be given treatment'. Personal kit included the inevitable cigarettes, matches, a torch and camouflage cream. Each section commander and his second-in-command would carry a compass and binoculars.

Bonciani, writing about the preparations, said that of the equipment, 'All quite two-thirds are almost always lost on landing... In point of fact, the only things one really bothers about are one's arms and ammunition. Of course it nearly always turns out that one of these things, usually the smallest to which one has never given a second thought, suddenly becomes priceless. Even a piece of toilet paper, on which a scribbled order can be sent to a couple of men on their own in a forward position, may save the lives of the whole section.'

Describing the way that problems seemed to build up before an operation he joked 'There comes a time when one feels strongly tempted to toss everything aside and jump in the nude, armed only with a knife.

'That'd make things a lot easier,' laughed Major Ramsay, who was working like a slave on our behalf; 'it'd be all right about the knife, but jumping in the nude would cause too much scandal in dear old England!'

What the men of No 1 ISAS did not know was how close the operation had come to being delayed or cancelled due to serious supply problems. Ramsay noted, 'More trouble and anxiety were caused and time wasted over the non-arrival of essential stores than over anything else ... On 18 April I was called by HQ 15 Army Gp and ordered to have tps [troops] ready to operate on night 20/21 Apr. Many stores were still outstanding which could have prejudiced the operation, but duplicate orders were sent out to attempt to cover the deficiencies.' The stores finally began to arrive on the morning of 18 April and by 15.00 hours the hard-working RQMS (Regimental Quarter Master Sergeant) and his storeman clerk, who dumped them on the counter of the stores tent for collection by the paratroops, could report that they had issued the bulk of them. At the end of the day Ramsay was relieved to know that the paratroops had all their kit.

In the sunshine the patrols broke down the ammunition loads and primed grenades. A photograph shows the men of 'F' Recce Squadron priming No 36 grenades next to a stack of plastic explosives. It might not be according to the training manual, but they were by now experienced veterans, well acquainted with the hazards of high explosives.

As they boarded their aircraft a USAAF photographer caught the moment as they paused by the steps and then looked into an aircraft that was carrying Patrols V and W from 'F' Recce Squadrons to photograph the men as they sat knee to knee in the cramped interior. The clothing and equipment might be British, but the expectant and confident faces beneath the distinctive rimless paratrooper's helmets were unmistakably Italian. On the left of the picture the spare face of Sergeant Piero Piatti smiles confidently at the photographer. The men are dressed in khaki serge battledress with a lightweight plain grey-green parachutist's Over Smock Mod 1942. While most wear the issue Helmet Airborne Troops Mk II Mod 1942, some have the rimless Helmet Despatch Riders Mk I Mod 1942 – an indication, perhaps, of some last-minute improvisation by the RQMS.

The aircraft carrying No 1 Italian SAS were to fly on corridors hugging the contours on the outward leg and at safer heights on the return. The emergency landing fields that had been alerted for the operation read like names from a travel brochure – Forli, Rimini, Ravenna, Florence, Pontedera and Pisa – but this would be a challenging and risky operation.

To the west the aircraft in corridors A, B and C flew due north until they reached the town of Borgo a Mozzano, with the distinctive feature of the 1,026-metre-high Monte Barbona. Here the aircraft in corridor A continued almost due north to the Initial Point (IP) of the city of Reggio nell' Emillia; the aim was that the final leg of the flight would be close to last light and the 'time over target' (TOT) as soon after darkness as possible. Their DZs, or in USAAF terminology Targets, would be numbers 30 to 34. The aim was to have a minimum of 20 minutes' separation time between drops on DZs in the same area.

For the aircraft in Corridor B the IP was the town of Modena with the DZs 26 to 29. Finally, the pilots in Corridor C would have a more difficult IP of the town of Spilamberto; the other two IPs were on Route 9, the distinctive arterial road running from Milan through Bologna to Rimini. The IP of Spilamberto was to the east of a bend in the River Panaro but lacked the obvious features of a city and major road. Significantly, it would be the pilots on Corridor C who would experience problems with navigation on the mission. The pilots were assigned DZs 15 to 25 and their return flight would take them back to the east of their outward journey.

To the east Corridor D had a different outward and return leg. At the town of Faenza on Route 9 here the aircraft would fly due north to the distinctive navigation mark of the coastal Lake Comacchio and then swing west; the IP would be the northwest shore of the lake and the DZs assigned to the pilots were 1 to 12. Over DZs 2 to 7 the USAAF aircraft would drop 150 dummy paratroops.

This deception plan had been used effectively at D-Day in Normandy where in the darkness or half light the sound of the transport aircraft reinforced the impression that the half-size figures descending on parachutes were real paratroops. The British made 'Paradummies' were known as 'Ruperts', while those dropped by the Americans were 'Oscars'. They stood about three feet tall and were constructed from tough hessian material stuffed with straw or wood shavings. The dummies were fitted with an incendiary charge intended to prevent the enemy discovering their real identity on the ground; others had pyrotechnic charges to simulate gunfire. It was hoped that if the enemy came upon the burned fabric and harness, they would assume that the soldier had destroyed his parachute and was now hidden somewhere in the vicinity.

On D-Day in 1944 two SAS teams were dropped along with 'Paradummies' in a deception plan codenamed Operation TITANIC. It was a large-scale operation in which a force of 40 RAF Hudsons, Halifaxes and Stirlings dropped dummies as well as dropping bundles of Window radar-reflective jamming strips and the two SAS teams. TITANIC was designed to confuse the Germans as to where the main weight of the Allied airborne assault was directed, so 200 dummy parachutists were dropped near to the base of the Cotentin Peninsula, 50 more east of the River Dives, and 50 to the southwest of Caen.

In the end the operation appeared to live up to its inauspicious name when seven men of 1 SAS were dropped south of Carentan, Normandy. Prior to the operation Captain John Tonkin remembered the two officers emerging from Colonel Paddy Mayne's tent at Fairford, Gloucestershire 'as white as sheets' after they had received their orders for TITANIC. They were instructed that if they took prisoners they were to allow some of them to escape, to spread alarm by reporting landings by hundreds of Allied parachutists.

The landing early on the dawn of D-Day was widely scattered and the men were unable to locate their weapons containers. Without them they could do little and so went into hiding. On 10 July they were discovered by a patrol and in the firefight three of them were wounded. Later a larger group of German paratroopers returned; 'they were heavily armed with light machine guns, Schmeissers and rifles. They were all young with 'white faces and appeared jumpy'. To resist would have been hopeless and the group were surrounded and obliged to surrender. Fortunately they were not subject to the 'Commando Order' and executed.

At the time it must have felt like a failure, but combined with the scattered night drop by the men of the US 82nd and 101st Airborne Divisions, Operation TITANIC convinced General Kraiss, the acting commander of the German 352nd Division held in reserve behind Omaha Beach, that a major airborne threat had developed behind him. He called out his reserve regiment and at 0300 hours they bicycled off in the darkness to search the woods south-east of Isigny. The regiment was therefore not available to launch what would have been the *coup de grace* counterattack against the American soldiers trapped close to Omaha Beach.

A little less than a year after D-Day, on 14 April 1945 Ramsay visited the HQ of 64th Troop Carrier Group and conferred with the Operations Officer, Lt Col Priest. Fourteen aircraft would be used, with two available as back-up; radar navigation had been considered but discarded in favour of visual. Ramsay and Priest discussed the height of the drop, time spacing and parachuting drill. Since the aircraft would have to take off at five-minute intervals this would inevitably mean there would be a loss of surprise, since some paratroops would be over their DZs almost an hour after the first men had landed. For the Germans, who had lost any control of the air space in Italy as far back as 1943, any aircraft was hostile and could safely be engaged with anti-aircraft fire as would be brutally evident on the night of 20 April.

That evening between 20.35 and 21.15 hours at the prescribed five minute intervals the 14 USAAF C-47 Dakotas thundered down the runway at Rosignano. Six carried the men of *Nembo* and eight those of 'F' Recce Squadron. Before the take-off they had a final parade and Ramsay read them two more messages wishing them good luck from General Mark Clark and General McCreery and emphasising the importance of the mission. It was McCreery who had seen the potential of the little force as part of the Allied Spring offensive and now the men of No 1 Italian SAS were determined to prove him right.

49 Bonciani.
50 'F' Squadron.
51 *Airborne Equipment: A History of its Development*, John Weeks.
52 'F' Squadron.

Chapter 8

Operation HERRING

Just show me a man willing to jump out of an airplane
and I'll show you a man who will fight for his country.

General James M. Gavin
US 82nd Airborne Division

On the morning of 21 April it appeared that Operation HERRING had got off to a good start, with one exception. At HQ 1 ISAS Major I. G. MacPherson signalled to SO (M):

All HERRING parties successfully despatched night 20/21 with exception RAMSAY's aircraft which returned due flak and navigation trouble.

Alex Ramsay's problems would be a pointer to navigation errors that would beset many of the pilots. Captain Robert Morris Jr, USAAF, the pilot of Ramsay's Dakota, carrying two patrols commanded respectively by Lt Alfio Cavorso and Sergeant Major Carlo Scalambri, filed a detailed report of the mission. For him and other pilots the fog and smoke on the battleground below made navigation and flying difficult and the flak extremely hazardous.

'After definitely establishing myself at the (I.P.)', wrote

Morris, 'I took up a heading to my target. Due to heavy flak encountered I was forced to fly at altitude of two (2) to three (3) hundred feet above the terrain. The conditions of the ground base, smoke and the inaccuracy of the navigational charts made it extremely difficult to definitely pinpoint myself.' Morris returned to his IP and made several runs on his target but failed to locate it. He radioed for Rhubarb radar navigation but since he was now having to fly at about 600 feet he was too low for the radar to track him. By now the men destined for DZ 16 must have realised that the mission was not going well and they had been in the air longer than anticipated. Morris sent one of his crew back to Ramsay and in the cramped confines of the cockpit the Captain explained to the Major that he could not definitely pinpoint the target. Morris said to Ramsay 'I could drop him on an ETA [Estimated Time of Arrival] and place him within a few miles of target. The Major stated that he would prefer not to jump unless I could definitely pinpoint him on the target. On his suggestion I returned to base.'

The pilot had spent almost one and half hours trying to locate the DZ and returned to the airbase at 01.30 hours. The diligence of Captain Morris would give the lie to those pilots who would later state that there was insufficient time over the target area to ensure an accurate delivery of the paratroops aboard. While the fact that Ramsay and Morris had English as their common language would have ensured clear communication between the two officers, the fact remains that the pilots appear to have thought they were roughly in the right area and that seemed good enough to order men into jump into very hostile territory. Italian accounts state that the mission was aborted despite protests from the two patrol commanders and their men.

Captain Julian Caston, USAAF, who was flying the Dakota with sticks destined for DZs 14 and 15, filed a confident report that reflected the attitudes of his fellow pilots. Using the city of Ferrara as a navigation point, his navigator instructed him to turn left and, estimating the location of the two DZs, Caston reported that he dropped his two sticks in an area of the designated DZs. In reality they landed in comparatively open countryside almost due west of Ferrara. The designated DZs were actually SSW of the city on the road running south to Bologna where the SAS patrols would have been well placed to ambush German traffic.

When the operation was over it emerged that one of the sticks had been dropped almost 30 miles from their designated DZs. Following an angry telephone call from his superior, Lt Colonel Priest, the Operations Officer, submitted a report on 3 May to the Commanding General of the 51st Troop Carrier Wing.

Colonel Priest, who had piloted the second aircraft to take off and had dropped his stick exactly on target, interviewed the pilots and requested they submit a written report explaining the navigation errors. The most significant fact was the old problem that had beset them when they had dropped the 2nd Bn 509th Parachute Combat Team at Avellino on the night of 14-15 September 1943 [See Appendix 2]. In the darkness the terrain features and checkpoints seen below looked like those of the designated DZs. He further explained that the pilots had had insufficient time over the target area to positively identify the DZs. He explained:

'4 In the Tactical Air Plan for Operation 'HERRING' it was stated a minimum of twenty (20) minutes time separation was required. In normal supply operations it has been found necessary to allow thirty (30) minutes or more on moonlight, clear nights and up to forty five (45) minutes on dark nights. This permits time to fly a course from two or more known fixes such as towns, rivers etc or DZ in order to positively fix the proper position. It was decided on operation 'HERRING' that the time element was more important than absolute accuracy and a time limitation of two hours and forty minutes (2 +40) was designated. This necessitated departing from IP on a heading, check distance and by time, and drop as soon as memorised ground features were recognised. All crews for this operation were carefully picked and with the crews selected twenty (20) minutes would have been insufficient accuracy. The time allowed made it necessary to take off at five (5) minute intervals.

5 Other features were:
a Visibility restricted due to dust and smoke from battle. Weather reconnaissance ship reported visibility one half (½) mile
b Wind report as received not accurate
c Evasive action, necessary due to flak and ground fire, caused error in time and direction to target
d Smoke and haze cut down light from moon and made check points difficult to see. Vertical visibility only.
e Low altitude required for edge of safety limited range of vision'

In the last paragraph he wrote:

'7 *It is my conclusion that consideration should be given to the limitations and requirements of the mission to be performed. Accuracy can be obtained with thirty (30) to forty five (45) minutes time over target area in favourable weather. This mission was performed with a minimum of time, restricted visibility, and harassed by enemy activity.'*

Priest had put up a strong case to justify or at least explain the pilot error; perhaps he did not know that on 16 April his CO, Colonel John Cerny, had put on record a 'get out' paragraph for the operation in a letter to the Commanding General of 51st Troop Carrier Wing. 'It is understood that the Commanding Officer, 64th Troop Carrier Group reserves the right to cancel any or all targets not deemed tactically sound depending on the ground and air situation and weather at the time of the planned execution'.

In his report on the operations of the *Nembo* Parachute unit dated 19 May, Colonel Umberto De Martino, Chief of Staff of the *Folgore* Group was more direct. 'Owing to the enemy flak and the insufficient experience of the pilots, the groups were dropped somewhat widely apart instead of being close together at the four pre-arranged points. Some areas where they landed were nearly 40 Kms, as the crow flies, from the pre-arranged points.'

The British Intelligence Officer who debriefed the patrols noted 'The wideness of the drops is very disappointing, especially as all crews except that briefed for zone 16 reported having made a correct drop. In addition it is reported that one aircraft accelerated and took avoiding action while the jumping was in progress. That inaccuracy in dropping did not in all cases cause interference with the work on the ground is due to the fact that being natives, they quickly ascertained from local inhabitants exactly where they were and took advantage of local targets.' Though their orders stated that men should be dropped from between 600 and 1,000 feet, giving the parachutes enough time to deploy but ensuring that the men were in the air for a minimum of time, some pilots dropped their paratroops from 1,000 feet or higher, which meant that the paratroops were were hit by ground fire as they descended.

Ultimately the reason that the drops were so inaccurate was that the mission required highly-trained specialised pilots with plenty of experience. The pilots of 64th Troop Carrier Group had demonstrated their ability in daylight drops with big formations and re-supply missions, but HERRING was just too complex and too hazardous for them. These men were not bomber pilots who had encountered flak on almost every mission. Flying at a steady speed, straight and level at 600 feet must have felt almost like suicide – they wanted to get the job done and get out of danger. For the pilots there must also have been the strong feeling that the war was almost over and was it worth dying to allow a bunch of crazy Italian paratroops make a low-level jump – though these sentiments would remain unspoken.

The rough spread of the drops had put the bulk of 'F' Recce Sqdn in a triangle southwest of Ferrara. They were in a position to interrupt German movement along Route 64 and the minor roads running north from Bologna to Ferrara. However, there was one spectacular exception; Patrols C and D were dropped way off to the west, close to the River Panaro. The men of *Nembo* had a similar experience; while some landed around Poggio Rusco near the Po, others were scattered to the south and one stick landed not far from Modena, completely outside the designated area of operations. For the men who had just jumped into the Flak-filled darkness, the realisation of how badly off target they had landed must initially have come as a shock – it says volumes for their drive and courage how quickly they adjusted and began offensive operations.

On the morning of Saturday 21 April the officers at HQ 1 ISAS and SO (M) had no idea that the operation had got off to such a disastrous start. With no radios, the SAS teams on the ground could not report their locations or that they had been dropped well away from their DZs.

However, with the exception of the men destined for DZ 16, everyone jumped, though some did hesitate when faced with the tracer-filled void below them. Moments before they exited the aircraft, the three bomb cell equipment containers had been dropped – they would become the rallying point for the sticks after the men had landed.

As he descended, a paratrooper would see the canopies of the other members of his stick and this would give him an idea of where they would land and where the containers would be located. Parachuting at night, it is hard to estimate the speed of descent and the ground comes up in a rush. The shock – similar to that of jumping off a 15-foot wall – was absorbed through braced knees and ankles and spread through the body as the paratrooper rolled onto his side. There was a moment to catch his breath, glance around at the terrain and then pull in his leg bag with his pack and retrieve his weapon. The next drill was to cut off four lengths of rigging line from his parachute and stow it in the leg bag. Once he had hidden the leg bag and parachute in a ditch or under a hedge he would then start to walk in the direction of the container – linking up along the way with the other members of his stick. For many of the men the silk or nylon parachutes were well worth retrieving after the fighting was over.

The men had also been trained on how to react to an opposed landing – if there was fire from the ground the parachutes and container would be left. Each man would make his way to the prearranged rendezvous (RV), an idea that was fine in theory but terrifyingly difficult in the darkness ripped apart by flashes of gunfire and explosions. It was here that the reply to the challenge of '*Folgore*' would mean life or death. Ramsay had explained that if the enemy had been alerted, the patrol commanders were to find alternative targets to attack. Two factors that had not been considered in the planning were to prove a problem – the bright moonlight and barking farm dogs that are a feature of rural life in most countries. Trying to move quietly and evade the alerted Germans was therefore made a little harder.

It was good that many problems had been anticipated because even before the men of No I SAS hit the ground the problems came at them thick and fast.

Back at HQ 1 ISAS the first indicators of how the operation was shaping up came on 23 April. In a terse signal, V Corps, HQ 6th Armoured Division reported that they had found four men on 22 April, the patrol who had brought in six prisoners and had been passed down the line to the Division's Tactical HQ. The message ended 'Four of this party were killed by Bosch on landing'. A day later Major Villiers of the Grenadier Guards, the No 6 Special Force Staff Section liaison officer attached to 6th Armoured Division, sent a more detailed report to the Eighth Army.

Ref HERRINGS. One Gds Bde found six dropped near POGGIO RENATICO. Claim forty Hun killed amn dump Poggio blown. Led in by civilians after hiding from Hun. Two six Bde found four, later taken off by Cpt Maitland. Six one Bde found five at 0382 dropped north of Poggio. Claimed Huns fired at them during drop and gave instant chase killing one and four POW. Rest OK but had to hide. Saw Hun Tpt and tank going North; put bombs on road but no bang. Bde reported to Birch [the Squadron liaison officer] *who collected. F. Recce seem to have matter in hand.*

Based on these preliminary reports the effort expended on training, equipping and flying in No 1 Italian SAS in Operation HERRING appeared to have been wasted. It would only be later, when the patrols were collected and debriefed, that a full picture emerged, and one that heartened the men at the HQ 1 ISAS at Fiesole. The intelligence officer who collated the reports added his footnote.

Considering the conditions of drop, the perseverance with which several of the parties went about their harassing task seems highly commendable. The tone of several reports has been considerably modified, as the natures of some of the men concerned is to deal in superlatives although without any intention of distorting the truth.

While some groups would lie up in the countryside in drainage ditches or farmland as had been proposed in the original planning, most found friendly farmers and used their houses and outbuildings as a base. It was helpful that those buildings that had been requisitioned by the Fascist authorities had a notice to that effect nailed to the front door. For many of the men of No 1 ISAS their temporary bases gave a glimpse of rural Italy that seemed unspoiled and a reminder of what they were fighting for.

The nine men of Patrol V, 'F' Recce Squadron, commanded by Sergeant Piero Piatti and destined for DZ 13(a) took off at 20.35 hours and reached their DZ about an hour and a half later. They landed on their designated DZ in open ground to the west of the Ferrara-Bologna road and near a road junction that put them in an excellent position to ambush traffic on two vital north-south axes. As they floated down, tracer fire arced up from the darkness below and 25-year-old paratrooper Pierino Vergani was wounded before he had even landed; as he struggled out of his parachute harness on the ground he was captured and killed. With an alert enemy in the area it was difficult to link up, but by morning, once the patrol was assembled, they went into action. Word quickly spread among the local population that thousands of Anglo-Italian paratroops had landed in the area. The men of No 1 ISAS were happy to fan the flames of the rumours. On the first night, when they heard the shouts of 'Achtung *Fallschirmjäger!*' as German troops attempted to hunt them down, they simply joined in – this not only threw their hunters off the scent, but also helped to reinforce the idea that this was a mass parachute jump.

The first target of Patrol V was a German command post on the road from the village of Poggio Renatico, which they attacked with incendiaries and grenades – as the Germans ran from the blazing building, they were raked with sub-machine gun fire. This attack may have been the one reported on 24 April by the Grenadier Guards Major with No 6 Special Force Staff Section as an attack on an ammunition dump. The next target was a small convoy of three vehicles that were set on fire – in the firefight that followed it was estimated that 60 Germans were killed or wounded and ten shaken survivors surrendered. The Germans were using a minor road parallel to Route 64 as they attempted to escape north. The patrol linked up with 6th Armoured Division at the little village of Gallo on Route 64 just north of the River Reno where they handed over their prisoners.

The aircraft carrying the ten men of Patrol W commanded by Sergeant Major Dante German and destined for DZ13(b) had taken off five minutes earlier, and reaching its DZ there was a delay when seeing the tracer fire, one man hesitated. Four men failed to link up with the patrol and were reported missing, presumed dead; they had in fact landed in trees and been captured. They managed to escape from a column of prisoners in Padua and made their way back to join the unit on 30 April. Despite this the patrol drawn from 'F' Recce Squadron set to work – wrecking four telephone circuits and then ambushing two trucks loaded with German troops. Under heavy automatic fire and exploding grenades, the trucks caught fire; some men died in the flames and others were caught in small-arms fire. In the light of the flames the Italians counted 27 dead and rounded up nine prisoners who were passed on to 6th Armoured Division. In their reports the Italians used the distinctive 6th Armoured Division insignia of a knight's armoured gauntlet to describe the formation – they had linked up with troops of the 'Armoured Fist'.

The ten men of Patrol F under Second Lieutenant Aldo Trincas, destined for DZ 14, landed close to buildings where German troops were resting. Two men, 26-year-old Gino le Mangia and 23-year-old Joseph Tiracorrendo, were killed in the firefight that followed, but two other members of the patrol managed to break contact in the dark. When the fighting was over, the local community buried the paratroopers in the courtyard of the Sant' Andrea farmhouse. A plaque to the two men was unveiled in May 2008.

Undeterred by these losses, Trincas' patrol set off, and after reaching the road between Bondeno and Vigarano, they ambushed three trucks, which caught fire. Moving away, they then buried a plastic explosive charge linked to a pressure switch in the road. However, they more than fulfilled their mission when they reached a bridge over a canal, probably the Cavo Napoleonico to the east of Bondeno, attacked the demolition party and ripped out the charges. The enemy toll from these attacks was 20 killed and 31 prisoners who were handed over to a tank squadron of 6th Armoured Division.

Patrol U from 'F' Recce Squadron, commanded by Sergeant Aurelio Asperges, was also dropped away from the designated DZ 14, landing near the village of Mirabello, north of the River Reno. The men had moved to the door when the pilot of the Dakota, panicked by the tracer fire and flares, opened up the throttles and consequently they had the frightening experience of jumping from an accelerating aircraft. The stick landed at 22.45 hours but was scattered; after it had assembled, the patrol decided to move south to link up with the approaching Allied forces. Arriving at a crossroads they took up a defensive position and then sent out patrols, cutting four telephone lines. On 22 April they located a house in which German troops were resting and in the attack that followed, they knocked out trucks and killed 18 soldiers; 16 more were captured and passed over to British troops later that day. The patrol suffered no casualties during their operation.

It took Captain Julian Caston, the pilot of the aircraft flying to DZ 15, an hour to reach the location for the Drop Zone, the Borgata Madonna Woods near Mirabello, at map grid reference 047765. The ten men from Patrol I, 'F' Recce Squadron, commanded by 2nd Lieutenant Carlo Scaranari, received the order to jump and as they descended they saw below them the jewel-like streams of tracer fire. If they had been delivered to the correct location, they would have been close to the bridge over the River Reno, which was, without doubt, a demolition target for the Germans and vital for 6th Armoured Division. They were actually dropped at grid 020842 along a road, possibly the N486 between Bondeno and Ferrara, that was busy with vehicles and marching troops. 26-year-old Paratrooper Silvio Infanti was killed by ground fire as he descended. Two paratroopers failed to reach the containers and were reported missing, and in the initial after-action report one man was reported to have landed on the canvas canopy of a German truck; in reality two had landed on trucks and were taken prisoner – however, they were able to rejoin the unit a few weeks after the operation. On the ground, after they had assembled, the group broke down into two patrols; one, commanded by 2nd Lt Scaranari, attacked a column of vehicles and marching troops, inflicting about 25 casualties. During the night the second patrol dug a plastic explosive charge with a pressure switch into the N255, the road between Mirabello and Agostino. Scaranari was a tough veteran of the fighting near Florence where he had been badly wounded. He had refused to take sick leave and returned to the squadron with four or five splinters still lodged in his liver. There were fears that the shock of a parachute landing might trigger a haemorrhage; his reply was: 'Seeing that we're going to end up in a cloud of lead anyway, why should I bother about a few small bits I can't even see?'

Not far away, at about the same time as Scaranari's men went into action, the men of 8 Battery, Werfer Regiment 71 commanded by *Oberleutnant* Hans Golda, had had a run-in with the partisans, who had already started to attack and delay the Germans. Having fired salvoes from their *Nebelwerfer* six-barrelled rocket launchers in support of the men of 278th *Volksgrenadier* Division, who were attempting to hold the line of the River Reno, the battery had pulled back. They rendezvoused at Sant' Agostino and were ordered to make for Bondeno, but word came that it was already in enemy hands – this may have been a rumour or simply that partisans were in control of the area. The British 6th Armoured Division actually reached Bondeno on 23

April. New orders were issued to the German troops to head for Finale Emilia on the River Panaro. When his battery was about two and a half miles away from the bridge, they found the road blocked with immobilised trucks and horse-drawn vehicles. They were trapped in the darkness, unable to move off the road since there were deep drainage ditches on both sides. 'It made a pathetic picture', wrote Golda. 'In the direction of Finale we could hear the sounds of battle. Officers of all levels were wandering around. Nobody took any decisions.' Word was that partisans were holding the bridge.

Golda took a bold and very risky decision – on his orders his men unhitched the Nebelwerfers and the young battery commander made rapid calculations for range and elevation. Too short and his rockets would explode among the German troops crowded in the darkness further up the road. 'I must say I had never before felt as pale or shaken so much as I did at that moment, as the tubes stared into the night and the gunners waited for the order to fire. I stood in the corner of an empty shed, whispered in God's name and yelled out. The whole battery – fire!'

With a roar the rockets streaked into the night and exploded around the bridge and buildings down the road. It drove off the partisans and suddenly the traffic began to move. Eventually the battery reached the wooden bridge across the Panaro and quickly crossed it, since as Golda recalls, 'Every minute was precious. We had to get as far away as possible before the Jabos [ground-attack fighters] came.'

Meanwhile, the men of 'F' Recce Squadron Patrol Q under Lt Georgio Ganzini, destined for DZ 17(a), had a similar disorientating experience as those of 15 – happily without meeting enemy opposition. The grid for their DZ was 000913; open ground to the south of the Po that would have put them in position to intercept east-west traffic between Bondeno and Ferrara. Their pilot, distracted by anti-aircraft fire, had dropped them at 923862, near the town of Cento. As they descended one man mishandled deploying his leg bag, and when it broke free and slammed into the ground, an incendiary stowed inside burst into flames, illuminating the DZ. The stick assembled and their first target was two trucks that caught fire after they were hit by grenades. After they had cut telephone lines (the drill for cutting telephone lines was to cut in two places so that a long length was removed – this made it very difficult to splice the wire together quickly) they took cover in a farmhouse to fight off a large group of German soldiers. For the next six hours they were under sustained attack – incredibly, the Italians suffered no casualties and the Germans broke off the attack as American ground forces began to approach the area. Patrol Q killed an estimated 11 Germans and were able to round up 130 prisoners, whom they handed over to a Brigade commander of 6th Armoured Division.

The Dakota carrying the men of Patrol N, under Maresco Abelardo Iubini, to DZ 18(a) took off at 21.00 hours, and an hour and twenty minutes later the paratroops from 'F' Recce Squadron received the order to jump. When the stick had landed and assembled around its container they realised that they had been dropped in the area of Sant' Pietro in Casale, about nine miles away from the designated DZ and south of the Reno. Worse still, this was a busy road junction that was on the railway line from Bologna to Ferrara and consequently the enemy, who were in considerable numbers, were alert and moved rapidly towards the DZ. On the road vehicle-mounted crew-served weapons opened fire – possibly 2cm or 3.7cm anti-aircraft guns – and a firefight followed. 'F' Recce Squadron patrol managed to disengage without casualties, though they were scattered, and, operating as two sections, ambushed a convoy of nine vehicles, setting three on fire and probably wrecking another. As the shocked and exhausted German soldiers tumbled from the vehicles, the paratroopers rounded up 60 prisoners and counted 25 dead or severely wounded. The prisoners were handed over to the partisan command who had taken control of Sant' Pietro in Casale. Remarkably, patrol N suffered no casualties.

For the men of Patrol O under 30-year-old 2nd Lt Angelo Rosas, destined for DZ 18(b), the night would be short and grim. The pilot dropped them nine miles off target, close to the N64. The original after-action report stated that three men landed in a concentration of German soldiers bivouacked for the night and their fate was unknown. The report goes on to note grimly, 'Two more are believed to have been hit while dropping and finished off by the enemy.' In the darkness the patrol could hear one of their number fighting a lonely battle for several minutes before the firing stopped. The remaining four grouped themselves together and shot their way out of the village, claiming that they had inflicted an estimated 30 casualties on the enemy. Analysis after the war has produced two versions of what happened that night. The one which was the basis for citations for gallantry decorations drafted in 1946 stated that the patrol was in a firefight as soon as it landed; the fighting lasted for about an hour. Eighteen-year-old Private Amelio De Juliis, seeing that the patrol commander was in danger, broke cover, ran to the officer and though wounded in the right arm continued to throw hand grenades. Thirty-year-old Sergeant Major Aristide Arnaboldi, seeing the two men, raced towards them but all three died moments later, crushed by the volume of fire. The other version of the short life of the ill-fated patrol states that Arnaboldi had been killed while he was still in the air and that Rosas and De Juliis fought separately, and that De Juliis did not throw any grenades. When they had surrendered, both men were clubbed to death by the Germans.

The second version of events sounds closer to the grim reality of the action – it would have been hard for men to rally in the dark in a firefight, let alone give covering fire; moreover, the original after-action report speaks of one man firing. Bonciani would say of Rosas, 'He fought as all Sardinians fight, but the outcome was inevitable.' As a partisan, 16-year-old De Juliis, who would be awarded a posthumous MOVM for his part in Operation HERRING, had encountered 'F' Recce Squadron during a night patrol in foul weather in the Abruzzi. The son of peasant farmers from Pizzoferrato, he knew the area well. He had led them to safety along a remote track and then pressed Captain Gay to be allowed to join the Squadron. It took a week of pestering and then he was taken on strength. The men had been reluctant to see him take part in parachute training for HERRING but Arnaboldi had promised to look after the young man and told Gay 'Don't worry about him, sir. I'll keep him right beside me. We'll take good care of him.' The two are commemorated by a plaque in Maccaretolo San Pietro in Casale – at 18 De Juliis remains the Italian Army's youngest recipient of the MOVM. His official citation ends 'Great example of a strong spirit'. It may have been the survivors from this patrol who went to ground and were picked up by 26 Bde, 6th Armoured Division as reported by Major Saunders.

Happily for the men of 'F' Recce Squadron Patrol L under Sergeant Major Joseph Turolla and Patrol M under Lieutenant Aldo Temellini, who jumped over DZ 19(b) and 19(a), their pilots dropped them accurately and on time. However, both groups came under fire as they descended. 'Temellini had landed in the garden of a villa which housed a German H.Q., and owed his survival solely to the surprise and alarm his sudden appearance out of the sky caused to the two sentries on duty at the time.'

On landing, the patrol was immediately attacked and scattered, and 22-year-old Gianni Biasi, 22-year-old Giovanni Valle and 27-year-old Gaetano Aldeghi were killed in action. Two of the casualties were men killed attempting to cross the Reno – their bodies were only recovered at the end of 1945. Two men who had gone to ground were captured and though one was able to escape, one was killed by his captors. The men of L Patrol mined a road and then seized the critical village of Sant' Venánzio, which assisted by local partisans, they held for six hours against desperate German attacks by men intent on reaching the crossing over the Reno a few miles to the north. At the end of this small epic they were relieved by British forward units who had reached the area. During the fighting, the patrol had captured 14 prisoners who were handed over to the British forces, and inflicted at least 15 casualties on the enemy. They had also dug in a plastic explosives charge on the road.

The ten-man Patrol M, destined for DZ 19(b), landed at 23.10 hours. They had come under fire but suffered no casualties except the dignity of Lieutenant Temellini, who became entangled in a tree. Three men set off on a reconnaissance patrol and linked up with the local partisans; they cut seven telephone wires and then attacked a German billet, killing, wounding or capturing the platoon that was resting in the buildings. As the day progressed more prisoners were taken and when the Italians linked up with the British they handed over a total of 56. Two vehicles were destroyed with incendiaries. Arguably for the Germans, surrendering to the men of No 1 ISAS, who wore British uniforms and were therefore part of a formed and disciplined force, was a much better option than the risk of execution following surrender to the partisans. The patrol lost two men, 27-year-old Privates Lino Mottadelli and Francis Fulci, who were killed as they attempted to cross the River Reno to avoid being trapped by German troops.

The aircraft carrying the two 'F' Recce Squadron patrols C and D under Captain Carlo Gay and Lieutenant Francesco Serra, who would jump over DZs 23(a) and (b), took off at 21.50 hours and after about an hour's flight dropped them 12 miles west of their intended DZ. When he saw anti-aircraft fire the pilot had panicked and opened up the throttles just as the men were exiting from the aircraft, and at this point one parachutist hesitated. This led to the patrols being widely scattered on the ground and some men, including Gay, who had landed on a house, being injured.

Happily there was no opposition on the ground but some of the patrol would not link up for 11 hours. However, in many ways theirs would be a textbook operation. As they landed, some of the group were met by partisans. Bonciani recalled the disconcerting replies to their questions that followed the initial delighted greetings:

'Where do you come from?'
'I come from Nonantola, but I live here now.'
'Well, then, what's the name of 'here'?'
'Ravarino. We're just a couple of kilometres out of the village.'
'Ravarino. How far away are Finale dell' Emilia and Cento?'
'Oh, a good way from here, about twenty or twenty-five kilometres.'
Obviously the pilot must have been tight when he told us to jump!'

Patrol C linked up with the local partisans of the 'Achilles' Battalion, who were led by a former Italian Navy Petty Officer, and the joint force urged the local population to rise against the retreating enemy. German forces were driven out of the villages of Ravarino and Stuffioneto between Route 12 and the N568 – north-south axes from Modena to the Po. The two liberated villages were then held for nine hours against attacks by German troops attempting to escape north. When the forward patrols of the US 88th Infantry Division, II Corps finally reached the area they found that it was already secure. In all, the SAS patrol captured 450 prisoners, whom they held at the HQ of the partisan commander in Ravarino – and handed over to US troops after OC 'F' Recce had received a signed receipt for the prisoners. At the conclusion of the operation the receipt was passed on to Major Ramsay. The patrol also attacked and killed the German demolition guard at a bridge across the Panaro, at Camposanto, and saved the bridge. On 21 April they ambushed a six-vehicle convoy, knocking out one, which caught fire and later attracted roaming Allied fighters which strafed the convoy. The bare facts of the ambush come alive in Bonciani's account.

> *'We had just reached the verge of the road, when two, four, then six, headlights suddenly appeared further down it. We flung ourselves into the cover of the ditch, and soon saw that three light trucks and a lorry were approaching.*
>
> *'Don't all fire at the first. The lorry's the most important,' ordered Gay.*
>
> *The first two vehicles crashed into the hedge, but the third contrived to slip past and drove off at top speed, its headlights out. The lorry was full of soldiers. It was hit with incendiary grenades and, after skidding violently, turned over completely. Then there were wild, confused cries, and we made off over the fields, just as men from it were beginning to open fire haphazardly. Shouting Germans streamed out of a small villa nearby and paused for a moment, probably to give first aid. Then we heard orders being shouted, and directly afterwards they began to follow us. However, they mistook the direction.'*

The following day at Palazzina Stuffione the patrol attacked and blew up a German ammunition dump.

One stick of men from the *Nembo* Company, destined for DZ 25, were dropped ten miles to the west of the correct location near Quattrocase, close to Route 12 in the northwest corner of the operational area. A second stick were, in the words of the after-action report, 'scattered over the Magnacavallo area, MR 7805'. The drop had been seen by the Germans, who quickly moved into the area and captured several of the troops as they landed. However, 2nd Lt Amillio Rafone of 1 Section, II Platoon managed to link up with 11 other members of the patrol. Taking a soldier with him, Rafone set off to reconnoitre enemy positions. They were captured, but the young officer was clearly an enterprising soldier, managing to escape at Padua and making contact with local partisans. He took command of the group and they rounded up 400 prisoners as well as weapons and equipment, which were handed over to the Eighth Army. Rafone, who had been slightly wounded when he was behind enemy lines by Allied air strikes, eventually reached the 1 ISAS base on 3 April, having, like the rest of the stick, marched and hitch-hiked back to base in Fiesole because no transport had been provided by the Fifth Army.

The failure of the Fifth Army to pass men of Operation HERRING back down the line came despite Operations Memorandum No 12 from Fifteenth Army Group HQ, which had been issued by Major General A. M. Gruenther, Chief of Staff Fifteenth Army Group, by command of General Clark. It stated that:

Armies will warn units when Operation HERRING is taking place, and will ensure that ISAS personnel falling into the hands of our own troops are passed by the quickest means to the nearest
Allied unit or formation HQ for return to their own unit. If there is doubt as to their bona fides, they will be passed back by the quickest available means to Army Refugee Interrogation Posts for identification by security personnel.

The Eighth Army and Fifth Army both received two copies of the Memorandum and a total of 38 were distributed down the chain of command.

A day before the operation was launched, by command of Lt General Truscott Operations Memorandum #14 was issued by Brigadier General Don Carelton, the Chief of Staff to the Fifth Army. In greater detail it explained that the men from Operation HERRING would be in British uniform and would be carrying the special Eighth Army unit identification card. In the fourth paragraph it stated 'Army G-4 will evacuate parachutists from the Army cage to HQ No 1 ISAS FIESOLE as rapidly as practical on returning empty supply convoys.' The memorandum was distributed to II Corps, IV Corps and 92nd Division and 85th Division. It appears that the message never reached the men in the front line, or perhaps this small-scale Anglo Italian Special Forces operation was disregarded by the US Forces because it was 'not invented here'.

However, in fairness the flow of traffic was northwards and the only vehicles driving south were those carrying PoWs. So Gay's group made their way home, hitching rides with trucks alongside their former enemies. When they reached Florence they found that despite their identity cards they were in grave danger of being held by the US Army in the PoW camp at Soffiano. 'But after a fiery argument with a wooden-headed American major we were eventually allowed to go on'.

Sergeant Major Giovani Bordin, who had taken command of 8 Section, III Platoon, was not to know of these communications failures when he led the patrol in attacks against enemy transport in the Quattrocase area close to Route 12, operations that yielded 100 prisoners.

The group, who had been destined for DZ 25, were all prepared to take the war to the enemy, even in small numbers – Sgt Major Antonio Villanti and Sergeant Francesco Pompo, who had been isolated from the patrol, took command of partisans near the crossroads village of Schivennóglia to the west of Route 12 and led attacks against transport, capturing 260 prisoners. However the coup was the attack by a 11 Section, IV Platoon commanded by Sgt Major Piscioneri on an anti-tank gun battery position. The guns that had probably been sited to cover the withdrawal across the Po at Ostíglia Révere were captured and their crews passed over to advancing units of II Corps, Fifth Army.

In comparison with some sticks, when the men of 12 Section, IV Platoon landed at what should have been DZ26 at 23.00 hours and discovered that their pilot had dropped them only 2½ miles off target, they might have considered themselves to have been lucky. However, some of the men had deployed their leg bags too fast and they broke loose, so when 2nd Lt Franco Bagna assembled the fourteen men, he found to his consternation that some of them were unarmed. Happily they were able to link up with 10 Section under Sergeant Major Libero Iop and then reconnoitred Route 12. The Germans, it appeared, had wisely moved off this main axis and were using side roads to withdraw, and thus the patrol saw no traffic. However, on the night of 21-22 April, the paratroops were lucky, ambushing trucks and horse drawn transport on the road.

It was on the morning of 22 April, in fighting for a remote farmhouse at Cassellone Nuovo that the men of Operation HERRING would suffer their highest casualties.

The British report about the action is terse and reflects the "fog of war". It records that the patrol took over a farm, was attacked, took prisoners, was surrounded and suffered heavy casualties with only two men escaping. Carlo Benfatti's *L'Operazione HERRING No 1* gives a much more detailed account, but even with the benefit of time and careful research there are still conflicting versions of the events at the Martinelli farm.

The patrol had moved into the barn alongside farm on 22 April and a German Senior NCO and soldier had been killed in the area. In the early hours of the morning of 23 April four German soldiers came to the farm – they were either looking for their missing comrades, or another version has it that they were looking for food. The young farmer Clito Martinelli may have been killed at this point or later as the Germans were eating. The soldiers were seated at the table in the farm when Bagna decided that he would take them prisoner. He and Iop burst into the kitchen with a shout of '*Alto le mani!*' but the Germans reacted quickly and in the close-range firefight that followed Bagna was hit in the chest and killed.

With a total of six Germans now dead the *Folgore* patrol now discussed whether they should remain at the farm or go to ground and await the arrival of Allied forces. It was perhaps a reflection of their inexperience that they opted to stay at the farm, since by now the Germans were alert and with daylight, well-armed fighting patrols were scouring the area and soon launched a succession of attacks against the farm. In the fighting that followed six men from Bagna's patrol were killed or mortally wounded, along with seven men from 10 Section. Incredibly, Paratroopers Renato Migheli and Giovanni Timossi from

11 Section and Sergeant Major Iop and Paratrooper Angelo Di Bernardo from 10 Section managed to escape, and an hour later made contact with advanced units of the Fifth Army. These survivors eventually reached the No 1 ISAS base on 27 April, having been passed through the Prisoner of War system. After the war Bagna would be posthumously awarded the MOVM. His official citation reads: 'A shining example of the courageous paratrooper spirit'. Bagna was not an obvious hero – a member of an old Piedmontese family, the studious young man had read classics before concentrating on an engineering degree. He had been called up in 1940 and after serving with the 9th Engineers Regiment had completed a paratroop course three years later, transferring to *Folgore* fighting in Sicily and Italy.

Like many of the other patrols the men of 1 Section, I Platoon commanded by Lt Ugo Bodon, who were to jump at DZ 27, encountered anti-aircraft gun fire in the final leg of the flight and this may have been a contributory factor in an example of spectacular pilot error. When, soon after 23.00 hours, they had finally orientated themselves, they realised that they were at Sant' Damaso – 25 miles away from their designated DZ. The British after-action report notes rather tartly, 'This error is all the more surprising an error in that the zone of arrival is to the South of the MODENA-BOLOGNA road.' The men had been dropped southeast of Modena, close to the River Panaro; outside the area delineated for Operation HERRING and much closer to the German front line.

They were under fire as they descended and German patrols began to sweep the area, making assembly difficult and drawing the patrol into firefights before they had time to exit the area. One man was killed when his parachute failed to open and two men were wounded and captured but managed to escape.

It was difficult for the patrol to operate effectively on the first night but they managed to attack single vehicles and cause casualties. On the following day some of the men shed their uniforms for civilian clothes and entered villages on the outskirts of Modena, where they planted incendiaries in enemy trucks and, working with local partisans, took 15 prisoners. Early on the following night the patrol laid three plastic explosive charges fitted with pressure switches on Route 9, the Modena-Bologna road. They had the satisfaction of seeing two detonate under German vehicles and the patrol then closed in at short range, taking on the wrecked vehicles with their sub-machine guns. When the firing was over, 15 terrified German soldiers staggered out with their hands up. By the close of their operations, Bodon's group had killed or wounded 40 enemy and taken 52 prisoners, who on signature of a receipt by a Major were handed over to the 133 Infantry Bn of the US IV Corps. Like other HERRING patrols who had landed in the US Fifth Army area, there was no transport available for them to return to base and so it was on 1 May that Bodon's group finally arrived back in Fiesole.

When Lt Guerrino Ceiner's 2 Section I Platoon, who should have landed at DZ 28(a), rolled up their parachutes and moved towards the containers minutes after 12.00 hours, they discovered they were actually near Sant' Giácomo, close to Route 12. Some of the patrol had been scattered and linked up with partisans, taking command of the force and attacking German forces as they withdrew.

The main body under Ceiner ambushed vehicles on Route 12 between Medolla and the market town of Mirandola. putting six vehicles out of action and taking prisoners who were passed on to soldiers of the II Corps, Fifth Army when they reached the area.

When Second Lieutenant Vincenzo De Santis' 4 Section, II Platoon, destined for DZ 28(b), landed at 22.30 hours, they discovered that not only were they eight miles off target on the western edge of the operational area between the villages Sant' Próspero and Lorenzo, close to Route 12, but worse still, part of the stick had been dropped on the far bank of the River Secchia, so making it impossible to assemble. Finally, their misfortune was compounded when one leg bag broke loose as its owner exited from the aircraft – it hit the ground and exploded, alerting the Germans. At dawn the party was still scattered in small groups in the area. However, the enterprising commander, equipped with false documents obtained from the partisans of Sant' Próspero and dressed in civilian clothes, conducted a reconnaissance of the area, cutting telephone lines and crucially, assembling his scattered men. That evening at 21.00 hours, the party split into two groups and put in an ambush on Route 12 between the hamlet of Osteria il Cristo and Casa Tusini. After waiting for about an hour and a half a vehicle column came down the road and the ambush was sprung. It proved a textbook action in which the lead vehicle was hit and rolled over, blocking the road. As dawn broke, the paratroops realised that five vehicles were trapped, and almost on cue, roaming Allied ground-attack fighters, the dreaded Jabos, appeared and strafed the traffic jam.

The patrol took command of 150 partisans in the area and

the joint forces rounded up 189 prisoners. By now the German retreat was turning into a rout and De Santis' patrol captured six armoured vehicles, possibly from the LXXVI Panzer Korps attempting to extricate themselves from their positions north of Lake Comacchio. The vehicles had been set on fire by their crews and the men were now trying to escape north on bicycles. The prisoners were held in the Consorzio Agrario in Sant' Prospero until US troops arrived and they could be handed over. Captured weapons were distributed to the partisans to allow them to mop up the area. The patrol was obliged to wait for almost a week in the area because the Fifth Army would not provide transport and they eventually arrived back at at Fiesole on 29 April.

For some of the 1 Italian SAS patrols Operation HERRING lasted over 72 hours instead of the 36 initially foreseen; however, it was a clear success. Assisted by local partisans, whose help had proved invaluable, the damage inflicted by the Italian paratroops was reported as:

481 enemy killed and 1083 prisoners captured

44 vehicles destroyed or immobilised

150 vehicles captured, including six armoured cars, two tanks and five guns

77 telephone lines cut and demolition charges removed from three bridges.

On the evening of 29 April the Fifteenth Army Group HQ transmitted the cease-fire orders throughout northern Italy, and the remaining Axis forces were ordered to down their arms within the next 48 hours.

For the Allied armies, the Po Valley offensive was the climax of the long and bloody Italian campaign. At the beginning of the spring offensive, it initially appeared that it might be a repetition of previous operations, and become another slow, arduous advance over rugged terrain in poor weather against a determined, well-entrenched and skilful enemy. However, by April 1945 the combat-hardened Allied Fifteenth Army Group, a truly multinational force which, even though inferior in numbers to Army Group C, more than made up for this with its firepower, mobility and crucially MATAF's complete air superiority, had proved victorious.

Opposite them the Axis forces had been worn down by years of combat on many fronts; and were plagued by disastrous political leadership as well as shortages of nearly everything needed to wage a successful defensive war. By April factors such as terrain, weather, combat experience, and able military leadership, that had for months allowed the Axis to trade space for time in Italy could no longer compensate for the simple lack of manpower, air support, and materiel. By the end of the first two weeks of the campaign both sides realised that the end of the war in Italy was in sight, and that all the Allies needed to complete the destruction of Axis forces was the skilful application of overwhelming pressure, a feat that had largely been accomplished within ten days, by 2 May 1945.

'The Allied victory evoked no euphoria', wrote Graham and Bidwell, both veterans of the campaign in Italy, 'no sense of triumph, no victory parades. The fighting troops after a good sleep were fully occupied in collecting, disarming and making arrangements to administer 145,000 prisoners of war, demobilising the partisans and restoring the public utilities of towns wrecked by bombing. The older men could remember the first air-raid sirens of 1939, the victory and defeat in France and the beaches of Dunkirk. The younger men, most of them veterans of 24 or 25, had known nothing but a state of war during their adult lives. It was, at first, hard to grasp that it was all over.'

During the entire Italian campaign, total Allied losses exceeded 312,000, of whom 60 per cent, or about 189,000, were sustained by the Fifth Army, the remainder being British and Commonwealth troops, Brazilians, Poles, Frenchmen, CIL Italians and members of the Jewish Brigade. German losses in Italy were estimated at over 434,600, including 48,000 killed in action and over 214,000 missing, the majority of the latter presumed dead. In Northern Italy the partisans took a brutal revenge against the Fascists or those who were thought to have been Fascists – the numbers killed vary. At least 15,000 died but the figure may have been double.

Somewhere in this grim butcher's bill are the casualties of No 1 Italian SAS – 19 men from the '*Nembo*' company and 12 from 'F' Recce Squadron were killed, and around ten wounded. For Lt Guerrino Ceiner the losses from the '*Nembo*' company cut deep but for Captain Carlo Gay the hurt was more intense – 'F' Recce Squadron was a close-knit group with bonds stronger than the tie of family or blood. For Major Alex Ramsay the losses were also keenly felt – No 1 Italian SAS was his command and in the few weeks that they had been together the force had been shaped and trained by him. However, for all the men, the most tragic death was that of De Juliis – the 18-year-old's enthusiasm had seemed an optimistic pointer to a new post-war Italy.

On 29 April Lt Col Beevor sent to London a copy of the preliminary report on Operation HERRING. He gave a short resume of the intention behind the operation and added 'From preliminary reports it appears that a substantial measure of success was achieved and the Italian paratroops carried out their task with distinction'. A day earlier a Top Secret encoded signal from the Main HQ Eighth Army was very upbeat about the success of the operation, so much so that it stated that there was a role for more such operations by the Italian SAS. A new formation, No 2 ISAS, should be formed, using 20 men from 'F' Recce Squadron and up to 300 from *Nembo*. Stores, weapons and equipment were to be delivered by 1 May at the latest to the Sant' Severo area. Training would be condensed and the weapons would be similar to those carried in Operation HERRING. The tone of urgency in the signal can still be sensed nearly 65 years later – however, the war would end before No 2 ISAS would come into existence; it was to have been dropped in the Trieste area.

Nembo would live on after the war, initially as Mechanised Infantry, until 1991, when it returned to its origins, being reborn as the 183th Parachutist Regiment '*Nembo*', based in Pistoia (Tuscany), part of the *Folgore* Parachute Bde that had been formed in 1960. *Folgore* was expanded to a regiment in 1993, and, as Light Infantry with an air portable and airborne capability, has consistently been deployed in all of Italy's overseas military operations. These include peacekeeping in Lebanon in 1982. In 1991 a Parachutist Tactical group deployed to Kurdistan in the humanitarian aid mission ITALFOR AIRONE. A year later the Brigade supplied personnel to the operation VESPRI SICILIANI. *Folgore* had a particularly challenging assignment in Somalia between 3 December 1992 and September 1993 as part of Operation RESTORE HOPE.

Operations closer to home took elements of the Brigade to the Balkans as part of IFOR/SFOR in Bosnia, KFOR in Kosovo and the MNF in Albania and troops were also sent to serve in INTERFETD in East Timor. In 2005 *Folgore* participated in Operation BABYLON in Iraq.

In August 2007 it took part in Operation LEONTE 2 in Lebanon under the aegis of the UN (Resolution 1701), following the war between Israel and Hezbollah in the summer of 2006.

In 2001 Italy committed troops to the ISAF operations in Afghanistan. On 17 September 2009 *Folgore* paratroops were escorting a convoy in central Kabul when it was hit by a car driven by a suicide bomber. Two Lynx armoured vehicles were destroyed, with six paratroopers killed and four wounded. At the time these losses brought to 21 the deaths suffered by the 3,200-strong Italian contingent in Afghanistan.

Like many Allied Special Forces formations at the close of the war including No 1 and 2 SAS Regiments, 'F' Recce Squadron had served its purpose and was disbanded. As a formation it was too small to have an effective role in a modern peacetime army, but perhaps also it was too closely associated with the Eighth Army for the Italian High Command. After the war in Britain the formation designated No 1 Italian SAS was buried away in the files of the National Archives at Kew. British and American historians studied the Eighth and Fifth Army battles, but the Italian contribution to the final victory, and particularly that of No 1 Italian SAS, received little or no mention.

On 25 June 1945, at the final parade of 'F' Recce Squadron held appropriately at the Teatro Romano di Fiesole, General Harding, the GOC XIII Corps, stood stiffly to attention in front of the Squadron colours, emblazoned with its 19 battle honours, as he took the salute. He then presented each man with a personal letter of commendation.

Farewell Message from the G.O.C., 13th Corps, to ...... of 'F' Recce Squadron

It is with profound regret that I send you this farewell message to mark this sad and moving occasion, which brings to an end the long co-operation between 'F' Recce Squadron and 13th Corps. 'F' Recce Squadron was the first Italian unit to take up arms against our common enemy and to show by its spirit and deeds that Italy would fight alongside the Allies to regain its liberty. Ours was a real brotherhood of arms. 'F' Recce Squadron, commanded with zeal and dash by Francesco Gay, has carried out, invariably with great courage and success, every task assigned to it. The laurels of the squadron were won by the valour of its soldiers in the snows of the Maiella, above the ruins of Cassino, amidst the vineyards of Tuscany, and in the wintry mud of the Apennines. Your final operation, your jump over the Po valley, was the culmination of your ambitions and the complete expression of your spirit. Some of you fell in action. Let us hold them in remembrance. You have written a bright page in the history of the liberation of your country, a page which, in the future, will often be re-read. Now we must all look towards the future. Now that the war is over many of us are about to return to our homes. The men of 13th Corps will never forget you. In their name, as well as in my own, I wish you God-speed and good fortune.

John Harding, Lieut-Gen,
G.O.C. 13th Corps

It was fitting that Captain Carlo Gay received a personal letter from General McCreery – the modest general who had the vision to see a role for the force that would become No 1 Italian SAS.

To the C.O. 'F' Recce Squadron

Now that the Italian campaign has been brought to a victorious conclusion and 'F' Recce Squadron is about to leave the allied forces, with which it has fought in so distinguished a manner, I wish to express to you and all the officers and men of the Italian unit my gratitude for your great contribution towards the bitter struggle against our common foe and my appreciation of the courage which you have displayed continuously throughout the two years you have spent under command of the British 8th Army.

The first group of some twenty volunteer parachutists was formed in October 1943. Encouraged and enlarged as a result of its excellent results in action, it was made into a squadron in January 1944.

Particularly noteworthy were the patrols which 'F' Recce Squadron carried out in the spring of 1944, both in the line and behind the enemy's lines in the Campobasso area, and in the Maiella where you yourself were wounded. 'F' Recce Squadron also played a distinguished part in the liberation of Rome, Arezzo and Florence. It came to know all the battlefields of Umbria and the Apennines, where it shed its own blood generously in the cause of freedom of nations.

Its brilliant operational record was brought to a close by its operational jump in the area between Ferrara and

Modena during the final stages of the Italian campaign,
which, in co-operation with the local patriots, led to the
infliction of heavy casualties on the Germans, the capturing
of more than eight thousand of the enemy, and the disruption
of the enemy's lines of communication during his retreat.

The parachutists of 'F' Recce Squadron can be justly
proud of their achievements. The allied troops in Italy, who
have watched them fighting beside them, have learnt to
appreciate and recognise the value of their work and their
quality as soldiers

Signed
R.L. McCreery Lieut-Gen,
G.O.C. 8th Army

Both Gay and Ceiner were awarded the MAVM – the Silver
Medal for Military Valour. Gay continued his career in the
Italian Army and later both officers were honoured by the
Italian government with the rank of General of the Paratroops.

Memorials remain to these brave men. At Ponte a Ema,
Florence where 'F' Recce Squadron buried its dead after
heavy fighting for this important road and rail junction, a
memorial stone was erected. In the days that followed, the
women of the small community would place fresh flowers
on the graves. When after the war the Italian military dead
were collected and grouped together into larger cemeteries
the men of 'F' Squadron were moved, but the stone that
had been placed in the original cemetery was retained and
stands, bordered by flowers, on the steps of the town.

Each year on 25 April a service of remembrance is held
at the modern church of Our Lady of the Paratroopers at

Cà Bruciata, Poggio Rusco and the elegant modern Dragoncello which records the names of the men who fought and those who died in Operation HERRING. The battle fought for the town, a community that can trace its origins back to pre-Roman times, has become a battle honour for the modern *Folgore* with the 3rd Battalion having the title 'Poggio Rusco'.

With each year the service and celebration of the courage of this select group of Italian paratroops has attracted greater numbers. In April 2008 Silvano Bordoni of W Patrol, 'F' Recce Squadron and Settimio Cencetti of 8 Section III Platoon, *Nembo* were guests at the celebration when a travelling exhibition was opened at Castello Estense di Ferrara; 'Operation Herring - Italian paratroopers' contribution to the liberation of our country'.

It was an opportunity for veterans, serving soldiers and community leaders to honour men who, as No 1 Italian SAS, not only jumped into battle but some of whom subsequently gave their lives for the liberation of Italy.

53 Hans Golda memoir.
54 'F' *Squadron*.
55 Ibid.
56 Ibid.
57 *Tug of War*.

Appendices

Appendix 1

The Commando Order

This notorious order was promulgated by Hitler soon after Operation BASALT, a raid mounted on Sark on 3/4 October 1942 by men of the Small Scale Raiding Force (SSRF).

There were numerous probes by Commando forces against the Channel Islands, but Operation BASALT, undertaken by seven men of the SSRF and five from No 12 Commando, led by Captain Geoffrey Appleyard and Lieutenant Anders Lassen, may have prompted the Commando Order. In Peter King's *The Channel Islands War 1940-1945* he explains that five prisoners from a German engineer detachment were captured in bed in the Discart Hotel on Sark. With their trousers around their ankles they were bound with the Commando's toggle ropes. (six foot long with a wooden toggle spliced in at one end and an eye at the other. They were used for climbing cliffs or building simple rope bridges). Despite these restraints a running fight developed. Two Germans escaped, though one of them was wounded and two soldiers, Esslinger and Bleyer, were killed.

Inflamed by this news, on 18 October Hitler issued the secret *Kommandobefehl* - The Commando Order.

Der Führer SECRET No.003830/42g.Kdos.OKW/Wst
F.H. Qu 18.10.
12 Copies Copy No.12

1 For a long time now our opponents have been employing in their conduct of the war, methods which contravene the International Convention of Geneva. The members of the so-called Commandos behave in a particularly brutal and underhand manner; and it has been established that those units recruit criminals not only from their own country but even former convicts set free in enemy territories. From captured orders it emerges that they are instructed not only to tie up prisoners, but also to kill out-of-hand unarmed captives who they think might prove an encumbrance to them, or hinder them in successfully carrying out their aims. Orders have indeed been found in which the killing of prisoners has positively been demanded of them.

2 In this connection it has already been notified in an Appendix to Army Orders of 7.10.1942 that in future, Germany will adopt the same methods against these Sabotage units of the British and their Allies; i.e. that, whenever they may appear, they shall be ruthlessly destroyed by the German troops.

3 I order, therefore:-
From now on all men operating against German troops in so-called Commando raids in Europe and Africa, are to be annihilated to the last man. This is to be carried out whether they be soldiers in uniform, or saboteurs, with or without arms; and whether fighting or seeking

to escape; and it is equally immaterial whether they come into action from Ships or Aircraft, or whether they land by parachute. Even if these individuals on discovery make obvious their intention of giving themselves up as prisoners, no pardon is on any account to be given. On this matter a report is to be made in each case to Headquarters for the information of Higher Command.

4 Should individual members of these Commandos, such as agents, saboteurs, etc., fall into the hands of the Wehrmacht through any other means - as, for example, through the Police in one of the Occupied Territories - they are to be instantly handed over to the SD. To hold them in military custody - for example in POW camps etc., - even as a temporary measure, is strictly forbidden.

5 This order does not apply to the treatment of those enemy soldiers who are taken prisoner or give themselves up in battle, in the course of normal operations, large scale attacks; or in major assault landings or airborne operations. Neither does it apply to those who fall into our hands after a sea fight, nor to those enemy soldiers who, after air battle, seek to save themselves by parachute.

6 I will hold all Commanders and Officers responsible under Military Law for any omission to carry out this order, whether by failure in their duty to instruct their units accordingly, or if they themselves act contrary to it.

(Sgd)
Adolf Hitler

Appendix 2

No 1 Italian SAS
'F' Recce Squadron

Patrol 'C' DZ 23
Cap. GAY Carlo Francesco
Cap. BONCIANI Carlo
S.Ten.Med. SAVONUZZI
Giorgio
Serg.Mag. DALL'ASTA
Modesto
Parac. BACCAN Luigi
Parac. GUGLIELMO Romolo
Parac. CIOTOLA Edoardo
Parac. MASCARETTI
Gianfranco
Parac. WELPONER Paolo

S.Ten SERRA Francesco
Serg. GIOVANNANGELI
Tonino
Serg. CHIODINI Tito
C.le Mag. BIANCHIN
Giovanni
C.le Mag. ZARATTI Giuseppe
Cap.le SEGNALINI Gastone
Parac. PAGLIARUSCO Luigi
Parac. CARNEVALI Mario
Parac. BIONDOLILLO Ugo
Parac. GOMISCEK Eugenio

Patrol 'I' DZ 15

S.Ten. SCARANARI Carlo
C.le Mag. MARCUZ
G.Battista
C.le Mag. ANTONIACONI
Eligio
C.le Mag BIALE Attilio
C.le Mag CINQUINO Paride
Parac. BALESTO Rino
Parac. CAPRETTI Angelo
Parac. CIPOLLAT Luigi
Parac. MARCHIORETTI
Tommaso
Parac. INFANTI Silvio
Killed in action 20 April 1945
at Madonna Boschi-Poggio
Renatico

Patrol 'F' DZ 14

S.Ten. TRINCAS Aldo
Serg. PANIZ Duilio
C.le Mag. MANGIA Gino
Killed in action 20 April 1945 at
Mirabello di Sant'Agostino
MAVM and CGVM

C.le Mag. POLESE Luigi
C.le DELLA GIOVANNA
Ennio
Parac. TIRACORRENDO
Giuseppe
Killed in action 20 April 1945 at
Mirabello di Sant'Agostino
MAVM
Parac. DREOSTO Pietro
Parac. SCATTOLO Nello
Parac. CAMARRA Nicola
Parac. GANDOLFI Rino

Patrol 'U'

Serg. ASPERGES Aurelio
C.le Mag. BONIZZONI Luigi
C.le Mag. FALETTI
Gaudenzio
C.le Mag. FABBRI Vasco
C.le MARASCA Lorenzo
C.le MACIOCE Bruno
Parac. CAMICIOTTOLI
Dagoberto
Parac. LANATI Giuseppe
Parac. POIRE Elio
Parac. IGLIORI Ugo

Patrol 'Q' DZ 17

Ten. GANZINI Giorgio
Serg. RUVOLI Rino
C.le Mag. FENOGLIO
Angelo
C.le Mag. TRAVAINI Celso
C.le DI STEFANO Ildefaro
C.le VERONA Antonio
C.le LUPINI Celso
Parac. FATICANTI Spartaco

Parac. PERELLI Giulio
Parac. BORSETTI Antonio

Patrol 'L' DZ 19

Serg.Mag. TUROLLA
Giuseppe
C.le BIASI Gianni
Killed in action 20 April 1945 at
Poggio Renatico MAVM
C.le VALLE Giovanni
Killed in action 20 April 1945 at
Poggio Renatico MAVM
Parac. ALDEGHI Gaetano
Killed in action 20 April 1945 at
Poggio Renatico MAVM
Parac. BARSANTI Benso
Parac. DAL RE Paolo
Parac. DOLZAN Mario
Parac. COLANGELI Mario
Parac. ALDEGHI Gaetano

Patrol 'M' DZ 19

Ten.TEMELLINI Aldo
Serg. COSTA Umberto
C.le BONA Giovanni
C.le TOCCAFONDI Franco
Parac. VALENTINI Primo
Paracad. DESIDERI Amedeo
Parac. FLUMÌNI Ernesto
Parac. TONON Domenico
Parac. MOTTADELLI Lino
Killed in action 20 April 1945 at
Poggio Renatico
Parac. FULCO Francesco
Killed in action 20 April 1945 at
Poggio Renatico

Patrol 'V' DZ 13

Serg. PIATTI Piero
C.le FREGONI Luigi
C.le MERLO Pietro
C.le RONCORONI Angelo
Parac. FILPA Franco
Parac. PEROLFI Alfredo
Parac. SALVEL Luigi
Parac. TEDESCHI Antonio
Parac. VERGANI Pierino
Died 23 April 1945 at Lendinara

Patrol 'W' DZ 13

Serg. Mag. TEDESCO Dante
Serg. BAIOCCHI Franco
C.le PIRELLI Mimmo
Parac. GUIDA Arturo
Parac. RICCI Guido
Parac. ROSSI Dino
Parac. TANTERA Abele
Parac. LENZI Giovanni
Parac. GIANNINI Calafo
Parac. BORDONI Silvano

Patrol 'N' DZ 18

Maresc. IUBINI Abelardo
Serg. Mag. PERSEVALLI
Piero
C.le Mag. IACOBONI Ettore

Parac. DUS Francesco
Parac. GIARDINI Gino
Parac. BORIN Mario
Parac. NIRONI Enzo
Parac. ZIRALDO Olivo
Parac. ANSELMO Giuseppe
Parac. SUPPO Edoardo

Patrol 'O' DZ 18

S.Ten. ROSAS Angelo
Killed in action 20 April 1945 at
San Pierro in Casale MAVM
Serg.Mag. PECORARO
Giuseppe
C.le Mag. ARNABOLDI
Aristide
Killed in action April 20, 1945 at
San Pietro in Casale MAVM and
MAVM
C.le TRUZZI Primo
C.le SISTI Roberto
Parac. ARBIZZANI Sergio
Parac. LIBERATORI
Armando
Parac. PODANA Osvaldo
Parac. DI BARTOLOMEI
Enzo
Parac. DE JULIIS Amelio
Killed in action 20 April 1945 at
San Pietro in Casale MOVM

'Nembo' Company

I Platoon

1 Section DZ 17
S Ten BODON Ugo
Serg Mag ZARA Massimo
C le Mag MORETTI Michele
C le Mag COSSALTER
Ernesto
C le GAIA Giusseppe
Parac. FRANCIO Callisto
Parac. FIORUCCI Orlando
Parac. ZANCARLI Renzo
Parac. DE PERON Giusseppe

2 Section DZ 28
Tenente CEINER Guerrino
Serg Mag MARRONE
Romano
C le CENERI Dino
C le MAGI Alfonso
C le MAGNANI Armando
Parac. PACE Carlo
Parac. FURLAN Efraim
Parac. SILVESTRI Franco
Parac. SORI Edgardo
Parac. MELIS Tarcisio

3 Section DZ 27
Serg Mag USSI Giorgio
C le Mag FIUMI Roberto
Paracad LUNESO Giovanni
Parac. CONGIU Franco
Parac. MULAS Gian Maria
Parac. NASTASIO Aldo
Parac. SETTEMBRE
Armando

Parac. FILIPPINO Giuseppe
Parac. TAGLIERINI
Salavatore
*Died under interrogation 20
April 1945 at San Damaso*

II Platoon

4 Section DZ 28
S Ten DE SANTIS Vincenzo
Serg Mag MARIANI Luigi
C le Mag VARA Mario
Parac. GREPPI Cirillo
Parac. SALIS Giovanni
Parac. CRESCIOLI Antonio
Parac. ZANINOTTI Mario
Parac. DE VALERIO Mario
Parac. COLLI Raimondo
Parac. VIGNA Alfredo

5 Section DZ 28
Serg Mag MAGLIONE Polito
C le Mag CARNIATO Armido
C le Mag VAILATI Frederico
Parac. MORELLI Giovani
Parac. ACCORDINI Aldo
Parac. MOBILIA Luigi
Parac. PENNA Mario
Parac. DE ZORZI Giovanni
Parac. MAGILI Lino
Parac. ALBANESE Gastone

6 Section DZ 24
Serg Mag MARTINETTO
Benedetto
C le GRILLETTI Angilo

Parac. MACCARI Pietro
Parac. TOMASI Giorgio
Parac. VENTURI Enzo
Parac. PRACUCCI Gino
Parac. ZANIN Gerolamo
Parac. POMANTE Nicola
Parac. IMBERTI Giovanni

Parac. CAVALIERI Ettore
Parac. ZENNARO Aurelio
Parac. SPALLUZZI Giovani
Parac. FRANCINI Alfiero
Parac. SADOCCI Riccardo
Parac. DE PELLEGRINI
Rinaldo

III Platoon

IV Platoon

7 Section DZ 25
S Ten RAFFONE Aurelio
Serg Mag PARUZZO Antonio
C le Mag MURGIA Sestilio
C le Mag ZOCCASTELLO
Luciano
C le CECCHETTO Alfredo
C le ZECCHI Giuseppe
C le DELL'ERA Vincenzo
Parac. FALSONE Mauro
Parac. BARALDINI Bruno

10 Section DZ 26
Serg Mag IOP Libero
C le GELLI Gelsomino
Killed in action on 23 April 1945
at Dragoncello di Poggio Rusco
C le CUCCHI Enea
Killed in action on 23 April 1945
at Dragoncello di Poggio Rusco
MAVM
Parac. BIAGGI Fiorenzo
Killed in action on 23 April 1945
at Dragoncello di Poggio Rusco
Parac. BERTACCO Pietro
Killed in action on 23 April 1945
at Dragoncello di Poggio Rusco
Parac. CARRETTO Giovanni
Killed in action on 23 April 1945
at Dragoncello di Poggio Rusco
Parac. EDUARDO Domenico
Killed in action on 23 April 1945
at Dragoncello di Poggio Rusco
Parac. PECILE Tarcisio
Killed in action on 23 April 1945
at Dragoncello di Poggio Rusco
MAVM
Parac. DI BERNARDO Angelo

8 Section DZ 25
Serg Mag VILLANTI Antonio
Serg POMPO' Francesco
C le Mag MILANO Carlo
C le Mag BORDIN Giovanni
Parac. CENCETTI Settimio
Parac. PUPI Giorgio
Parac. BELLINI Mariano
Parac. CERUTI Gino

9 Section DZ 25
Serg Mag MONTALBANO
Antonio
C le Mag GAUIDIO Tullio
Parac. TROI Giacinto

11 Section DZ 26
Serg Mag PISCONERI
Vincenzo
C le Mag VIETTI Gian
Battista
Killed in action on 22 April 1945
at Malcantone di Sermide
Parac. PRANDI Pasquino
Killed in action on 22 April 1945
at Malcantone di Sermide
Parac. LANDI Olinto
Killed in action on 22 April 1945
at Malcantone di Sermide
Parac. STEFANELLI
Guiseppe
Killed in action on 22 April 1945
at Malcantone di Sermide

Parac. DI NATALE Carmelo
Parac. FINOTTO Ermes
Parac. SERRA Antioco

12 Section DZ 26
S ten BAGNA Franco
Killed in action on 23 April 1945
at Dragoncello di Poggio Rusco
MOVM
C le Mag MONDADORI
Ernesto
Killed in action on 23 April 1945
at Dragoncello di Poggio Rusco
MAVM
C le OTTINI Luigi
Killed in action on 23 April 1945
at Dragoncello di Poggio Rusco
Parac. FADDA Angelo
Killed in action on 23 April 1945
at Dragoncello di Poggio Rusco

Parac. GUGLIEMETTI
Antonio
Killed in action on 23 April 1945
at Dragoncello di Poggio Rusco
Parac. MARINI Nicola
Killed in action on 23 April 1945
at Dragoncello di Poggio Rusco
Parac. MERELLA Salvatore
Killed in action on 23 April 1945
at Dragoncello di Poggio Rusco
Parac. MIGHELI Renato
Parac. TIMOSSI Giovanni

Appendix 3

Weapons and Equipment

3 in Mortar

The Ordnance M.L. Mortar 3 inch Mk 2, to give it its full designation, would prove a potent and versatile weapon for the SAS. It was the standard British Infantry Battalion support weapon that had a minimum range of 125 yards and maximum of 2,750 yards. The HE and smoke bombs weighed 10 lb and an experienced crew could fire 15 bombs a minute. The mortar could be broken down into three loads – base plate, 36lb barrel, 42lb bipod and sights (45 lb) and carried by men or mules, which allowed the SAS to engage targets from remote locations that were hard to spot and engage with counter-battery fire.

Hawkins Mine or Grenade

The official designation for this ingenious little device was Hand Grenade Anti-tank No 75. It weighed 36oz, of which just over 18oz was explosives. It had two crush igniter fuses which were inserted under the striker plate and could either be thrown in front of a tank or placed as a mine. If it was thrown it was designed so that it would land on a face that ensured that the crush igniters worked. The charge was powerful enough to cut a track or destroy a wheeled vehicle, though by the end of the war they were laid in clusters. Since it measured 4¾ x 3¾ x 2¼ ins it could be carried by soldiers in their 37 Pattern ammunition pouches.

If they were laid as a minefield, the Army Pamphlet No 13 recommended that there should be a gap of three feet between them to prevent sympathetic explosions, with the striker plate upwards and a covering of a thin layer of earth.

2.36in Rocket Launcher

Universally known as the 'Bazooka' after the curious musical instrument played by American comedian Bob Burns, the rocket launcher fired a 3.4 lb rocket that could penetrate 4.7 inches at 0°. Its greatest attraction was that the launcher weighed only 13.25 lbs. The M1 launcher was 5ft 1in, but the M9 folded into two sections, reducing the length by half. The only drawback was that rocket gases were ejected from the rear when the weapon was fired; however, there was no recoil. As well as HEAT, smoke and incendiary rockets were produced.

Bren LMG

The Bren Light Machine Gun (LMG) was the British Infantry Section automatic weapon. Weighing only 22.12 lb and being 45.5 in long, it was an ideal weapon for partisan groups. It was easy to clean and maintain and was an air-cooled gas-operated weapon with a 30-round box magazine. It had a slow rate of fire; about 500 rpm; but was very accurate, with sights set out to 2,000 yds. The first guns, built at the Royal Small Arms Factory at Enfield, were based on the ZB 26, a LMG design from the Czechoslovakian small-arms factory at Brno. The names of the two factories were combined to produce the Bren, a superb LMG that would soldier on from World War 2 to the first Gulf War in 1991.

Vickers MMG

The Vickers 0.303in Medium Machine Gun (MMG) was a veteran of World War 1 and would soldier on with the British Army until 1974. It was a three-man load, so, like the 3-inch Mortar, could be carried to remote locations. With water in the cooling jacket, the gun weighed 40lb and the tripod 48.5lb. It had a comparatively slow rate rate of fire of 450 to 500 rpm and a maximum range of 3,600 yards. Using a dial sight that was introduced in 1942, the gun could be used for indirect fire, which Farran's men employed effectively against German positions out of sight in dead ground.

75 mm Pack Howitzer

The American M1A1 Pack Howitzer weighed 1296 lbs and so could be towed by a Jeep, mules or broken down into six loads, or, with the M1A1 on Carriage M8, into nine loads for parachute delivery. The howitzer fired a handy 13.7 lb M41A1 HE shell to a maximum range of 9,760 yards.

Ammonal

Ammonal is an explosive developed in World War 1 and used principally for cratering. Though effective, it is very hygroscopic and can be neutralised when water penetrates the mixture, which is composed of ammonium nitrate, TNT and aluminium powder. Ammonal has a detonation velocity of approximately 4,400 metres per second.

Thermite

Thermite, discovered in 1893 by a German chemist, is a compound that burns at temperatures of around 2,500° C

(4,500° F). In grenade form it is used against artillery pieces and vehicles, since the extremely high temperatures generated will fuse metal together. A Thermite grenade could be used to weld the breech of an artillery piece or cut through an engine block. For the men of No 1 ISAS, the added attraction of Thermite grenades was that though they generated intense heat and light they were almost noiseless. It was probably these grenades that were so effective setting fire to trucks in the ambushes sprung by No 1 ISAS. Similarly the Fire Pot, a shallow cylinder of 5.25lb of magnesium alloy and 1lb of thermite, seven of which had made up the payload of the obsolete RAF 25lb Mark 1 Incendiary bomb, had been modified to be a silent sabotage weapon for use against stores dumps and parked vehicles. One of the aims of Operation HERRING was to create traffic jams as targets for MATAF ground-attack aircraft, and smoke and flames produced by these incendiary devices as they consumed German motor transport would have proved very effective as a marker.

PE 808

PE 808 plastic explosive was a British invention perfected at the Royal Ordnance Factory at Bridgewater just before the war, and was to revolutionise covert operations and sabotage. It was composed of cyclotrimethylene-tritramine, a powerful but sensitive explosive which the British called Research Department Explosive or RDX. Mixed with plasticising oil, it was made more stable and became a waterproof, shock-proof and putty-like material. It was a yellowy-brown colour and was packed in waxed paper cartridges. PE 808 had a characteristic marzipan smell, and if handled and inhaled would give the user a splitting headache, known as a 'gely (gelignite) headache'. Plastic explosives were incredibly versatile, since unlike earlier slab explosive like Gun Cotton, it could be moulded against a target or used to fill containers as improvised anti-personnel and vehicle devices.

Cordtex

Cordtex, also known as Detonating Cord or Det Cord, is a waterproof, flexible hollow plastic cord containing pentaerythritoltetranitrate, an explosive that detonates at 2000 metres a second. It can be used to link several charges together in a ring main, or to fire a charge that is located away from the booby trap switch and detonator.

Booby Trap Switches

The Switch No 4 Pull Mk 1 was a brass cylinder about four inches long with a spring-loaded firing pin – when a trip wire was attached and a pull of 6 to 8 lbs exerted, the pin was released and hit a .22 cap, that would in turn fire a No 27 Mk 1 flash detonator. The Switch No 5 Pressure Mk 1 was a useful device for attacking both railway locomotives and trucks plus other wheeled vehicles. To attack rolling stock, a PE charge was buried in the gravel ballast on a curved stretch of track. Early designs used a spring-loaded firing pin held back by a shear pin, which broke under the pressure of the train on the track that would flex it slightly. The later, more sophisticated Switch No 5 Pressure Mk 1 had an extension rod, which was positioned so that it touched the track, while the charge and mechanism were hidden in the ballast. When the track flexed as the train passed over it, sufficient pressure was transmitted to the extension rod to release the spring-loaded firing pin.

The Pressure Switch operated under pressures of between 22lb and, with the extension in place, up to 66lb. The Fog Signal was an adaptation of a peacetime spring-clip explosive device that could be fitted to a railway track to warn drivers that there was fog further down the line. As the locomotive's wheels crushed the shallow cylinder of explosives, the detonation would alert the driver and fireman to the hazard. The SOE took the Fog Signal and added a sleeve that would take a Flash Detonator – the detonator was in turn linked to a length of Cordtex at the end of which was a PE charge.

X Type Parachute

Developed by Raymond Quilter of the GQ company, which had been manufacturing parachutes since 1934, the X Type was a simple and reliable military parachute. The parachute measured 28ft across with a circular 22in vent in the centre. All earlier types were made of silk but later, cotton parachutes known as 'Ramtex' were introduced. Nylon canopies were manufactured towards the end of the war. There were 28 rigging lines each 25ft long made of nylon or silk with a minimum breaking strength of 400 lbs. The web harness supported a minimum breaking strength of 1.3 tons. All metal fittings were of forged stainless steel. Men who had jumped with the X Type said that the shock of landing was similar to jumping off a 15-foot wall.

Mitra Beretta MAB38

Introduced in 1938, the 8.8 mm MAB 38 was based on the Villar Perosa. It had two triggers, one for semi-automatic and one for automatic fire. It fired from 10-, 20- or 40-round magazines that could be loaded by hand or by specific tools. It was 947mm long, weighed five kilograms and fired at 500 rounds per minute. The muzzle velocity was 420 metres per second and the maximum range for the pistol-sized bullet (the same as the Beretta 34 pistol) was reported as 1000 metres; in reality the effective range was around 100. The Moschetto Automatico was manufactured in the Beretta factory located at Gardone Valtrompia, Brescia. It was used both by the Allies and German forces. Until 1943, it was only available to parachute units, Carabinieri and Polizia Africa Italiana. It became more widespread in the Armed Forces of the Republic of Salò, partisans and Italian units fighting under Allied command. Its later version, called MAB 38/42, was lighter, shorter and had a higher rate of fire. It served well into the 1970s with Carabinieri and Police.

Fairbairn Sykes Fighting Knife

The elegant double-edged knife was named after Captains William Fairbairn and Anthony Sykes, who had served in the Shanghai Municipal Police before the war and had developed a keen knowledge of armed and unarmed combat. They taught these skills to Commandos in training in Scotland and developed the knife based on fencing foil designs. The FS Knife is 11 inches long, with a tapered 7-inch dagger blade and has a distinctive bottle-shaped grip that is designed to fit into the natural crease between the palm and ball of the thumb. Fairbairn's wartime publication *All-in Fighting* describes in detail vulnerable points on the human body where a thrust or slash would be lethal. FS Knives were widely issued to Commandos and SAS troops during the war. The knife features as the insignia of several operational special forces formations around the world.

C.L.E. Container

C.L.E. stood for Central Landing Establishment, where the container was developed, and was used to deliver supplies from aircraft. During an airborne landing the containers would be dropped immediately before the stick of parachutists left the aircraft. The container might have the packs of those jumping with the heaviest loads as well as spare weapons and ammunition. The Mk.1 had a metal framework covered with plywood, whilst the Mk.1T was covered with a metal skin and the Mk.3 had either covering. It was made of two halves that were hinged along its length to make an approximate cylinder when closed. It could be carried and released from a 500lb or a universal bomb carrier which earned it the nickname 'Bombcell'. Thus it would be carried under the wings of the Dakota transport aircraft, and in the bomb bay of bombers such as the Stirling. One end of the container was domed to form a crushable head on which it landed, while housed at the other end was the parachute bag and pack. The weight of the C.L.E. container and parachute was between 103½lbs net and 350lbs.

The 64th Troop Carrier Group USAAF

The 64th Troop Carrier Group USAAF had a varied and distinguished war. It began as the 64th Transport Group, constituted on 20 November 1940 and activated on 4 December at Duncan Field, Texas. A redesignation to 64th Troop Carrier Group in July 1942 marked a change in role to providing airlift for paratroop and glider units and other airborne forces.

The Group was adjudged ready for combat duty on 20 July 1942 and in August it deployed to a base at Ramsbury, England.

The Group was in England for a short time. Instead of serving with the Eighth Air Force, to which it had originally been assigned on arrival in the European Theatre, on 14 September 1942 it was posted to the Twelfth Air Force. This assignment meant that it would have a role in Operation TORCH, the invasion of North Africa. On 10 November the air echelons flew to Africa from England via Gibraltar. Anti-aircraft gunners fired at the 34 aircraft as they passed over the Algiers waterfront, but the troop carriers landed their passengers, the British 3rd Parachute Bn The Parachute Regiment, at Maison Blanche, the Algiers airfield, at dawn on 11 November. A crew chief and a paratrooper were wounded.

At 06.00 hours on 12 November, 26 of the Group's aircraft took off with more than 300 British paratroopers and dropped them, some two and a half hours later, at

Bone; the British troops were received by the French garrison, if not with enthusiasm, at least without opposition. The troop-carrier aircraft and their escort of 12 Spitfires returned safely.

Bad weather prevented an attempt on 15 November to carry out a drop on Souk-el-Arba, about 60 miles southeast of Bone, but at 11.00 hours on the following day 32 aircraft with fighter escorts set out again for Souk-el-Arba, and dropped almost 400 British paratroopers on or near the airfield. All aircraft returned safely to Maison Blanche at about 16.00 hours.

A little after noon on 29 November, 18 aircraft of the 64th Group, along with 26 from the 62nd Troop Carrier Group set out, with fighter escort, carrying more than 500 men of the British 2nd Parachute Bn. By the time the DZ at Depienne was reached, the formation was ragged and loose; consequently there was much dispersion in the drop. It would prove to be a hard fight and after several days, of the 530 who had dropped at Depienne, more than half had been killed or captured.

No more airborne missions were flown in North Africa. Throughout the winter and spring the 64th Group operated from its base at Blida, Algeria. In June, however, the Group moved to Zena II, Kairouan, Tunisia, to train for its next troop carrying mission: participation in Operation HUSKY.

The first HUSKY mission called for the 64th to join with four other troop-carrier groups in dropping 3,405 men on the high ground northeast of the Sicilian port of Gela between 23.40 hours on D-1, 9 July and 00.30 on D-Day. The troop carriers began taking off at 20.15 hours. At some fields the clouds of dust created by the take-offs could be seen from five miles and many of the pilots had to take off on instruments.

The group committed two aircraft more than its scheduled 49 and was the only one of the five involved that succeeded in keeping its formation. At 00.25 hours the 2nd Bn 505th Parachute Infantry Regiment was dropped *en masse*. The paratroopers were under fire during and after the drop, but they succeeded in clearing out the enemy forces and completed their assembly before noon. During the course of the day they defeated strong enemy forces, captured the town of Sant' Croce, Camerina, and took 200 prisoners. The aircraft all returned safely, although some landed at fields other than the intended landing place.

The 64th contributed three C-47s, with crews, to Operation FUSTIAN, a glider and parachute attack by 1 Bn Parachute Regiment on 13-14 July to capture the Simeto Bridge near Augusta, Sicily. Although this mission was in many respects badly executed, the prime objective was achieved and the bridge was captured intact.

On 26 July the Group moved from Zena II to El Djem and at the end of August to Comiso, Sicily. On the night of 14-15 September the Group flew its first combat mission to Italy. Forty aircraft carried the 2nd Bn 509th Parachute Combat Team to Avellino. The paratroopers were to destroy bridges and find any other way possible to disrupt the German lines of communication, thus adding to the logistical difficulties of supplying the enemy troops surrounding the Allied beachhead at Salerno.

The pilots returned believing that the mission had been successful, but it emerged that only 15 aircraft had dropped their sticks within four or five miles of the DZ. Eleven aircraft had dropped their sticks 10 miles from the

DZ, at a locality that resembled the Drop Zone, 12 more from between 10 to 26 miles away from the DZ and finally two aircraft loads were still unaccounted for, a full month after the operation. In the after-action report the Group acknowledged that 'The parts in the failure played by inadequate training, a difficult route, an obscure drop zone, inadequate pathfinder facilities, and loss of equipment are hard to estimate, but it seems clear that the mission was a failure.' These navigation errors would be repeated in Operation HERRING two years later.

For several months the Group carried stores and passengers over much of Africa, all of southern Sicily, and parts of Italy. In the spring there was an opportunity to make amends for the Avellino mission. On 1 April the four squadrons of the 64th Group were notified that they, along with the 4th Squadron of the 62nd Group, were to leave forthwith for detached service in the China-Burma-India (CBI) Theatre of Operations.

The 35th Squadron was the first to take off and left the air base at 06.00 hours on 2 April 1944. The other squadrons followed, and the last aircraft got away on 5 April. In theatre the 16th and 17th Squadrons began operations from Lalmai, Lower Bengal, and then from Dinjan, Upper Assam, and with 216 Squadron RAF working out of Chandina, between April and June the Group was instrumental in supplying the men of 5307 Composite Unit (Provisional), better known as Merril's Marauders in the Ft. Hertz Valley and 170,000 British and Indian troops holding Imphal.

The 64th's C-47s frequently flew as many as three round trips a day into the Imphal Valley. Every sortie meant two payloads. Reinforcements, food, ammunition, and other supplies were flown in; casualties and 'useless mouths' were flown out. The 'useless mouths' were 'the administrative and logistic personnel, military and civilian, who had been needed when Imphal was a supply base but who had so little combat capability that they were a burden when the Plain became a battlefield.'

The Group lost seven aircraft during its operations in Burma.

The Tenth Air Force awarded 197 Distinguished Flying Crosses,including three Oak Leaf Clusters; 294 Air Medals, including 90 Clusters; and five Purple Hearts to members of the five AAF Squadrons that participated in the Burmese operations.

Although the 64th's Detached Services in the CBI were originally intended to end in May it was mid-June 1944 before they returned to their base at Comiso, Italy. Just over a month later they were committed to Operation DRAGOON (originally ANVIL): the invasion of southern France. On the night of 3-4 August, the Group flew a simulated major night parachute mission, carrying troops of 2 Parachute Bde and using Rebecca, MF (medium frequency) beacons and lights as navigational aids. On 12 August came a practice glider mission. In the final rehearsal the lead aircraft, after the formations had made a long over-water flight, dropped dummy paratroops at dawn on 13 August.

The operation began on 16 August. The 64th's first role in the operation was participation in ALBATROSS. The Group committed to the mission a lead serial of 36 aircraft and a second serial of 27; the first of these aircraft took to the air at 0211. The Group made a good drop, although the concentration of troops and supplies was not all that might have been desired. The 64th did not participate in Operations BLUEJAY or CANARY, glider and paratroop missions respectively flown later in the day; but it did play an important part in the fourth airborne operation of the day, a glider mission codenamed DOVE. This involved the towing of more than 300 Waco gliders carrying the 550th Glider Infantry Battalion and other troops to the number of about 2,250. Great quantities of materiel were also transported. The first of the 64th's aircraft committed to this mission took off from Ciampino at 15.10 hours. The flight to the target was apparently uneventful, but the landing zone was found to be obscured by smoke, and the gliders were released on detecting the signal from a Eureka beacon that had been installed earlier in the day. The 64th was the only group that had to use navigation aids other than visual on this mission. Because of obstructions placed in the landing fields by the Germans, all of the gliders released were damaged or destroyed on landing. Eleven glider pilots were killed, and more than thirty pilots and about 100 glider-borne troops were injured. The materiel delivered suffered surprisingly little damage. All of the Group's aircraft returned safely; no enemy aircraft were sighted, but there was some damage from Flak.

Operation DOVE was recorded as the 64th's last troop-carrying mission of the war. The post-war USAF official history does not regard Operation HERRING as a troop-carrying mission since it states that the men of No 1 Italian SAS were not dropped as a single formation.

The Commanders of the 64th were Lt Col Malcolm S. Lawton, c. Dec 1940; Col Tracey K Dorsett, unkn; Lt Col Claire B. Collier, c. 1 Mar 1943; Col John Cerny, 16 May 1943-1945.

The aircraft employed in Operation HERRING was the Douglas C-47 Skytrain known to the RAF, which operated over 1,200 in World War 2, as the Dakota. It had began life as the Douglas DC-3, a commercial airliner manufactured at the Santa Monica plant in California. Fitted with folding bench seats, it was used as a troop transport carrying 28 fully-armed soldiers ,while with a reinforced floor and wider doors it was used for 2.6 tons of cargo, a representative load being two Jeeps, a 6-pounder anti-tank gun, or 14 freight baskets. The Dakota had a wingspan of 95ft, was powered by two 1200hp Pratt and Whitney 'Twin Wasp' R-1830 engines and had a top speed of 230 mph. Total production reached 10,123 and as a ground-attack aircraft armed with Gatling guns it operated during the Vietnam War, with the grim nickname of 'Puff the Magic Dragon'.

Allied order of battle
August 1944 – May 1945

Allied Forces HQ Mediterranean

Supreme Allied Commander Mediterranean:
General Sir Henry Maitland Wilson (until 12 December 1944)
Field Marshal Sir Harold Alexander (from 12 December 1944)

Deputy Supreme Allied Commander Mediterranean:
Lieutenant-General Jacob L. Devers (until September 1944)
Lieutenant-General Joseph T. McNamey (from September 1944)

Chief of Staff:
Lieutenant-General Sir James Gammell (to 12 December 1944)
Lieutenant-General Sir John Harding (from 12 December 1944
to 24 March 1945)
Lieutenant-General John K. Cannon (from 24 March 1945)

Commander in Chief:
General Sir Harold Alexander

Chief of Staff: Lieutenant-General Sir John Harding

Commander: Lieutenant-General Mark Wayne Clark
Chief of Staff: Major-General Alfred M. Gruenther

US Fifth Army

Commander:
Lieutenant-General Mark Wayne Clark (until 16 December 1944)
Lieutenant-General Lucian K. Truscott (from 16 December 1944)
US II Corps
Major-General Geoffrey Keyes
US 34th Infantry Division (Major-General Charles Bolté)
US 88th Infantry Division (Major-General Paul W. Kendall)
US 91st Infantry Division (Major-General William G. Livesay)
US 85th Infantry Division (Major-General John B. Coulter) (until April 1945)
Italian Legnano Combat Group (from 1945)

US IV Corps
Major-General Willis D. Crittenberger
US 1st Armored Division (Major-General Vernon E. Prichard)
6th South African Armoured Division (Major-General Evered Poole)
US 85th Infantry Division (Major-General John B. Coulter)
(from April 1945)
1st Brazilian Division (General Mascarenhas de Morais) (from November 1944)
US 10th Mountain Division (Major-General George P. Hays)

(from February 1945)
British XIII Corps (until January 1945)

Independent units under Army HQ
US 92nd Infantry Division (Major-General Edward M. Almond) (from November 1944)

British Eighth Army

Commander:
Lieutenant-General Sir Oliver Leese (until 1 October 1944)
Lieutenant-General Sir Richard McCreery (from 1 October 1944)

British V Corps
Lieutenant-General Charles Keightley
British 1st Armoured Division (Major-General Richard Hull)
(until 25 September 1944)
British 4th Infantry Division (Major-General Dudley Ward)
(from October to November 1944)
Indian 4th Infantry Division (Major-General Alan Holworthy)
(until October 1944)
British 46th Infantry Division (Major-General John Hawksworth until 6 November 1944, then Major-General C.E. Weir) (until December 1944)
British 56th Infantry Division (Major-General J. Y. Whitfield)
British 78th Infantry Division (Major-General D. C. Butterworth until 10 October 1944 and then Major-General Keith Arbuthnott) (from March 1945)

British 6th Armoured Division (Major-General H. Murrey)
(from 18-23 April 1945)
Indian 8th Infantry Division (Major-General Dudley
Russell)
(from March 1945)
Indian 10th Infantry Division (Major-General Denys Reid)
(from October 1944 to February 1945)
New Zealand 2nd Division (Lieutenant-General Sir
Bernard Freyberg) (November 1944 to 14 April 1945)
Jewish Brigade (from February to March 1945)
Italian *Cremona* Combat Group (from 1945)
Italian 28th *Garibaldi* Brigade (from 1945)

British X Corps (until December 1944 and from February
1945)
Lieutenant-General Sir Richard McCreery (until 6
November 1944)
Lieutenant-General John Hawkesworth (from 6 November
1944)
Indian 10th Infantry Division (Major-General Denys Reid)
(until October 1944)
Jewish Brigade (from March 1945)
Italian *Friuli* Combat Group (from 1945)

British XIII Corps (from January 1945)
Lieutenant-General Sidney Kirkman (until 25 January
1945)
Lieutenant-General Sir John Harding (from 25 January
1945)
British 4th Infantry Division (Major-General Dudley
Ward)
(to September 1944)
British 6th Armoured Division (Major-General Horatius
Murray) (from August 1944 to March 1945)
Indian 8th Infantry Division (Major-General Dudley
Russell) (until March 1945)

Indian 10th Infantry Division (Major-General Denys Reid)
(from February 1945)
British 1st Infantry Division (Major-General Charles
Loewen)
(until January 1945)
British 78th Infantry Division (Major-General D. C.
Butterworth until 10 October 1944 and then
Major-General Keith Arbuthnott (from October 1944
to March 1945)
New Zealand 2nd Division (Lieutenant-General Sir
Bernard Freyberg) (from April 14, 1945)
Italian *Folgore* Combat Group (from 1945)

Canadian I Corps (until February 1945)
Lieutenant-General E. L. M. Burns (until 10 November
1944)
Lieutenant-General C. Foulkes (from 10 November 1944)
Canadian 1st Infantry Division (Major-General Chris
Vokes until 1 December 1944 then Major-General H. W.
Foster)
Canadian 5th Armoured Division (Major-General Bert
Hoffmeister)
British 4th Infantry Division (Major-General Dudley
Ward)
(from September to October 1944)
New Zealand 2nd Division (Lieutenant-General Sir
Bernard Freyberg, Major-General C. E. Weir acting
commander 3 September -17 October 1944)
Greek 3rd Mountain Brigade (Colonel Thrasyvoulos
Tsakalotos) (from September to October 1944)

Polish II Corps
Lieutenant-General Władyslaw Anders
Polish 3rd Carpathian Rifle Division (Major-General
Bolesław Bronisław Duch)
Polish 5th Kresowa Infantry Division (Major-General
Nikodem Sulik)
Polish 2nd Armoured Brigade (Brigadier-General
Bronislaw Rakowski)

Other Units
2nd Commando Bde (Brigadier Ronnie Todd) (1945)
2nd Parachute Bde (UK) (to December 1944)

The Italian Co-Belligerent Army

Cremona Combat Group (of British V Corps, 9 April 1945)
7th Italian Artillery Regiment [-1Bty]
21st Italian Infantry Regiment [3 Bn]
22nd Italian Infantry Regiment [3 Bn]
144th Italian Engineer Bn
Folgore Combat Group (of XIII Corps, 9 April 1945)
Nembo Regiment [3 Bn]
San Marco Regiment [3 Bn]
57th Italian Field Regiment [-1Bty, 1Trp]
154th Italian Field Regiment
184th Italian Artillery Regiment
184th Italian Engineer Battalion
Friuli Combat Group (of British X Corps, 9 April 1945)
35th Italian Artillery Regiment
87th Italian Infantry Regiment [3 Bn]
88th Italian Infantry Regiment [3 Bn]
120th Italian Engineer Bn
Legnano Combat Group (of US II Corps), 9 April 1945)
11th Italian Artillery Regiment
51st Italian Engineer Battalion

68th Italian Regiment Infantry
69th Italian Regiment Infantry
Legnano Combat Group (enlarged and reassigned to US
Fifth Army, 23 April 1945)
HQ, *Legnano* Combat Group
Legnano Ordnance Field Park
Legnano Mechanical workshop
34th *Carabinieri* Section
51st *Carabinieri* Section
51st Supply and Transport Coy
51st Medical Section
51st Italian Engineer Bn
52nd British Liaison Unit
244th Field Hospital
332nd Field Hospital
11th Italian Artillery Regiment
68th Italian Infantry Regiment
  1st Infantry Bn
  2nd Infantry Bn
  3rd Infantry Bn
  405th Mortar Coy (3-inch)
  56th Antitank Coy (6-pounder)
69th Italian Special Infantry Regiment
  1st *Bersaglieri* Bn
  2nd *Alpini* Bn
  3rd *Alpini* Bn
  15th Mortar Coy (3-inch)
  16th Antitank Coy (6-pounder)

Appendix 6

German Army Group C

Commander:
Field Marshal Albert Kesselring (until 25 October 1944, from January 1945 until 9 March 1945)
General Heinrich von Vietinghoff (from 25 October 1944, until January 1945 and from 9 March 1945)

German Tenth Army
General Heinrich von Vietinghoff (until 25 October 1944)
Lieutenant-General Joachim Lemelsen (from 25 October 1944 to 15 February 1945)
Lieutenant-General Traugott Herr (from 15 February 1945)

German LXXVI Panzer Korps

Lieutenant-General Traugott Herr (until 26 December 1944)
Lieutenant-General Graf Gerhard von Schwerin (from 26 December 1944 to 25 April 1945)
Major-General Karl von Graffen (from 25 April 1945)
German 1st Parachute Division (Lieutenant-General Richard Heidrich until 18 November 1944, then Brigadier Karl-Lothar Schultz)
German 5th Mountain Division (Major-General Max-Günther Schrank to 18 January 1945, then Brigadier-General Hans Steets)
German 71st Infantry Division (Major-General Wilhelm Raapke) (until December 1944)

German 162nd Infantry Division (Major-General Ralph von Heygendorff)
German 278th Infantry Division (Major-General Harry Hoppe)

German LI Gebirgs Korps

Lieutenant-General Valentin Feurstein until March 1945 and then Lieutenant-General Friedrich-Wilhelm Hauck
German 44th Reichsgrenadier Division *Hoch und Deutschmeister* (Major-General Hans-Günther von Rost) (until November 1944)
German 114th Jäger Division (Brigadier-General Hans-Joachim Ehlert to 15 April 1945, then Brigadier-General Martin Strahammer)
German 305th Infantry Division (Lieutenant-General Friedrich-Wilhelm Hauck until December 1944, then Brigadier-General Friedrich von Schellwitz)
German 334th Infantry Division (Major-General Hellmuth Böhlke)
German 715th Infantry Division (Brigadier-General Hanns von Rohr) (until January 1945)

German Fourteenth Army
Lieutenant-General Joachim Lemelsen (24 October 1944 until 17 February 1945)
Lieutenant-General Frido von Senger und Etterlin (October 1944)
Lieutenant-General Heinz Ziegler (24 October to 22 November 1944)
Lieutenant-General Traugott Herr (22 November to 12 December 1944)
Lieutenant-General Kurt von Tippelskirch (12 December 1944 to 16 February 1945)

German I Fallschirm Korps

Lieutenant-General Alfred Schlemm (to 30 September 1944)
Lieutenant-General Richard Heidrich (from 1 November 1944
to 23 January 1945)
Major-General Hellmuth Böhlke (from 23 January 1945 to February 7, 1945)
Lieutenant-General Richard Heidrich (from 7 February 1945)
German 4th Parachute Division (Major-General Heinrich Trettner)
German 356th Infantry Division (Major-General Karl Faulenbach
to October 1944)
German 362nd Infantry Division (Major-General Heinz Greiner)

German XIV Panzer Korps

Lieutenant-General Frido von Senger und Etterlin
German 26th Panzer Division (Major-General Eduard Crasemann to 29 January 1945, then Brigadier-General Alfred Kuhnert to 19 April 1945, then Major-General Viktor Linnarz)
German 65th Infantry Division (Major-General Helmuth Pfeiffer)
16th SS-Panzergrenadier Division *Reichsführer-SS* (SS-Gruppenführer Max Simon until 24 October 1944 then SS-Brigadeführer Otto Baum)

Army Group Liguria

General Alfredo Guzzoni
German 42nd Jäger Division (Major-General Walter Jost)
German 34th Infantry Division (Major-General Theobald Lieb)
Italian *Monterossa* Mountain Division
Italian *San Marco* Infantry Division

Army Reserve

German 29th Panzergrenadier Division (Major-General Fritz Polack)
German 20th Luftwaffe Field Division, re-designated German 20th Luftwaffe Sturm Division in June 1944 (Brigadier-General Wilhelm Crisolli until 1 June 1944 then Brigadier-General Erich Fronhöfer)

Independent Units
German LXXXV Corps (Italian-French border)

Lieutenant-General Hans Schlemmer
German 148th Reserve Division (Major-General Otto Schönherr) (to August 1944)
German 90th Panzergrenadier Division (Major-General Ernst-Günther Baade to 9 December 1944, then Lieutenant General Gerhard von Schwerin to 26 December 1944, then Brigadier-General Heinrich Baron von Behr)
German 157th Mountain Division, re-designated German 8th Mountain Division in February 1945 (Major-General Paul Schricker)

Adriatic Coast Command

German 94th Infantry Division (Major-General Bernhard Steinmetz)
German 188th Mountain Division (Major-General Hans von Hölin)

Abbreviations

AAI – Allied Armies in Italy
AFHQ – Allied Force's Headquarters (Mediterranean)
AMG – Allied Military Government
AMGOT – Allied Military Government of Occupied Territories
BBC – British Broadcasting Corporation
CIL – *Corpo Italiano di Liberazione*
CLN – *Comitato di Liberazione Nazionale*
DSO – Distinguished Service Order
DZ – Drop Zone
G1 – Personnel (General Staff)
G2 – Intelligence
G3 – Operations and Training
G4 – Logistics
GS – General Staff
J – SOE Italian Section head
MAAF – Mediterranean Allied Air Forces
MATAF – Mediterranean Allied Tactical Air Forces
MC – Military Cross
MM – Military Medal
MO1 (SP) – Cover name for SOE
MP – Member of Parliament
No 1 SF – SOE in Italy
OKW – *Oberkommando der Wehrmacht*, German High Command
OSS – Office of Strategic Services
PE – Plastic Explosives
PPA – Popski's Private Army
RAF – Royal Air Force
SAS – Special Air Service
SBS – Special Boat Squadron
SD – *Sicherheitsdienst*, SS Intelligence Service
SRS – Special Raiding Squadron
1 SF – No1 SF

SOE – Special Operations Executive
SO (M) – Special Operations Mediterranean
USAAF – United States Army Air Force

Bibliography

AAVV, *The Tiger Triumphs – The Story of Three Great Divisions in Italy*, HM Stationery Office India, 1946

Arthur, Max, *Forgotten Voices of the Second World War*, Ebury Press, London, 2004

Bailey, Roderick, *Forgotten Voices of the Secret War*, Ebury Press, London, 2008

Benfatti, Carlo, *L'Operazione Herring No 1*, Editoriale Sometti, Mantova, 1998

Bradford, Roy and Dillon, Martin, *Rogue Warrior of the SAS*, John Murray, London, 1987

Buckley, Christopher, *Road to Rome*, Hodder and Stoughton, London, 1945

Danchev, Alex and Todman Daniel (editors) War Diaries *1939-1945: Field Marshal Lord Alanbrooke*, Weidenfeld & Nicolson 2001

Darman, Peter, *A-Z of the SAS*, Sidgwick and Jackson, London, 1992

Deakin, F. W., *The Brutal Friendship: Mussolini, Hitler and the fall of Italian Fascism*, Pelican, London, 1962

Dear, I. C. B. Editor, *The Oxford Companion to the Second World War*, OUP, Oxford, 1995

Farran, Roy, *Winged Dagger*, Collins, London, 1948 *Operation Tombola*, Collins, London, 1960

Ford, Ken, *Battleaxe Division*, Sutton Publishing, Stroud, 1999

Gooderson, Ian, *A Hard Way to Make a War*, Conway, London, 2008

Graham, Dominick and Bidwell, Shelford, *Tug of War: The Battle for Italy 1943-45*, Hodder & Stoughton, London, 1986

Harrison, Derrick, *These Men are Dangerous*, Cassell & Co, London 1957

Hinsley, F. H., Thomas, E. E., Simkins, C. A. G., Ransom, C. F. G., *British Intelligence in the Second World War Vol 3 Part 2*, HMSO, London 1988

Holland, James, *Italy's Sorrow*, Harper Press, London, 2008

Kluger, Steve, *Yank: the Army Weekly*, Arms and Armour, London, 1991

Lee, Michael, *Special Operations Executed*, William Kimber, London, 1986

Marshall Cavendish Books, The War Years 1939-1945 Eyewitness Accounts, Marshall Cavendish, London, 1994

Messenger, Charles, *World War Two Chronological Atlas*, Bloomsbury, London 1989

Ministero della Difesa, *Gruppi di Combattimento Cremona – Friuli-Folgore-Legnano-Mantova-Piceno (1944-1945)*, Roma, 1973

Mortimer, Gavin, *Stirling's Men*, Weidenfeld & Nicolson, London, 2004

Pitt, Barrie (Editor), *History of the Second World War*, Purnell & Sons, 1966

Rigden, Denis (Introduction), *SOE Syllabus*, The Public Record Office, 2001

Scagell, Robin (Editor), *Images of War*, Marshall Cavendish Partworks, 1990

Seaman, Mark (Editor), *Special Operations Executive*, Routledge, London, 2006

Stevens, Gordon, *The Originals*, Ebury Press, London, 2005

Warner, Philip, *The Special Air Service*, William Kimber, London, 1971

War Office Field Engineering and Mine Warfare Pamphlet No 7, Booby Traps 1952

Weeks, John, *Airborne Equipment*, David and Charles, 1976

National Archive
Air 51/20 Operation Herring HS 6/792 Support of military and naval operations. Herring paratroop drop for sabotage and harassing enemy retreat WO 204/1521 Operation Herring operational cables WO 204/6851 Operation Herring minutes of meeting and planning papers WO 204/7890 Operation Herring: minutes of conference and operations memorandum WO 204/8024 Operation Herring: organisation and training of Italian parachute troops. Operational directives: reports and summary of results WO 218/215 Operation Tombola Report March–April 1945

Websites
www.history.army.mil/
www.commandosupremo.com/Herring
www.milhist.net/ordbat/italcobel.html
www.squadronef.it/

SAS OPERATIONS IN ITALY 1943-45

Brenner Pass

SWITZERLAND — AUSTRIA

COLD COMFORT
17 FEB 54

Turin ● Milan ●

Venice ● Trieste ●

HERRING
7 APRIL 45

● Fiume

Genoa ● **GALLIA**
27 DEC 44

● Reggio Emilia

TOMBOLA
4 MAR 45

Y U G O S L A V I A

SPEEDWELL
7 SEPT 43

● Ravenna

Spezia ●

BAOBAB
27 JAN 44

Allied Line
March 1945

Rimini ●

● Florence

● Sibenik

Ancona ●

**MAPLE-
DRIFTWOOD**
7 JAN 44

● Split

CORSICA

POMEGRANATE
12 JAN 44

JONQUIL
26 SEPT 43

SAXIFRAGE
14 DEC 43

Terni ●

BEGONIA
2 OCT 44

SLEEPY LAD
18 DEC 43

**MAPLE-
THISTLEDOWN**
7 JAN 44

CANDYTUFT
27 OCT 43

● Rome

Anzio ●

Cassino ●

Commando operation
with SRS 2 sas
3 OCT 43

A L B A N I A

Allied Line
March 1944
7 January 1944

Naples ●

Foggia ●

Tirana ●

SARDINIA

HAWTHORN
7 JULY 43

Bari ●

D Sqdn 2SAS
with 1 AB Div
9 SEPT 43

Salerno ●

MARIGOLD
30 MAY 43

Ginosa ●

● Taranto

SRS
12 SEPT 43

● Bagnara

Messina ●

● Reggio

S I C I L Y

CHESTNUT
10 JULY 43

**SRS raid
coastal Btys**
12 July 43

Bizarta ● Tunis ●

Pantalleria ●

Augusta ●

SNAPDRAGON
28 MAY 43

● Syracuse

NARCISSUS
10 JULY 43

N

T U N I S I A

M A L T A

SAS operations in Italy. These ranged from the offshore islands
of Sardinia, Pantelleria and Sicily to the mountain passes on the
Austrian border. While some met with success, others saw
casualties, capture and execution for the lonely brave men
deep behind enemy lines.

THE END IN ITALY

The final thrust that took the Anglo-American armies from Rome to the Swiss border. The Germans had hoped to hold on the mountain line and deny the Allies the free movement of the Po valley but had plans to defend the southern Alps.

THE SPRING OFFENSIVE – April 1945

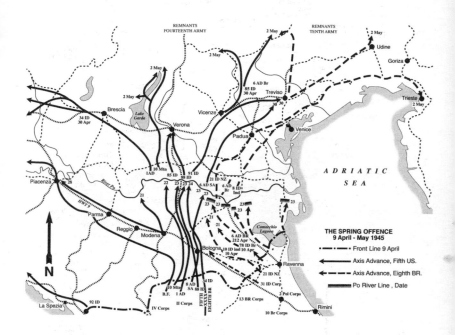

Above: The Allied spring offensive in 1945 – the men of No 1 Italian SAS would land in the centre of the 5th and 8th Army thrust towards the River Po and make a valuable contribution to the confusion and disruption suffered by German forces.

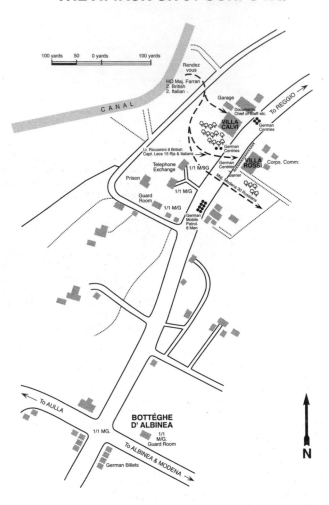

OPERATION *TOMBOLA* – THE ATTACK ON 51 CORPS HQ

The attack on the German 51 Corps HQ. Farran had devised a simple but effective plan that inflicted casualties on an important HQ as the Allies were about to launch their spring offensive.

INDEX

The Secret War in Italy